D1333267

new world wines

new world wines

the complete guide

Julie Arkell

WARD LOCK

Created and produced by
FOCUS PUBLISHING
The Courtyard
26 London Road
Sevenoaks
Kent TN13 1AP

Publishing Director Guy Croton
Managing Editor Caroline Watson

Art Director Glen Wilkins

Location photography by Cephas Picture Library
Studio photography by Laura Wickenden

Map artwork by Glen Wilkins

This edition first published in the United Kingdom by

WARD LOCK
Illustrated Division
The Orion Publishing Group
Wellington House
125 Strand
London WC2R 0BB
First published 1999

Distributed in the United States of America
by Sterling Publishing Co., Inc.
387 Park Avenue South, New York, NY 10016-8810

A CIP catalogue record for this book is available from the British Library

ISBN 0 304 35160 1

Colour separation by Tenon & Polert Colour Scanning Ltd.
Printed and bound by South China Printing Co. Ltd, Hong Kong

Frontispiece: The sun setting over a vineyard in the Carneros district, Napa County, California, USA.

Contents

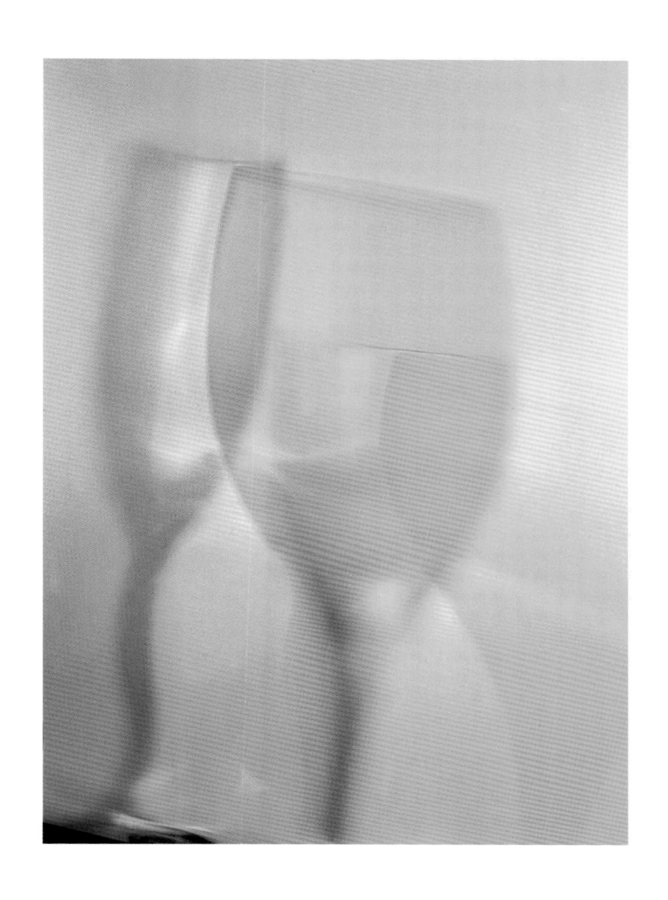

Introduction

The New World wine revolution

Of all the developments in winemaking this century, the most exciting is the explosion of the industry in what has come to be known as the New World. The sheer speed at which winemaking has developed here simply takes the breath away.

Let me take you back to 1981. I had just joined the wine trade and I soon signed up to take London's Wine and Spirit Education Trust examinations. Heavily biased towards Europe, just one paragraph of the first course book was dedicated to the New World – and, incredible though it might now seem, Canada and New Zealand were not even mentioned. The second course book was marginally better; 14 pages on the New World this time (still no reference to New Zealand, though Canada was acknowledged, at least), with the greatest emphasis placed on the United States – not surprising, as Robert Mondavi had already kicked off the Californian renaissance back in 1966. Even so, these few pages contained no sense of excitement nor any hint of the dramatic revolution which was about to unfold. Incidentally, Australia was awarded approximately the same number of words as Cyprus, North West Africa, Hungary and even England!

This tale serves to underline how far the New World has come in such a short space of time. Is there any wine lover nowadays who does not regularly drink the wines of Australia, New Zealand, South Africa, North America and South America? This is particularly true of the new breed of wine consumer in the United Kingdom. New World wines form only one per cent of sales in mainland Europe, yet we in Britain have embraced with fervour the fresh, clean, fruit-driven flavours of New World wines, flavours made possible by top-notch viticultural practice, state-of-the-art winery technology, and most importantly, the skills of highly trained viticulturists and winemakers; the British have welcomed the ease with which we can choose these wines, thanks to varietal labelling and clear branding; and we have recognized the excellent value for money which the New World offers in relation to many of the established Old World 'greats', even at the costlier end of the price scale.

The phenomenal rise to glory of the New World has certainly given the Old World something to worry about. It speaks volumes that the European Union has recently announced subsidies totalling

ECU1.2 billion for vineyard replanting and the installation of new winemaking technologies. This is most ironic, given that the New World wine culture was established by the Old World in the first place.

Europe already possessed a winemaking history spanning some 11 centuries when its first explorers set sail to colonize the New World. The early settlers were deeply accustomed to drinking wine and, of course, the fledgling Spanish colonies needed it for sacramental purposes, and so the vine travelled with them. The often stuttering vinous history of each New World country is fascinating, chronicling see-saw patterns of boom and bust driven by the effects of war, Prohibition, diseased vineyards, Gold Fevers, politics, fashion, the rediscovery of forgotten vineyards, and a variety of other factors peculiar to each region.

Strangely enough, though, while Old World methods obviously supplied the original role models, each failure and each renaissance provided the New World with the opportunity to improve upon and update viticultural practice and harness the latest winemaking technology, and it has been this willingness and ability to adapt and to experiment which has arguably been the most significant factor in the development of the modern-day, forward-thinking, New World wine industries.

This has been more than helped by the absence of inhibiting rules and regulations pertaining to appellation systems which still bind the majority of the Old World to its past. Indeed, there is huge resentment amongst many New World producers of the European doctrines which are currently being forced on them by the European Union (in true protectionist style), whereby New World countries must register delimited wine-producing areas if they wish to continue to market and sell their wine within the Community.

Spring flowers in the vineyards of Wendouree Cellars, near Clare, South Australia. These are not planted merely to make the vineyard look pretty, however. They act as an early warning signal of problems with pests and diseases which may affect the vine later. If the flowers wilt or die, then the grower knows that something is afoot and can take action before the vines are struck.

In fact, this happens to coincide with a movement within the New World to step back from merely pioneering new technologies and to take a closer look at the relationship between the grape and the land – a somewhat traditionalist Old World approach, one might say! This stemmed from the criticism that many New World wines were beginning to taste the same, and to a certain extent this was true of the first Flying Winemaker wines. Whichever winery they parachuted into, these mainly Aussie winemakers tended to make wine to a standard formula – albeit wine of much superior quality than had ever emanated from there before – riding roughshod over the nuance of local character.

But these early wines were made in Europe, most especially in the newly liberated countries of Eastern Europe, where old-fashioned winemaking practice and outdated equipment still prevailed. By the time the Flying Winemakers reached the unexploited parts of the New World, they had cut their teeth and had moved on from making one-dimensional wines. What matters most to my mind is that those consumers who had been so impressed by the flavours conjured from the Old World by the Flying Winemakers were more than willing at least to try the wines they were now making in somewhat strange places (Uruguay leaps to mind), simply on the strength of trust. One does wonder if the rise to popularity of many of these wines would have been so meteoric without the efforts of the Flying Winemakers, standardized or not.

Today, the travelling New World winemakers (and the equally important roving viticulturists) are far more sensitive to preserving the indigenous identity of the region, whether they be making wine in the New World or the Old. Many of these apostles have chosen to stay in Europe permanently, where they are raising the profile of many Old World wine regions by breaking away from hardened tradition. Some of them work in partnership with British wholesalers and retailers who wish to have direct control over the wines they are buying; others again are employed by New World companies who have actually gone as far as establishing their own vineyards and wineries in Europe.

Michael Brajkovic of Kumeu River Wines, Kumeu, Auckland, New Zealand.

Indeed, my crystal ball predicts that we are going see far more of this kind of activity, most particularly in the form of joint ventures between different New World countries, or between the New World and the Old. There are certainly signs that the current dichotomy between the Old World and the New is shrinking, and it will probably continue to do so for a number of diverse reasons – the further development of cool climate regions within the New World will deliver wines with more finesse than has been tasted before (far more European in style, if you like),

with concomitant European-style vintage variations; and the more innovative and progressive of producers within the Old World will continue to embrace and exploit New World technology.

We are also likely to see the expansion of winemaking interests in such disparate places as China, India, Japan, Kenya, Korea, North Africa, Vietnam and Zimbabwe. Most of these countries have centuries-long histories of grape-growing and winemaking, in fact, so they are Old World by classification. If the Flying Winemakers were to land there, however, the modern wine industries would likely emerge with the cutting edge of New World technology firmly in place and a definite New World imprint to the style of the wines.

In 20 years time, when people will look back at this book and say, 'How out of date!', I think we shall find that the phrase 'New World' will have developed well beyond questions of history and geography in terms of international winemaking. It will have come to mean the concept of pioneering new frontiers wherever they are taking place. But it will have been today's New World ideology and dynamism which will have led the way.

Julie Arkell, Somerset, May 1999

The New
World of
Winemaking

New World winemaking combines the best knowledge and experience from the 'Old World' with groundbreaking technology, careful planning and audacious experimentation.

Brave New World

A startlingly fresh and innovative approach ensures difference

The winemakers of the New World have never been afraid to experiment. Indeed, in many respects they have deliberately set out to overturn some of the Old World's most sacred cows of winemaking technique and practice. But does this mean their methods are better?

The argument goes round and round and seems destined to stay in orbit: is the character of wine ultimately determined by Terroir or Technology? More than any other, this issue of nature versus nurture has polarized Old World and New World winemaking philosophies.

The Old World 'terroirist' standpoint holds that each vineyard 'address' creates wine of a matchless, indelible flavour owing to the unique interaction between its soil, geography and climate. It is not something you can buy like technology; it is God-given and should not be interfered with. Nature is therefore allowed to take its course in the winery, where the winemaker is merely the midwife delivering an individual expression of fruit to the glass.

Merlot grapes on the soil at Frog's Leap Winery, Napa Valley, California, USA. Merlot gained popularity in the USA in the early 1970s and is now renowned for its soft, sweet cherry and brambly flavours and complex mint, cigar box and spice aromas.

Even the most ardent New World protagonists of technology will agree that this is an admirable doctrine if your vines happen to be planted at the perfect site, in perfect soils and in a perfect climate which will deliver perfect grapes to your winery door each and every year. However, they argue that nature is rarely so bountiful and therefore more often than not the tinkering hand of man is needed to craft wines which are going to be acceptable to both palate and purse.

Furthermore, extreme New World anti-terroirists will go as far as saying that terroir, and the concomitant establishment of restrictive appellation systems, is an invention of the marketing man, and they strongly resent being forced into a similar straitjacket by the machinations of protectionist European Union bureaucracy. We have all drunk enough appalling *Appellation Contrôlée* wine, for example, to

share sympathy with this view, but there have always been New World producers who are more than happy to give credence to the provenance of their grapes, acknowledging that the type of dirt in which they grow and the climate in which they ripen is every bit as important as the skill and tools of the winemaker. And, on the flip side, one only has to have a sip of a so-called Super-Tuscan wine, for example, to appreciate that not all of the Old World is glued to the concept of terroir. These delicious Italian wines can only claim *Vino da Tavola* status because all of the appellation rules have been broken – in the vineyard and in the winery – in the interest of creating better wine.

The floor of Corban's Stoneleigh vineyard in Marlborough, New Zealand, is strewn with large pebbles and rocks, abandoned by the river when it shifted course. These reflect sunlight during the day, but also absorb and store heat which is radiated at night, helping to keep the vines warm.

No doubt many producers will continue to hold their diametrically opposed views in this debate, but there are plenty of signs that Old World/New World differences are beginning to level out. New World technology is being embraced by winemakers in the warmer parts of the Old World – particularly by those who are prepared to risk a lower ranking in an appellation structure – while New World producers are becoming less aggressive in their appliance of science in the winery, recognizing that they have, quite literally, to go back to their roots if they are to achieve even greater glory.

In the Vineyard

Every vineyard has its own natural terroir – but it is what is done with it that counts. Ever since the first New World vineyards were planted, growers have recognized that good wine cannot be made without good fruit – indeed, as Charles Back of South Africa's Fairview Estate so aptly says, 'I like to do a lot of my winemaking in

A newly planted vineyard at Errázuriz in Chile's cool Casablanca Valley. Every detail was planned with painstaking care, from the exact spacing of the vines and the rows, to the amount of water which each vine is drip fed.

the berry' – and if this means that one has to meddle with nature, then so be it. To this end, the New World has pioneered new heights of viticultural technology, from the moment the vine is propagated in the nursery to the manner in which the grapes are delivered to the winery – and it has brought the fundamental importance of the viticulturist to the attention of the world along the way.

New World grape-growers have tremendous advantages over their Old World counterparts. For example, they have the freedom to plant whatever they like, often in virgin land, and there are no demanding regulations governing pruning methods or maximum yields and so on. Moreover, as each new vineyard is planted, every ounce of experience and each new technological advance can be harnessed to bring about even greater improvements in grape quality. Indeed, the art of vineyard management has now become the science of plot handling, whereby each block of vines within each vineyard is treated differently according to its individual requirements.

Global Positioning By Satellite (GPS) provides just one hi-tech example of how this can be achieved, most especially in extensive vineyards. During the harvest, the position of each of the mechanical harvesters can be pinpointed via GPS and its progress mapped to within just three metres. If an inferior batch of grapes reaches the winery, it is possible to track its precise source, giving the grower an unrivalled opportunity to investigate the problem. Is it the soil, the water supply, or has there simply been an error in the choice of picking date? Indeed, there are myriad computer monitoring schemes which can gather all kinds of vital information about natural conditions within vineyards, allowing growers to build up a database which can be used to predict trends and, therefore, the likely future demands for irrigation, spraying against disease and so on.

While the application of this type of technology is not the sole preserve of the New World, traditional Old World growers say that they have no need of it. Well, of course not. They have hundreds of years of empirical evidence on which to draw. They know the character and behaviour of their vineyards like the backs of their hands. The New World, however, must rely on technological short cuts to arrive at an equivalent understanding.

In the final analysis, there may be vast differences in the way it is accomplished, but progressive growers in both the Old World and New share a common goal: to procure grapes of the highest possible quality from their land. And as New World growers become even more selective in matching each grape variety to its optimum site, the gaps are bound to narrow even further.

A Site to Behold

We have a vine in our garden – or should I say that we inherited it when we moved in. I have no idea which variety it is, and because it is growing in a thicket of blackberry bushes so dense and wide that I do not even know where the vine actually springs out of the ground, it never receives any attention. Nevertheless, each year it produces plenty of bunches of grapes, probably because it is lucky enough to be growing in poor, well-drained soils on a very sunny, south-facing slope. Somehow, I don't think I am quite ready for the Viticulturist of the Year award!

In a way, this sums up large parts of the Old World; tracts of vine-populated land have been handed down from generation to generation over the centuries, and each guardian of that land has more or less had to coax the best from Mother Nature's provisions. In the New World, however, and with very few exceptions, growers have been able to choose where to site their vineyards, perhaps the single most important aspect of New World grape production.

So, how do growers set about selecting new sites? A number of different factors apply: elevated slopes attract more hours of sunshine than flat land, particularly if they are facing the Equator; soils need to be well-drained, relatively infertile and not liable to erosion; proximity to a large mass of water is important in marginal climates as it helps to modify temperatures. Indeed, the mesoclimate will determine if irrigation is required and, if it is, then the cost implications and the issue of water rights have to be taken into consideration. Much depends on the grape variety which is about to be planted (a decision which will always be driven by market forces to a certain extent) because each has different needs in terms of soil and mesoclimate. Finally, and though it may be obvious, there is little point in developing the perfect site towards the top of a mountain if there is no transport infrastructure to take your wines to market.

Once the land is purchased, it can then take anything up to three years to prepare it. The soil has to be surveyed for pests such as nematodes (microscopic roundworms) which, among other things,

In the New World, growers have been able to choose where to site their vineyards. This is perhaps the single most important aspect of New World grape production.

can spread destructive nepoviruses, and it may need to be fertilized or limed. The land needs to be ploughed (known as 'ripping' in viticultural circles), which breaks up compacted soils to improve drainage and to allow the vine's roots to penetrate deeper. A planting design must also be drawn up to map the spacing of vines and rows, a task which has to balance yields and quality alongside the space needed for the operation of machinery. Irrigation schemes need to be planned meticulously, taking into account the results of soil probes which measure moisture-holding capacity and thus the potential root zone of the vines. Historically, poor site preparation and imperfect planning have been the cause of most of the significant – and very often irrevocable – problems in new vineyards.

This time lag before growers can even stick a vine cutting into the ground often proves irrelevant. In the United States, for example, vines need to be ordered from the nursery one to four years in advance, particularly if popular clones and/or rootstocks are required (an impatient grower may decide to plant a variety more freely available, or choose inferior clones or rootstocks). There has been much talk about the limited availability of land for future vineyard developments, and as valid as this may be, I reckon that there are going to be even greater problems in supplying the vines to fill them, never mind the extra delay in waiting for the vine cuttings. However, this does give growers the time in which to save up to pay for them – $4 a vine at 1998 US prices. One needs an average of 2,224 to 3,212 vines per hectare in Long Island, for example, which gives an outlay of between $8,896 and $12,849 per hectare for the vines alone!

Grape Expectations

In the blinking of an eye compared with the Old World, the New World has not only embraced all of the classic noble grape varieties, but has seemingly made them its own. At least as far as the average consumer is concerned, that is.

Just look at Chardonnay, for example. Its most illustrious Old World rendition is white Burgundy, yet for centuries the French never declared this fact on their labels – the vineyard, village and producer always took priority. It was left to the New World to stamp the name of Chardonnay and other top grapes on wine-drinker's lips by introducing the concept of varietal labelling, a practice the Old World could not adopt quickly enough once it had witnessed the phenomenal success of this revolutionary marketing venture.

But the New World has not stopped at this achievement. The focus is now being directed towards identifying the most suitable rootstocks and clones for each variety within each country, within each region, within each vineyard, and even within each individual vineyard plot. As the New World wine industry matures, it is recognizing that this is the way forward to securing even greater heights of quality.

The topic of rootstocks is pretty straightforward, in fact. The root of the vinifera species of vine (responsible for all premium wines) is highly vulnerable to the predations of an extravagantly hungry louse called *Phylloxera vastatrix* – though to be

Darren de Bortoli of De Bortoli Wines, Griffith, New South Wales, Australia.

A more than 100-year-old Shiraz vine at Henschke's Hill of Grace vineyard, Eden Valley, South Australia. These gnarled old vines offer up tiny yields of highly concentrated and utterly delicious wines which sell out within minutes of release.

biologically accurate, we should now be calling it *Dactylasphaera vitifoliae*. To this end, most vinifera vines have to be grafted onto non-vinifera rootstock (generically known as 'American' rootstock), which is phylloxera-resistant. The precise choice of this rootstock, however, is proving to be of tremendous importance in the New World. For example, naturally vigorous rootstocks such as Dog Ridge, Freedom, Harmony, Rupestris St George, 99 Richter and 110 Richter are now giving way to those specially bred to limit vigour, such as Riparia Gloire de Montpellier, 101-14 Millardet et de Grasset and 3309 Couderc, while rootstocks such as 110 Richter and 140 Ruggeri can better tolerate drought conditions.

Clonal selection is also incredibly easy to understand once you think of Dolly the sheep or the propagation of house or garden plants. Where an individual vine has been noted for a particular quality – be it an ability to ripen early or an affinity to a particular type of soil, for example – then it is possible to physically reproduce thousands of identical copies of that vine by taking cuttings and growing them on. Using the correct clone in the correct site has an important impact on yields and grape quality. It is not uncommon, either, for growers to introduce a number of different clones to one site on the premise that clonal diversity gives greater complexity in the finished wine. Growers have to be careful, however. When the Cabernet Sauvignon Schleip 163 clone was first planted in South Africa, everyone was unprepared for the fact that the fruit ripened some four to six weeks earlier than anything they had planted before, which put tremendous pressure on unprepared wineries.

The generation of clonal material is achieved by purely physical procedures and is not at all the same as the highly

Gondolas full of harvested grapes at Montana's Brancott Estate vineyard in Marlborough, New Zealand's largest wine region. Companies such as Montana, who have on-site crushing facilities or wineries, gain a huge advantage because the fragile grape skins burst easily under their own weight when piled together like this, giving a slosh of juice and skins, which can lead to oxidation and over-extraction.

emotive subject of genetic modification. Vast progress has been made in Australia, California, Canada, France and South Africa over recent years in the development of transgenic vines. In essence, genes carrying DNA which has been 'typed' for its resistance to, say, frost, can be isolated from one grape variety and inserted into the genetic material of a different grape variety. In a rather loose sense, this is merely a man-made form of mutation, which the vine has quite happily been doing for itself over the centuries through natural selection.

However, the critical – and risky – difference now that man has stepped in is that there is not enough empirical evidence as yet to show how foreign genes behave in their new, unfamiliar homes over the course of time – or, indeed, how the host will react in the long term. Curing one problem may well create another unpredicted pattern of behaviour – for example, there is no point in increasing frost resistance in a vulnerable variety if it then refuses to produce grapes! No GM wines have been made to date, but it is surely only a matter of time before a producer takes the plunge and comes out with one – indeed, Canada's Château des Charmes have already planted their first GM vineyard.

These hi-tech considerations seem incredible compared with the approach adopted in the early New World days, when growers planted vines regardless of their suitability to the prevailing conditions. There are plenty of examples of farmers who simply replaced an unprofitable cash crop with vines in order to jump onto an apparently more propitious bandwagon. However, once it was realized that the vine is slightly more demanding in terms of where it is planted, growers were encouraged to think a lot more about varieties which would best enjoy their local environment. In parts of the New World, this has included the switch from native non-vinifera species such as *Vitis labrusca* and/or hybrid varieties, to the superior *Vitis vinifera*, the only vine species to have originated in Europe.

To date, it is market force which has driven the plantings of grapes such as Cabernet Sauvignon and Chardonnay, but the exploration of more obscure varieties is also proving its worth in the New World. Some commentators think that Chardonnay, for one, has had its day, and I am as bored with one-dimensional Chardonnay as the next wine-drinker. However, I think this argument specious; there will always be a market for what is usually an eminently drinkable wine, and there will always be the top-notch examples from this grape for which people will queue, if necessary.

Having said that, it is encouraging to taste the fantastic wines of those New World producers who are prepared to set the popular varieties aside in favour of grapes which they firmly believe are best adapted to their environment. The so-called Californian 'Rhône Rangers' spring to mind here; they are doing something really special, usually under-appreciated, and I am consequently looking forward to the day when we can drink more freely wines made from the Italian grapes (Nebbiolo and Sangiovese, for example) and those which hail from the New World's cool-climate regions, such as Gewürztraminer from Tasmania.

A Smart Move

We have all come to appreciate the efforts of the Flying Winemakers, but in their slipstream has come another equally important consultant, the Flying Vine Expert. As the New World is so fond of saying (and this is almost becoming clichéd now), good wine is made in the vineyard, an attitude which is now being grasped by parts of the Old World, too.

These experts zip in and out of vineyards, to assess how best to prune and trim the vines and to advise on suitable trellising systems (all summed up as 'canopy management'). There is some clear air turbulence in their contrail, however. Many believe that one has to work a vineyard for a full cycle to completely understand the nuances of its siting and to experience how the vines behave under year-round conditions.

Whichever side of the foliage wire you sit in this debate, there is no denying the fact that proper canopy management has been instrumental in maximizing potential flavours and assisting in the control of pests, most especially in cool humid areas where vine vigour is a problem, and the greatest exponent of this science is Australian viticulturist Dr Richard Smart, profiled in Chapter Two.

His research has proved that vigorous vines are easily capable of giving reasonable yields of high-quality grapes as long as the canopy is managed effectively, a view which is completely at odds with the traditional Old World belief that a vine has to struggle and be low yielding if its wines are to be of any worth.

Bearing in mind that the vine is a climbing plant, so it needs to be supported and kept in shape, this can be achieved by adopting a suitable trellis system such as Geneva Double Curtain, Lyre (or U), Minimal Pruned Cordon Trained, Ruakura Twin Two Tier, Scott Henry (invented by a former rocket scientist from Oregon), Smart-Dyson, Sylvoz (or Hanging Cane), Te Kauwhata Two Tier and Vertical Shoot Positioned.

Whichever training system is chosen, the focus is on achieving the correct distribution of foliage and grapes. There need to be enough leaves for photosynthesis – this provides vital sugar – but too many can block out the sunlight which the grapes require to ripen properly. An over-shaded canopy can therefore lead to reduced yields and poor grape quality with a strong herbaceous character, and it also has a knock-on effect for the following season, because the latent buds which will form next year's fruit are also masked from the sun.

An open canopy arrangement will also allow proper ventilation, which helps to protect the grapes from Flying Fungal Diseases, such as oidium (powdery mildew) or malevolent botrytis bunch rot, and in places where there is a high risk of frost, the vines can be trained high off the ground.

Irrigating a vineyard with overhead sprayers in Napa Valley, California, USA. In areas which are vulnerable to frost, this form of irrigation is a useful form of protection.

It is not simply a case of trellising, however. The density and spacing of vines in any given vineyard is also important in controlling yields, and overactive vine vigour can also be curtailed by planting companion crops such as chicory, clover, mustard and wild mint in between the rows. These also act as natural fertilizers, prevent soil erosion and encourage the birds that eat the insects which would otherwise feed on the grapes and leaves, or far worse, spread killer diseases such as leafroll virus or Pierce's Disease. The difficulty with this is that the birds can become an even greater pest in themselves. And on the subject of predators ... it takes more than cover crops or sound canopy management to protect vines from baboons, deer, squirrels, gophers, rabbits and kangaroos!

Drip Feeding

There are immense stretches of New World vineyards which rely on artificially applied water during the growing season – indeed, many of these vineyards would not even exist were it not for the fact that the land can be irrigated. Irrigation not only permits the cultivation and survival of the vines themselves, however; it provides tremendous opportunities for growers to influence the yield and the quality of their crop, and to many it forms an essential piece of kit in the vineyard management toolbox.

This contrasts completely with the attitude of the Old World, where even the word 'irrigation' is spat out in contempt by many growers. Such traditionalists believe that irrigated vines result in poor wines, but the cynic in me suggests this may be more a case of naked envy, because this practice is outlawed in European Union vineyards, with precious few exceptions. However, in the more northerly European countries, the point is utterly irrelevant; many years can be too wet quite naturally, much to the detriment of the grapes which become diluted and watery in character.

There is a bead of truth in the anti-irrigation argument, however, in circumstances where vineyards are over-irrigated, inadvertently or otherwise. Give the vine too much water and everything grows wildly – there are more leaves, more bunches per vine, more grapes per bunch and even the size of the grapes themselves is bigger, but the overall quality of the crop suffers. No two vines behave in exactly the same way (much depends on the weather in any given year, evaporation rates, soil permeability, individual vine vigour, the age of the vine and so on, even in some cool climate regions), so flood or furrow irrigation, where vineyards are drenched wholesale in water, allows very little control over the amount reaching each vine. It is nevertheless the cheapest method and is most useful in the production of inexpensive, everyday cask wines where high yields are the order of the day.

Spray irrigation is a more costly, but more controllable, form of applying water to vineyards as a whole. This works very well in areas which are particularly hot and dry because the chances of fungal infections (the chief hazard of any irrigation system) are reduced. It is also of benefit in spots which are vulnerable to spring frosts: according to basic principles of physics, a bud sprayed with water which then freezes is protected from frost damage by the insulating effect of its coat of ice.

Quite the best, albeit the most expensive, method of irrigation is drip or trickle irrigation where the pipeline becomes the lifeline. This system is far more sophisticated because it gives growers absolute control over the precise timing of irrigation. Moreover, all the grower has to do is to judge the optimum amount of water required for each vine to function at its most efficient and to balance yields against grape quality. And if the grower chooses that the vines should suffer mild levels of water stress – known as 'regulated deficient irrigation' (RDI) – then this is deemed all to the good in present-day thinking. It almost goes without saying that the more enterprising (and those who can afford it) use automated systems to measure soil moisture and to deliver the water to the vine, drop by drop.

Another advantage of drip irrigation is that it provides the most superior ready-made route via which fertilizers can be added to the soil. In unirrigated areas, vine roots usually have to dig deep and wide to find water, and will naturally absorb nutrients along the way. In irrigated vineyards, however, the root system tends to be huddled close to the surface (which is where the moisture is, after all), and so the vines often miss out on vital nourishment. This practice of mixing fertilizers with irrigation water is rather wonderfully described as 'fertigation'.

Irrigation is a word which is bandied about freely in the New World. Unfortunately, the water used to facilitate it is not. Some

Quite the best, albeit the most expensive, method of irrigation is drip or trickle irrigation where the pipeline becomes the lifeline.

Harvesting grapes in South Australia. A characteristic of New World methodology is to bring in the fruit when it is in peak condition.

countries are luckier than others – in South America, for example, meltwaters from the Andes provide limitless – and cheap – supplies of water to feed the irrigation infrastructure (first developed, incidentally, many thousands of years ago by the Incas), and in parts of Australia water can be diverted from the vast Murray-Darling and Murrumbidgee river systems at low cost.

In other places, however, the expense of conveying water to hillside vineyards and the thorny issue of water rights can make or break the potential of vineyard plantings and this may well prove to be an even bigger problem in the future, most especially if the model which predicts a global warming of 3–5°C (38–42°F) over the next 100 years proves to be accurate.

Reaping the Rewards

Given the choice, I would much prefer to sit at the wheel of a mechanical harvester than break my back picking grapes by hand. But is this actually the best way to bring in the crop? Does it make any discernible difference to the quality of the grapes, and therefore the wine?

This somewhat contentious issue is not a New World versus Old World debate, in fact, as both methods are practised in all areas, though it can be said that New World producers in particular have done much to champion the cause of mechanical harvesting (alongside mechanical planting, mechanical training, mechanical pruning, mechanical trimming and mechanical leaf-plucking for that matter).

To a large extent, this is because they are able to take advantage of economies of scale in so many of their vineyards. Unlike ancient Old World vineyards, New World vineyards can be planned properly and part of this planning is to plant the rows of vines at suitable distances apart to allow the ingress of motorized machinery, a procedure which is now being imitated in the new vineyards of the Old World. Furthermore, there are whole swathes of New World vines which are planted on dead flat land. It is impossible to use mechanical harvesters in sites located on steep slopes – indeed, as New World vineyards are gradually moving up onto the hillsides in the search for better quality, this problem is beginning to assert itself here, too.

As to the cost implications ... well the capital outlay may be considerable in terms of the vehicle itself and in constructing correctly dimensioned grape receival systems in the winery, but the mechanical harvester is usually cheaper to feed and house than a team of human grape-pickers. It can shake or beat grapes off vines at a rate of five man-hours per hectare compared with up to ten man-days per hectare, and it does not complain about working in the dead of night when it is cooler (critical to quality in hotter climates), or about working for 24-hour stretches. Furthermore, this speed gives producers an edge when it comes to deciding the exact timing of picking – the grapes can be harvested at the optimum moment.

Die-hard critics who reject mechanical picking (probably the ones who agree with the aphorism 'where ploughs go no vines should go') argue that a machine cannot select the best and the healthiest grapes for the job in hand – and to underline this, *Appellation Contrôlée* rules in France's Beaujolais and Champagne regions actually insist on hand-picking (mind you, some of their wines are made by pressing whole bunches, which would rule out mechanical harvesting anyway). This may have been true of the earliest models which harvested leaves as well as grapes (and often added a little protein to the crush in the form of snails and insects!), but these technical problems have largely been overcome.

The clear majority of scientific studies has proved that mechanical harvesting has no detrimental effect on grape quality and the consensus is that it offers more advantages than disadvantages overall, particularly with regard to costs – though this does not prevent even the staunchest of New World supporters of automation from milking every marketing opportunity to tell us about the 'superior' quality of their wines made from hand-picked grapes!

The clear majority of scientific studies has proved that mechanical harvesting has no detrimental effect on grape quality.

In the Winery

The Old World terroirist notion has always held that the winemaker is merely the custodian of nature's gift of grapes, which means in effect that the minimum is carried out by way of interventionist

Springtime mustard in a vineyard full of 100-year-old Zinfandel vines at Kenwood, Sonoma Valley, California, USA. The mustard is a highly rich source of nutrition.

Once the grapes have been unloaded and crushed, the juice (or for reds, the juice and skins) are pumped into the fermentation vessel. In the Old World, winemakers are more likely to rely on wild yeasts naturally present in the air to induce fermentation. New World winemakers, however, invariably inoculate their must with laboratory-cultured yeasts, which have a more predictable effect.

techniques when it comes to actually processing the grapes and making the wine.

Many New World winemakers, however, are forced to rely on technology if they are to make wines of quality, and moreover, they believe firmly in giving these wines their own personal stamp of flavour. As the late Max Schubert, creator of Australia's most famous, top-quality Penfold's Grange, once stated: 'It's so essential that a winemaker give some of his personality to his wine. His personality is part and parcel of the wine itself. The greatest wines have implanted in them the ideas of the winemaker as to what they should be. His character is part of the wine.'

To put these divisive points of view into some kind of balance one must consider two things. Firstly, the New World rarely experiences the Old World cultural legacy which dictates 'my father did it this way, and my grandfather, and his father before him, so this is the way I shall do it, too'. Of far more significance, however, is the fact that the majority of Old World wine producers have a cool climate on their side.

Long before the introduction of temperature-controlled fermentation (essential in preserving aroma and fruit flavours in white wines in particular), these winemakers had every chance of producing reasonable – if not fantastic – wines simply because low ambient temperatures in autumn kept fermentation temperatures in check quite naturally.

In the New World, however, where most of the vineyards and wineries are located in 'hot spots', the production of quality wine depends entirely on the artificial control of temperature. There is far more to the ethos of New World winemaking technology, of course, but I would suggest that temperature along the whole path of the winemaking process is the single most important factor to quality winemaking – without it, all other procedures render themselves quite pointless.

As in viticultural practice, New World winemakers are far less hidebound by tradition and strictly governed appellation rules and regulations, and in consequence they are more open-minded to innovation and experiment. Their approach is extremely scientific, but then one would expect that from highly trained oenologists who have learned their craft not at their father's knee, but rather at universities offering specialist winemaking degree courses.

The other advantage enjoyed by the New World is the fact that wineries can be purpose-built from scratch. Their design can accommodate serried rows of easy-to-keep-clean stainless steel tanks and tailored grape reception lines. Having said that, there are plenty of boutique wineries littering the New World which are primitive by anybody's standards, and there are very impressive state-of-the-art wineries in the Old World, too.

New World winemakers are the first to say that potentially fine grapes have often been mishandled by over-enthusiastic winemakers attempting to fashion them into styles of wine to which the grapes did not naturally lend themselves. They ended up with too much neutrality of flavour – the wines were indubitably well-made, fresh, clean and reasonably fruity, but the individual flair of character (an expression of terroir of all things, if you like) had been lost. We are now starting to see the adoption of winemaking procedures where the results bear an astonishing resemblance to those created by non-interventionist techniques – yet it has taken a deep understanding of technology to achieve this.

Honey, I Spoilt the Wine

When I contacted Randall Grahm of Bonny Doon in California to check that it was all right to profile him in this book, I asked him what his worst winemaking disaster had ever been. Honest to the very core, he named a few, but I was particularly intrigued by his reference to 'La Garrigue', a barrel-fermented Colombard which he chaptalized with 25 different types of honey. Sheer curiosity compelled me to question him more on this, and here is his reply:

'I had read, or more likely heard, about it being a particularly arcane Burgundian practice to chaptalize with honey (in homeopathic doses) to offer subliminal floral scents – those Burgundians always being up to something *hors de la carte*. Well why not push it a little bit further with a more substantial dose, I reasoned? The laws in California also bizarrely permit one to add honey but not sugar.

Literally the day after performing this exceedingly gooey operation on 40 or 50 odd barrels (odd being the operative word!) and creating the most unholy mess barrel sanitation-wise, I just happened to pick up Dr Chaptal's pamphlet extolling the virtues of the practice of sugar addition. The good doctor specifically mentioned that one can add cane sugar (preferred) and beet sugar (second choice), but *under no circumstances* should one ever add honey (there being problems with resultant clarity, filterability, etcetera, as I learned to my cost).'

Woodwork

Whether the wine is fermented in them or is simply aged in them, oak barrels across a wide range of sizes (typically holding anything from 225–1,200 litres/50–265 gallons) have always been part of the formula for premium wine production in the Old World. Astonishingly, however, oak barrels did not reach the New World until fifty odd years ago, pioneered by such luminary figures as Max Schubert in Australia and André Tchelistcheff in California.

Exactly what takes place remains one of nature's best-kept secrets, but the marriage between wine and wood is magical. Put wine into a barrel and it saps tannin, flavour and colour from the oak and, because wood is porous, it allows the wine to breathe, causing complex oxidative changes to its chemical make-up. The source of the oak itself also influences the porousness of the wood. The most-prized is French (from the forests of Alliers, Limousin, Nevers, Tronçais and Vosges) which contributes high levels of tannins and extract, though American oak is also popular, imparting a much sweeter and oakier taste to the wine.

However, New World winemakers experienced something of an uphill struggle to use oak to its best advantage at first. Many of the trailblazing oaked wines (whether they had been fermented and/or aged in it) tasted as if one was swallowing a floorboard. This owed much to the fact that the barrels were brand new (and possibly over-charred), which will always give big, toasty, vanilla flavours – previously used and/or bigger barrels reduce this effect.

But New World winemakers have also learned that each grape responds to oak in a different way. Riesling, for example, positively detests it and rolls over and dies if it even touches it. Many of the Italian varieties, such as Barbera and Sangiovese, prefer to keep a good distance from pale new oak or small-sized barrels. Good old Chardonnay, however, has a great affinity with it, to the extent that only relatively recently have we been able to buy unoaked Chardonnay from Australia.

The oldest working winery in Australia, dug in 1845 at Hardys Chateau Reynella.

It takes $600 or more to buy a 225 litres (50 gallons) barrique which will be used for four years only, so one of the huge advantages of New World winemaking freedom is that producers have been able to cut this cost by using inner staves (common in Australia and Chile, in particular) or oak chips (varying from shavings to one centimetre cubes, hence their jokey nickname *'Quercus Fragmentus'*). These are added during the fermentation process to give the oaky flavour and, used sensitively, can be perfect substitutes for the real thing in wines which are intended to be drunk young.

Such is the obsession with all things oaky, that an April Fool's Day jape run in *Decanter*

Pumping juice over the grape skin cap of Shiraz to extract colour and tannin. Brown Brothers' Winery, Milawa, Victoria, Australia.

magazine concerning oak 'tea bags' known as 'Chip Dips' was taken utterly seriously by many reputable companies! Perhaps this story serves to underline how utterly prepared we are to think that anything is possible in the New World....

Coming Over Hot and Cold

The New World may slowly be pushing into cooler viticultural areas, but the fact remains that the vast majority of its grapes still ripen under a very hot sun and temperatures are often rocket high at the time of harvest. One of the fundamental tenets of New World winemaking is to keep grapes in tip-top condition from the moment they are picked, so it is important that the grapes reach the winery as quickly as possible under these circumstances – the last thing that anyone wants is temperature-triggered premature fermentation before the grapes even arrive. Indeed, many New World growers pick their grapes at night when everything, including the grapes themselves, is much cooler.

In some cases, however, there is considerable distance between the vineyards and the winery, so the grapes have to be transported in refrigerated trucks or, indeed, the mountain is brought to Mohammed – field crushing facilities are becoming more of an everyday sight.

Once the grapes have been destemmed and crushed, the resultant must can be chilled to prevent oxidation and to postpone the onset of fermentation until it suits the winemaker (a delay which can often run into months in the case of some

Australian producers), a procedure which is particularly important in the production of white wine in hot countries. While this operation remains very much a New World speciality, its benefits are being recognized by producers in the Old World, too. The early 1990s witnessed the installation of France's first must chiller in the Languedoc region, for example, though I should point out that it was introduced by an Australian company making wine there.

Being able to hold unfermented white grape juice under refrigeration also allows the practice of cold stabilization whereby any remaining solid materials are given the chance to settle out. This has always been one of the hallmarks of New World winemaking, because it helps to give very clean and fresh wine. Some producers, however, are turning to cloudy juice fermentation in the belief that it adds complexity to the finished wine.

There is no point in carrying out all of the safeguards mentioned so far if fermentation temperatures are not carefully controlled, too. It is no accident that the very word 'fermentation' is derived from the Latin *fervere*, which means 'to boil'; left to nature, fermentation temperatures would reach runaway heights in hot countries and all aroma and fruit character would be driven off. Winemakers the world over now worship stainless steel for its ease of use in temperature control, though producers in the hot spots of the New World are particularly thankful because quality winemaking was simply not possible before its introduction.

After this praise for the merits of stainless steel, one might easily wonder why winemakers choose to ferment their premium wines in oak barrels. Quite simply, it is because the interaction between oak and fermenting wine gives superior flavours, though it must be said that temperature control is more difficult, especially in hot regions.

There is no doubt that refrigeration has empowered New World winemakers to make wines of internationally acceptable quality by mimicking the natural conditions of a cool climate. Many, if not all, of the above procedures are abhorred by Old World minimum interventionists.

A Breath of Fresh Air

Unlike many of their Old World counterparts, New World winemakers have a deep respect for air: it contains far too much of their arch enemy, oxygen, and to this end they attempt to exclude it as far as possible from every winemaking procedure when fresh, clean, everyday wines are being made (as ever, of course, there are the exceptions).

In hot regions, and most especially in areas where the vineyards are isolated from close-to-hand crushing facilities, this process begins as soon as the grapes are picked. This is particularly important for the more fragile white grapes; their thin skins are more liable to split during harvest, which exposes the pulp to air, and furthermore, their colour is very quickly affected by even a hint of oxidation. Blanket the grapes in inert gas, however, and

Barrels made in Spain of American oak, used for maturing 'sherry' at the Taylor Wine Company, Hammondsport, New York State, USA. In the hotter parts of the New World, barrels such as these need to be stored in an air-conditioned environment. Indeed, Giesen Estate in New Zealand has come up with a highly innovative system: they store their maturing wines in a series of refrigerated shipping containers, which means that they can individually control the temperature of each one.

oxidation is avoided. Indeed, protective measures such as this are far more important in white winemaking than red. Red wines are far less prone to oxidative change owing to higher levels of anti-oxidant phenolics gleaned from the grape skins – and it is harder to detect by colour, smell or taste.

'Reductive' techniques are all very well and good for the production of the 'anytime' standard of wine, but by the mid-1990s winemakers had begun to realize that, as long as it is controlled, a small amount of oxygen exposure prior to fermentation is essential to the crafting of fine wines, most especially those made from Chardonnay and Pinot Noir – indeed, a touch of the Burgundian Old World technique has crept in here. However, this was nothing startlingly new, really, even under New World winemaking methodology. After all, the oak barrel has been used throughout the New World for maturation purposes for around 50 years, so winemakers have always understood the mystical interaction between the wine which a barrel contains and the air which the oak breathes.

Which brings me to the downside of using inner staves or oak chips: the wines are denied the oxygen exchange which would happen naturally during a much longer period in barrel. While there are devices which can bubble oxygen through a wine in tank (a process called microboulage – just imagine tropical fish tanks), their supposed effect of simulating barrel ageing does not pass muster with me personally.

Keep it Clean!

You cannot feel them, you cannot smell them and you certainly cannot see them. But on every surface, at every touch and in every breath of air, there are zillions of microscopic bacteria, wild yeasts and fungi which, given the slightest opportunity, love nothing more than to feast on fermenting wine.

Without question, these little nasties can totally spoil wine, and what is worse, there is often no visible sign that it has been infected. This is especially true of warm, humid climates which demand even closer attention to winery hygiene. Bugs fester in these conditions and it only takes one to hop into the vat and a whole year's work can be ruined.

This is one of the reasons why New World winemakers adore stainless steel so much – it is so easy to clean. But it must be remembered that it takes a lot of water to keep it that way, and so the availability of an abundant supply of water is as critical to the winery as it is to the vineyard.

New World winemakers have long recognized the ratio of winery hygiene to wine quality, far more than many of their Old World cousins – this was one of the very fundamental improvements brought about by the Antipodean Flying Winemakers in parts of Europe, after all. Indeed, I shall never forget my first ever visit to a French winery where the owner quite nonchalantly threw the stub of his cigarette into an open-topped vat of fermenting wine. It gave a whole new meaning to the 'hints of tobacco' tasting note!

Finishing School

Freedom in winemaking is all very well and good, but each winemaker must adhere to his or her own country's set of regulations governing winemaking practices, permitted additives and so on, and furthermore, New World producers who wish to sell their wine within the European Union must also meet criteria which are often much stricter than those at home. The United States, for example, is currently in dispute with the European Commission over permitted maximum levels of sulphur dioxide, which are set much higher in the US by comparison with the EU.

In the ideal scenario, of course, where every grape picked is not only physiologically ripe, but is also chemically in balance, there would be no need for additives and other chemical tinkerings. The real world is not like that, however, and man very often has to intervene to put nature back in balance. After all, a cook in the kitchen has no qualms about adding a dash of salt or a sprinkling of pepper to a dish if it will enhance the naturally inherent flavours of the ingredients.

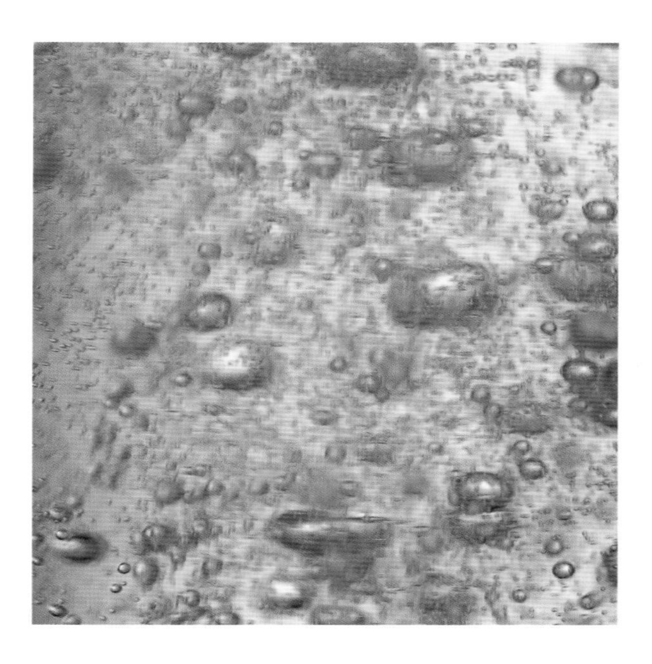

Too much oxygen is the scourge of the New World winemaker, but the carbon dioxide responsible for the bubbles in any sparkling wine deserves different consideration altogether.

Cork or Not?

An unacceptable face of the modern wine industry – New World or Old – is the growing problem of cork quality. Estimates vary depending on which propaganda report one reads, but anything between two and ten per cent of all wines are 'corked' at the time of opening. There is no missing this very nasty taint – the wine flaunts a truly offensive odour best summed up as dirty birdcage lined with damp cardboard, and you would have to possess a very poor sense of smell indeed to be able to bring the glass to your lips.

Spoilage is caused by the compound 2,4,6-trichloroanisole (TCA) which contaminates cork, though according to members of the cork industry, TCA has also been found in oak barrels. These same representatives also insist that no other bottle closure can match cork's elasticity, inertia, longevity, dependability and ability to protect wine from oxygen and/or leakage. Furthermore, they assert, cork is harvested from a renewable resource (the cork oak tree, *Quercus suber*) and it has an inimitable history as a stopper dating way back to 4,000 BC. As there was virtually no other way to close any type of bottle until the early part of the 20th century, this is hardly surprising, but if we were to extend the traditionalist argument to its logical conclusion, then we would still be drinking wine from amphorae and goatskins.

For centuries the humble cork was the only reliable seal for wine. This tradition is changing, as New World winemakers increasingly use plastic and other materials to bung their bottles. These new closures are completely airtight, which means that it is not necessary to store the bottles on their sides, a useful consideration in homes short of space.

The British retail wine trade in particular takes a rather more pragmatic view: if there is a more reliable form of bottle closure which will offer consumers a greater chance of drinking unspoiled wine, then it should be pursued with vigour. They have been lobbying the wine industry at large to change its closures and, to this end, thermoplastic elastomer stoppers, crown caps and screw tops are all options which are being explored.

In spite of the fact that the problem is a global issue, France is resisting the move away from cork by using the argument that wines will not mature in bottles closed with plastic corks because they cannot breathe through synthetic material. This is perfectly true, but trials have shown that bottle development is more likely to be the result of the oxygen which is dissolved in wine rather than the tiny amount of air which reaches it via the cork.

New World producers, however, are responding admirably – indeed, Australian wine giant Southcorp has very much been a pioneer in the research and market testing of alternative closures. No doubt they see the wisdom of keeping their British buyers happy, especially considering the importance of the United Kingdom market to their export trade. Nevertheless, their common sense runs deeper; why invest millions of dollars in top-grade vineyard development and hi-tech winery technology just to have their efforts – and reputation – ruined by a tiny, miserable piece of bark?

Influential Winemakers

New World wines could not have taken their formidable grip on the world market in such a short space of time without the strenuous efforts of a select band of men and women.

High-fliers

The winemakers behind the New World revolution

New World wines are clearly distinguished by two things in many people's minds – the fact that they are named after their grapes rather than châteaux, and the way that the same influential winemakers' names crop up time after time....

The cult of the winemaker is definitely a New World phenomenon. It began with people like Max Schubert in Australia, and André Tchelistcheff and Robert Mondavi in California in the 1950s and 1960s, consolidated later by the efforts of Australians such as Len Evans, Murray Tyrrell, Brian Croser, Dr Tony Jordan, Philip Shaw, Wolf Blass and so on.

But it was the 'Flying Winemaker' movement which did most to highlight the importance of the winemaker, a phrase first coined by Tony Laithwaite of *The Sunday Times* Wine Club in 1987. He formed an intrepid band of young, Australian-trained winemakers and sent them into under-exploited vineyards and wineries in obscure parts of Europe, and then into hitherto unexplored regions of the New World, where potential had never fully been realized. With the help of Australian technology and know-how, they provided a flying wine doctor service, turning low-grade bulk wine into good quality, exportable wonders.

As the concept expanded, other wholesalers and retailers commissioned independent winemakers to produce made-to-measure wines to suit their market needs, which in turn spawned a whole new generation of consultant winemakers and viticulturists (or winegrowers as they prefer to be styled). Nowadays, it is often the wineries themselves which will telephone for help, and nowadays it is not necessarily an Australian who will take the call. It will inevitably be New World attitude and technology which comes to the rescue, however.

The Flying Winemakers made all the headlines for their pioneering work in both the Old World and the New. But we should not overlook the quieter, less heralded efforts of New World winemakers who are achieving miracles within their own countries by pioneering new areas, new grapes and new techniques, and generally moving the industry forward on all fronts.

The following are just a few of the people whom I most admire for their pivotal work in bringing better wine to my table.

Peter Bright

A taste for the European lifestyle runs high amongst Australian winemakers, it seems. When Peter Bright first visited Portugal as consultant to João Pires Winery in 1978, it took him only two years to decide that he wanted to move there permanently. This must have made quite a change from Sydney and the outback, where he was raised, or Adelaide, where he studied viticulture and oenology at the famous Roseworthy Agricultural College (since merged with the University of Adelaide).

On graduation in 1977, Bright worked his winemaking magic for Hungerford Hill before taking his life-changing decision to leave Australia. However, you can take the man out of Australia, but you can't take Australia out of the man – his favourite wines, even after all this time, are based on Shiraz!

Once ensconced in Portugal, Bright continued to develop the João Pires range, and British consumers at the very least were soon being treated to wines such as João Pires Branco, Anfora and Bacalhoã, which did much to wean drinkers away from Mateus Rosé and other such Portuguese horrors.

In 1993, he left João Pires to set up his own company, Bright Brothers, and a year later he formed a joint venture company with Fiuza vineyard. Today, while Portuguese wines remain the crux of his business, the Bright Brothers portfolio has expanded to include wines from Italy and Spain, where he enjoys the challenge of crafting quality wines from local grape varieties – with great success, I might add. His most exciting developments, however, are taking place in Argentina, Chile and Uruguay, where he is producing a set of incredibly tasty wines.

Out of interest, I asked Bright what his greatest disaster ever had been: 'Becoming a winemaker. Now I don't know how to do anything else!' Well, wine-drinkers are very happy that he did and according to Bright we can expect to taste more Bright Brothers wines from all around the world in the future – particularly those from Australia.

Peter Bright, who feels that his greatest achievement so far has been 'in opening up the Argentine wine market in the UK, which was virtually nothing in 1994'.

Gaetane Carron

The bubbly and extraordinarily energetic Carron gained her degree in oenology from Dijon University in 1989, having quit her job to go back to university on discovering the joys of wine – 'It is never too late, *n'est ce pas*?' This action alone gives a clue to the personality of this Frenchwoman: she is not afraid to take risks, nor to work hard to achieve her goals.

After her first harvest in France, she headed across the Equator to work as a cellar hand at Australia's Rosemount Estate, where she learned most of the techniques which she so skillfully employs today. Of Rosemount she says, 'It was not like the Star Trek ship I had imagined, but you left the winery either hating it or hooked on winemaking forever.'

From there, Carron's travels took her to China, Oregon and California before she started working as an assistant winemaker during the 1991 vintage at Viña Errázuriz in Chile. Then it was back

Gaetane Carron, who describes Errázuriz in Chile as: 'Just like a scene from a Jacques Tati movie! I thought at the time that I had finally found an exciting challenge in life.'

Randall Grahm, who reckons that he will end up either as a very wealthy man, having made the world safe for Riesling and southern Italian grapes, or be clapped away in debtors' prison.

to Trimbach for a spell working on their 1991 vintage, too.

All this grounding proved invaluable on her return to Chile in 1992, when she was appointed resident winemaker at Viña Concha y Toro, in charge of two of their most prestigious wines. It was here that she started to make a name for herself and, though she would never say so herself, did much to transform the Chilean wine industry.

Carron then moved to Veramonte Estate in the Casablanca Valley in 1996 to do two harvests before returning to Europe, this time to the United Kingdom where she now works as Operations Manager for Western Wines – she had already spent her 1993, 1994 and 1995 annual holidays working for them in Italy and France! She now runs around Europe and South America, supervising the company's winemaking interests in Argentina, Chile, France, Greece, Spain and Portugal. Her mission is to raise the quality and broaden the diversity of wines in Europe by bringing her New World experiences to her job. Old World meets New World meets Old World.

I am left breathless by all of these achievements in just ten years – she also found time to have a baby! – but it is characteristic of Carron to end her résumé with, '*Voilà*! I think that is all!'

Randall Grahm

Something is afoot in California. One of the most entertaining and exuberant winemakers you will ever meet is beginning to think that 'The Rhône Ranger' epithet ascribed to him is 'a tad derivative'. Be that as it may, Grahm has been California's champion of classic Rhône grape varieties such as Grenache, Mourvèdre and Syrah in California. 'I am very proud of doing my bit to help conserve oddball, "ugly duckling" varieties,' he says, 'the world would be a poorer place for their disappearance.'

This crusade is not about one contrarian's dyspeptic view of Chardonnay, Merlot *et al*. Rather, Grahm feels that the fashionable grapes are not as well suited to California's Mediterranean growing conditions as the varieties of the southern Rhône, and has long sustained the argument for appropriateness in varietal plantings: 'We should be growing grapes in areas which best express themselves rather than seeking to exploit a momentary commercial opportunity.' He has certainly encouraged others to take a chance on the unknown by making the unknown a little less scary.

Grahm's winemaking career came about by accident. He majored in Liberal Arts at the University of California at Santa Cruz, and then found himself working in a wine store: 'Through exceptional fortune I was given the opportunity to taste a goodly number of great French wines and this singular experience turned me into a complete and insufferable wine fanatic.' Grahm returned to the University of California at Davis to complete a degree in viticulture in 1979.

He established his Lilliputian Bonny Doon facility in the Santa Cruz Mountains in 1983. The 'Great American Pinot Noir' for which he first strove proved elusive, but greatly encouraged by experimental batches of Rhône varietals – soon to become benchmark wines – he became ideologically committed to their prospects in California. The rest, as they say, is history – award was to follow award, and the Lowell Observatory even named the 'Rhône Ranger' asteroid in his honour!

As for the future, Grahm would like to be able to focus on one or two small things which he considers he can do very well, rather than being involved in the day-to-day operations of a winery ... 'I do hope that I will have the opportunity to prune grapevines and ride on a tractor again.'

Kym Milne MW

Every winemaker can woefully recount the tale of a particularly disastrous vintage, and Milne cites 1988 as his personal *annus horribilis*. At that time, he was chief winemaker at New Zealand's Villa Maria Estate – where he worked for eight years – and one week before they were due to harvest their Gisborne vineyards' Chardonnay, Cyclone Bola dropped nearly 41cm (16in) of rain on the crop.

This must have come as a true blow to a man heavily involved in turning Villa Maria from a struggling producer of mainly bulk wine into one of New Zealand's top sources of premium wines. It did his career no harm, however, as he was promoted to Chief Winemaker/Export Director of the Villa Maria Estate Group the following year.

Milne is actually Australian by nationality and prior to his move to New Zealand was employed as winemaker at Berri Estates Winery in South Australia, Australia's largest winery at the time. This was his first winemaking job on graduation from the celebrated Roseworthy Agricultural College where he gained his Bachelor of Applied Science (Oenology) in 1980. Eleven years later he passed the prestigious Master of Wine examinations at the first attempt, a very rare feat indeed.

While Milne is still a consultant for Villa Maria, in 1993 he based himself in the United Kingdom and launched several winemaking consultancy projects in France, Hungary, Italy (Puglia, Sicily, Trentino and Tuscany), South Africa and Spain. Indeed, he is proud of the fact that his winemaking projects on behalf of International Wine Services (of which he is a Non-executive Director) and Myliko have grown a business worth one million cases of sales in the UK in 1998 from nothing in 1993.

Kym Milne MW, who believes that winemaking is 'all about opening up new opportunities for suppliers, customers and, ultimately, consumers'.

Milne is not the kind of winemaker who whizzes round the world making wines which taste Australian. He prefers to work in partnership with the various wineries 'to make modern, accessible wines which maximize the fruit and varietal character of the vines as well as making the most of the climate, soil and so on'.

Dr Andrew Pirie

Pirie is one of the few Australian winemakers I know who does not look uncomfortable wearing a tie. He has the air of someone who is as happy in the boardroom as he is in the winery. His obvious business acumen has been proved with the recent acquisition of the Heemskerk Wine Group and the successful floating of his company, Pipers Brook Vineyard, on the Australian Stock Exchange in July 1998. The quality of his wines speaks volumes about the high standards of his winemaking.

So, canny Managing Director and talented winemaker rolled into one. But Pirie is no academic slouch, either – he trained as an agronomist at the University of Sydney (B.Sc. and M.Sc.) and has a Ph.D. in vine physiology.

One wonders why Pirie actively chose to make wine in Tasmania, a state whose name was hardly likely to be the first to roll off international wine-drinkers' tongues, particularly back in 1974 when the company was founded. He certainly could have selected a much easier environment in which to grow vines – this is cool climate territory, after all.

It was precisely this kind of cool climate, however, which provided Pirie with the conditions for which he was searching. His dream was to craft benchmark wines comparable to Burgundy and Bordeaux – ask him for his personal favourite style of wine and his reply is, 'An aged, complex Pinot Noir.'

Today, Pipers Brook is Tasmania's flagship wine company, producing a portfolio of internationally regarded premium estate wines. Furthermore, part of the magic of his wines is that Pirie is a passionate believer in the significance of terroir and regional authenticity: 'From the outset, Pipers Brook brands have been marketed with a distinctive regional identity, a philosophy which I believe has fostered the company's success.'

Pirie's plans for the future (this is a man who makes plans, after all) reflects ambition and utter dedication: 'We aim to be establishing Australian benchmark styles for Riesling, Gewürztraminer, Pinot Gris, Pinot Noir and sparkling wine. On the side, we have a large project to produce a Tasmanian Sauvignon Blanc which will rival the best of New Zealand.' Anyone who refers so nonchalantly to beating New Zealand at its own game deserves to be taken seriously.

Dr Andrew Pirie, who also holds a number of key wine and tourism industry positions. He is President of the Vineyards Association of Tasmania, is a member of the Australian Wine Export Council and is also a Director of Tourism Tasmania, a role which reflects his 'belief in the economic synergy of the wine and tourism industries'.

Ignacio Recabarren

Ignacio Recabarren, who recalls his first season at Viña Santa Rita: 'They made me work like a slave. I had a French winemaker on top of me at all times and he made me cry every day, but I just took it. I was afraid, but everything turned out great.' And somehow one can imagine those tears; Recabarren is an emotionally charged individual who thrives on nervous energy.

'The first thing a winemaker has to learn is to make mistakes; no winemaker is born completely wise.' This is an amazingly humble statement from Chile's most charismatic winemaker, whose list of honours runs to pages.

One wonders what would have happened if he had followed his first choice of career. Reading medicine at the Catholic University of Chile, he had the chance to study agronomy and winemaking soon took over his life. Five years of bulk winemaking in co-operatives led to a position at Santa Rita in 1978, and it was from here that he really started to make his mark.

In 1985, a longing for inspiration took Recabarren to California, Bordeaux (Châteaux Margaux and Lafite), New Zealand (Morton Estate and Cloudy Bay), and Australia, where he learned new skills from Philip Shaw at Rosemount and James Halliday at Coldstream Hills.

Charged with even more enthusiasm, he returned to Chile a year later, and has since made wine for Cono Sur, Viña Santa Carolina, Viña Casablanca, Viña Errázuriz, Viña La Rosa, Viña Porta and William Fèvre, and is currently making the 'Trio' brand for Concha y Toro. In particular, he championed Sauvignon Blanc at a time when it was deeply out of fashion.

Looking back on past achievements, Recabarren is most proud of his pioneering role in placing the Casablanca Valley onto the world wine map, and he is looking forward to making even better wines once he can utilize new clones and new grape varieties which have been grown in the right place. No doubt they will continue to emphasize the elegance, finesse and harmony between wine and terroir for which he restlessly strives.

Michel Rolland

At 52, and with five Bordeaux properties and an analytical laboratory to run, one might expect Rolland to have more than enough to do. But Rolland is also an inspirational winemaking consultant, finding time to advise other top Bordeaux producers, and to consult in Argentina, Chile, Hungary, India, Italy, Mexico, Morocco, Spain and the United States. All in all, he has about 90 clients.

His philosophy is simple: 'I like good wine! With good balance, fleshy, soft tannins, but powerful, deep. I love pleasure and charm. Sometimes complexity, if you cannot understand it, is boring.' In other words, he likes to make big, concentrated wines, but with the ripeness and accessibility to make them drinkable straightaway.

The very idea that a Bordeaux winemaker should hold such views surprises many. After all, this region is famous for wines which you keep forever before they are ready to drink. But Rolland took a

Michel Rolland, whose deepest regret is lack of time: 'Unfortunately, I am not able to work more. Time is a disaster. I am just beginning and I am already old.' But this does not stop him from saying, 'I would like to make more good wines everywhere in the world, with very different grapes. Winemaking is my hobby, but also every year is a new challenge because we have new grapes and different conditions. In five years, I will still be a winemaker looking for the best....'

more pragmatic approach when he started making wine at the family property in 1970, having completed his oenology degree: 'I began to think I'd chosen a rather boring career, since, in 25 years, I was likely to see only three great vintages, maybe fewer.' He realized that grape ripeness, low acidity and supple tannins were key to great wines, characteristics which form the Rolland signature. This signature has led to the criticism that all of his wines taste alike – not a view I share, incidentally – but Rolland is emphatic that he is careful not to lose regional character.

Rolland is Old World by geography, but New World in attitude. He is fanatical about winery hygiene and temperature control, for example, and recognizes the importance of harvesting good grapes. He nevertheless believes that wine should reflect its terroir and is not in favour of over-manipulation.

Dr Richard Smart

The 'Flying Vine Doctor', the world's most celebrated and experienced viticulturist, has dedicated over 30 years to the scientific study of grape vines, high vigour vineyards and canopy management. His seminal work, *Sunlight Into Wine*, turned traditional viticultural beliefs on their head by suggesting that yields can be increased without sacrificing quality, and he has done much to promulgate the maxim that good wine is made in the vineyard, raising the profile of the professional viticulturist – 'the real winemaker!' – along the way.

A former Dean at Australia's prestigious Roseworthy Agricultural College, Smart's list of qualifications is impressive: B.Sc. (Hons II) in Agricultural Science (Sydney), M.Sc. (Hons) (Macquarie), Ph.D. (Cornell) and D.Sc. Agric. (Stellenbosch) and he has authored or co-authored over 220 technical publications. His greatest satisfaction, however, derives from having been part of the scientific team led by the godfather of canopy management, Professor Nelson Shaulis of Cornell, which demonstrated the significance of canopy microclimate on wine quality, back in the 1970s. He is also proud of his work as Government Viticultural Scientist in New Zealand in the 1980s: 'I helped lay the technical foundations for an emerging, quality-oriented and internationally competitive wine industry.'

He left academia in 1991 to become a consultant, and Smart Viticulture now has over 200 clients in 16 different countries. His expert advice, most especially on trellis systems and pruning, has made a real difference to the way in which grapes are grown, especially where growers are actively seeking to improve quality.

It has not always been plain sailing. There are some who oppose his ideas, most particularly the French, who see Smart as a critic of the appellation system ... which is going to be interesting in light of part of his next perceived great challenge: 'I want to help some of the Old World producers use some better technologies and overcome some of their prejudices to make them more internationally competitive – this is beginning to happen in Iberia. And, of course, to continue to help the burgeoning New World, especially in the southern hemisphere.'

John Worontschak

It is typical of Worontschak's modesty that when you ask him what he feels his greatest achievement has been so far (he is only 38), he instantly replies, 'Becoming a father!' Prompt him more, however, and eventually he says, 'Without question, the impact that I had on the English wine industry. I had the knowledge to go to a totally unprofessional industry and improve on it'.

And he certainly has the knowledge. Born in Australia to Ukrainian immigrants, Worontschak was reading Geology at Adelaide University when a summer job at Petaluma winery was to profoundly change his life. He developed such a passion for wine and its production that he commenced a B.Sc. course in Oenology at the Charles Sturt University in Wagga Wagga in 1981.

On graduation, he consolidated his skills by working as assistant winemaker to Colin Campbell of Campbell's winery in Rutherglen and as a cellar hand at Saltrams in the Barossa Valley before embarking on a self-financed five-year world tour. By hemisphere-hopping to follow the seasons, Worontschak enhanced his knowledge at Yalumba and Penfolds in Australia, Clos du Bois in California, Hugel in Alsace, and Domaine Tim Marshall in Burgundy.

He settled in England, soon building up a successful business (now named Four Corners Consultancy) which was to revolutionize the English wine industry. Proximity to the continent fuelled a latent Europeanism, so it was no surprise that in 1993 the suitcases were out again and a Flying Winemaker was born. Worontschak's first venture was to the Czech Republic where 'to my surprise they understood my Ukrainian and to their surprise I didn't understand their communist ways!' Flying Winemaker projects have since taken him to Argentina, Canada, Chile, Mexico and Israel, and he is also a consultant for wineries in England, Mexico, Israel and South Africa.

Dr Richard Smart, who believes that: 'The most open-minded producers are in New Zealand, South America, and Australia; much of Europe is at the back of the pack, constrained by traditional beliefs.'

John Worontschak, whose philosophy is a hybrid of New World and Old. He believes that strict procedural and analytical controls should be blended with local ways where possible: 'I am not out to standardize, but to ensure a consistency of quality that must be expected in the late 20th century and combine this with the magic and excitement of discovering the unexpected and stimulating.'

Australia

This vast country has had an incalculable impact on the world wine market in recent years. Australia now produces some of the most exciting wines of modern times.

Wine Down Under

Quality and variety from the end of the earth

Of all the countries of wine's New World, it is probably Australia which has made the biggest impact in recent years. Blessed with an extraordinarily varied climate and topography, this huge country is responsible for some truly great wines.

Any first-time visitor to Australia who has had to resort to piling on yet another sweater to keep warm, or wring out their so-called waterproofs in the wake of a sudden torrential downpour, will agree that one soon shakes off any preconceived image that Australia is made up of one vast stretch of *Crocodile Dundee*, *Song Lines* and *Flying Doctors* territory. The outback is there in all its splendid glory, of course, but the country is fringed by a much cooler and greener land, especially in the extreme south and its corners and islands.

One can draw a similar analogy with Australian wines, too. Ask the average punter in the average British high street if he or she likes Australian wine and they will probably say 'yes' unhesitatingly. I am not being unkind here, but there will be few who will consider their answer and say something like, 'Yes, on the whole, but I prefer Tasmanian wines to those of Riverland.' These are random examples of just two Australian wine regions, but the difference between them is immense in every respect. The diversity of regional geography in Australia is enormous, and I cannot labour this point enough.

Interestingly, for many years the provenance of grapes was not of tremendous importance to many sectors of the Australian wine industry itself, either. As long as marketable styles of wines from popular grape varieties could be made to meet critical price points, the fruit was trucked into wineries from all over the country and blended together to produce glorious brands of bottled sunshine – and, in many instances, this still applies today.

There are arguments for and against this practice, of course. Winemakers are given the freedom to select the finest grapes for the task in hand, regardless of their origin. Some of the most popular brands are fashioned from fruit which hails from a number of different states (let alone regions). For example, Oxford Landing's only claim to origin is 'South Eastern Australia', yet it is a more than acceptable and highly reliable brand.

The ensuing loss of intrinsic regional identity, however, has led to accusations of an homogeneity of style and taste which owes far more to winemaking intervention and winemaker philosophy than individual terroir. Where this is true it seems such a shame because there is a largely unexploited treasure trove of highly individual, regionally-oriented wines just waiting to be discovered.

One of the most abiding strengths of the Australian wine industry is its dynamism and its willingness never to stand still. Australia may not be the oldest (or, indeed, the youngest) of the New World winemaking countries, but there is absolutely no doubt that it remains at the forefront and is one of the most technologically advanced wine industries in the world. A word of warning, however; no less than 84 per cent of the market is controlled by just ten very powerful companies (from a total of 1,101, though a new winery is born every 48 hours according to the latest issue of the *Australian & New Zealand Wine Industry Directory*), and the industry's four leviathans – Southcorp, BRL Hardy, Orlando Wyndham and Mildara Blass respectively – account for almost 70 per cent of the production of branded wine.

Over 680,000 bottles of wine now leave Australia every day, supplying 82 international markets (the United Kingdom represents the biggest export market, taking almost 46.8 per cent of all wine export sales and, at the latest count, nearly one in every ten bottles of wine drunk in the UK hails from Australia). Exports in 1998 rose in volume by 16 per cent against 1997 and domestic sales have increased by 1.6 per cent over the same period. 1998 saw 78,709 hectares of vines yielding 646,000 tonnes of premium grapes (68 per cent of the total crush), with Chardonnay, Shiraz, Cabernet Sauvignon, Semillon and Riesling leading the field.

After this build-up, you would be forgiven for thinking that Australia is top dingo in global terms, yet its influence is out of all proportion to its contribution to the world wine pool – Australia ranks as the tenth largest producer producing just 2.5 per cent of world wine share by volume. One Californian company alone, the wine supremo Gallo, makes half as much wine again as the whole of Australia.

The implementation of Strategy 2025 is expected to bring about strong growth in the future, however, and continued diversification will be an excellent marketing tool. Australia can optimize resources to produce a highly varied portfolio of wine styles; in this way, the industry can supply the full spectrum of market demands, keep pace with changes in market forces and challenge foreign competition by increasing market share.

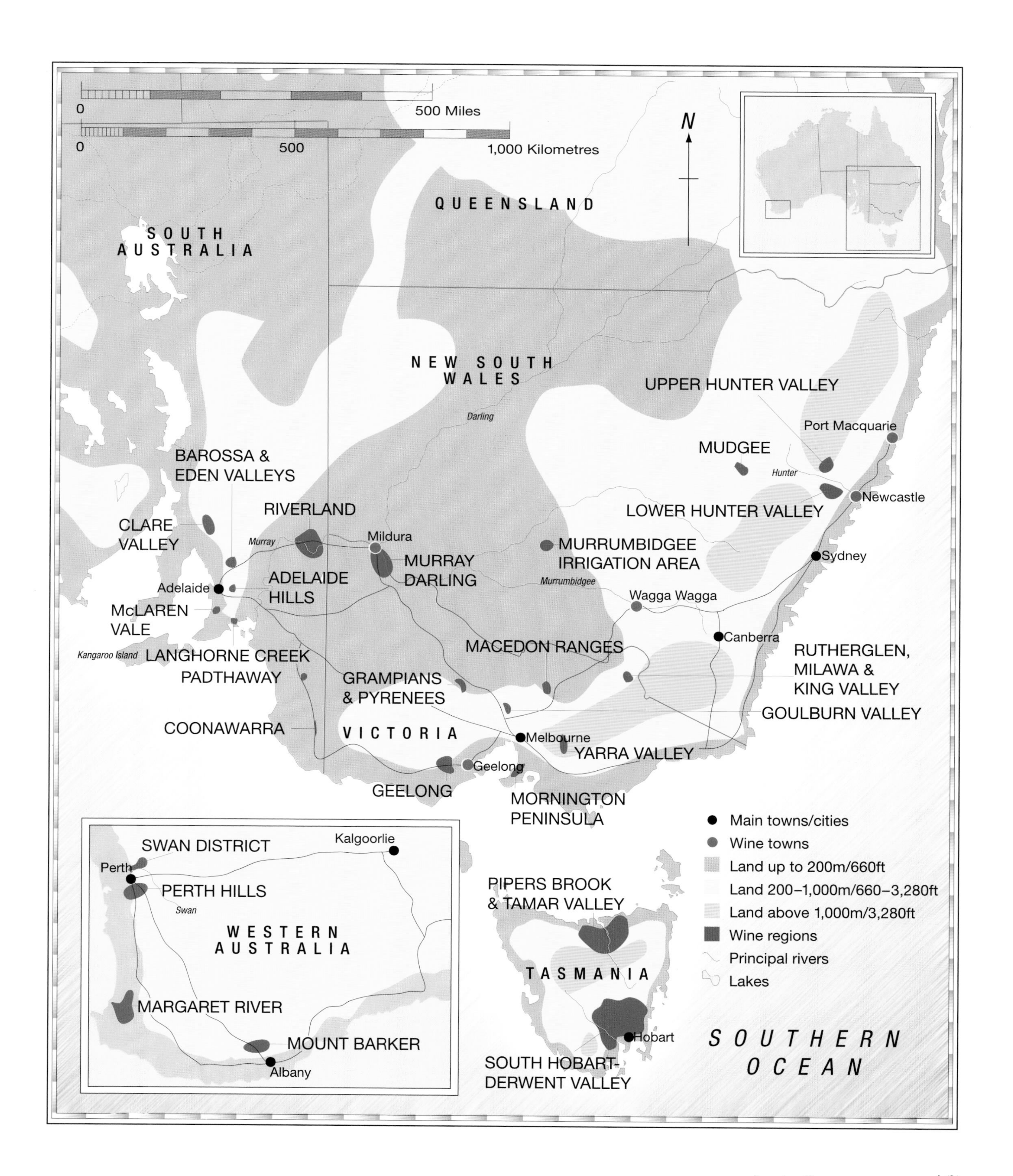
0
500 Miles
0
500
1,000 Kilometres
N
QUEENSLAND
SOUTH AUSTRALIA
NEW SOUTH WALES
UPPER HUNTER VALLEY
Darling
Port Macquarie
MUDGEE
Hunter
BAROSSA & EDEN VALLEYS
Newcastle
LOWER HUNTER VALLEY
RIVERLAND
CLARE VALLEY
Murray
Mildura
MURRUMBIDGEE IRRIGATION AREA
MURRAY DARLING
Sydney
ADELAIDE HILLS
Adelaide
Murrumbidgee
Wagga Wagga
McLAREN VALE
Canberra
MACEDON RANGES
RUTHERGLEN, MILAWA & KING VALLEY
Kangaroo Island
LANGHORNE CREEK
PADTHAWAY
GRAMPIANS & PYRENEES
GOULBURN VALLEY
COONAWARRA
VICTORIA
Melbourne
YARRA VALLEY
Geelong
GEELONG
MORNINGTON PENINSULA
SWAN DISTRICT
Kalgoorlie
Perth
PERTH HILLS
Swan
WESTERN AUSTRALIA
MARGARET RIVER
MOUNT BARKER
Albany
PIPERS BROOK & TAMAR VALLEY
TASMANIA
Hobart
SOUTH HOBART-DERWENT VALLEY
Main towns/cities
Wine towns
Land up to 200m/660ft
Land 200–1,000m/660–3,280ft
Land above 1,000m/3,280ft
Wine regions
Principal rivers
Lakes
SOUTHERN OCEAN

Highlights of History

1788

The very first Australian vineyard is planted at Farm Cove in Sydney Harbour (not far from where the Opera House now resides) by the colony's first Governor, Captain Arthur Phillip of the Royal Navy. En route to Sydney with the First Fleet, he has collected vine cuttings and grape seeds from such disparate places as Madeira, the Cape of Good Hope and Rio de Janeiro, so it is probable that they are the kind of hardy grapes used to make fortified wines. They are of immense significance as Australia has no indigenous grapes.

1800

In the desire to develop the Australian potential for winemaking (after all, it would be advantageous for Britain to have its own source of wine), the British Government despatches two French prisoners, de Riveau and Landrien, to Australia to establish vineyards and teach the skills of winemaking. The deal is that they spend three years here in exchange for their freedom. This is all very well and good, but a huge assumption has been made: that all French nationals know everything there is to know about viticulture and vinification, which is patently not true in this case! The best they can achieve is to create cider from peaches!

1803

Back in Sydney, a newspaper article promotes the value of drinking wine. By this stage, the country has become a nation of rum guzzlers and there is widespread drunkenness. The wines made are turned into a port style because this was the type of wine which the new immigrants were accustomed to drinking back in Britain.

1805

Captain John Macarthur, who has pioneered the Merino sheep industry, is given 3,400 hectares of land along with 34 convicts to work it. Forced to return to England in 1809, he uses his time in exile to study the French wine industry. On his return to Australia, he transports vine cuttings for further experimentation, and by the 1820s Macarthur is making wine on a commercial basis.

1823

Tasmania's first vines are planted by Bartholomew Broughton, a pardoned convict, at Prospect Farm in New Town, Hobart and, by 1827, he is able to offer 1,300 litres (286 gallons) of wine for sale. History does not record anyone actually buying any of it during Broughton's lifetime, but on his death in 1828, one Captain Swanston buys the property and, as production rises five-fold over the following 20 years, we can assume that the wines are indeed drinkable. In this year, Gregory Blaxland wins a silver medal in London for his fortified red wine made from grapes grown at his Parramatta estate.

1828

Vines are planted in the Upper Hunter Valley by George Wyndham at Dalwood and William Kelman at Kirkton, though early enthusiasm soon fades. The area is not to become important until the 1960s when Rosemount begins to plant new vineyards here.

1829

The first vineyards are established in the Swan District, though it is unclear who plants them. It is known that Captain John Septimus Roe grows table grapes at this time, but botanist Thomas Waters at Olive Farm may be cultivating grapes to make wine, too. Either way, the Swan District predates both Victoria and South Australia in viticultural terms, and for almost 150 years is the only significant wine-producing region in Western Australia.

1830

Following a wages dispute with Governor Darling, James Busby, who is generally credited as the 'father of Australian wine', returns to Europe and sets out on a vinous fact-finding tour. He returns with 570 different varieties of vine specimens which are distributed evenly between the Botanic Gardens in Sydney (which are subsequently lost through neglect) and his farm in the Lower Hunter River Valley, a location which he has recognized as being suitable for the cultivation of superior grapes. Of equal importance, however, is his zealous will to educate fellow vine-growers on improved methods of winemaking.

1835

William IV grants over 3,000 hectares of land in the Swan District to Henry Revett Bland, who sells it to three British army officers, Houghton, Lowis and Yule, even though they are stationed in India. Interestingly, while it is Yule who travels to Australia to set up and manage a winery (the state's first commercial example), its name is taken from the absent Colonel Houghton – indeed, he is never to visit Australia!

1837

Colonial surveyor Henry Fancourt White plants the first vineyard in Hastings Valley. Barton Hacl also establishes a vineyard near Adelaide in South Australia, though it is uprooted only three years later in the cause of urban expansion.

1838

John Reynell plants grapes at Reynella in the McLaren Vale and employs a labourer called Thomas Hardy, laying the foundations of the two dynasties which are to dominate the region for over a century to come. In the same year, William Ryrie plants the first Yarra Valley vineyard and viticulture spreads rapidly.

1840

Scottish merchant banker and philanthropist, George Fife Angas, buys 10,900 hectares of land in the Barossa Valley. He offers asylum to Lutheran Silesian peasant farmers who are seeking refuge from religious persecution (they have refused to annex their church to the State Church of Frederick III, King of Prussia), and a stream of other German settlers soon follow. Some seven years later, the vines which they have planted are flourishing and the first commercial wines are produced by Johann Gramp at Jacob's Creek, named after William Jacob who surveyed the area in 1841.

1843

After three years of medical practice in the Lower Hunter Valley, British surgeon, Dr Henry John Lindeman, is granted land at Cawarra and plants vines. In spite of a devastating fire which forces him to start over, he is to become a prominent and much-respected figure within the wine industry.

1844

Dr Christopher Rawson Penfold emigrates to South Australia from England and, for £1,200, purchases 200 hectares of farmland at Magill, in the foothills of the Mount Lofty Ranges, some eight kilometres (five miles) from the infant settlement of Adelaide. He plants the French vine cuttings which he has brought with him and starts to make fortified wine – but purely for medicinal use by his patients. As the demand for his wine grows, further vineyards are planted and at some point in the 1850s wine takes over from medicine as the family's chief source of income.

1847

The British Government allows non-British emigration to the colony for the first time. The impact within the wine industry is inestimable because it means that trained labourers can be brought in to work the vineyards and wineries.

1858

The first vineyards in Mudgee are planted by Italian-born surgeon and head of Sydney Hospital, Dr Thomas Fiaschi, though only one winery has survived come 1960. The revival of the Hunter Valley in the late 1960s is also to awaken interest in Mudgee.

1860

Chateau Tahbilk founds the first commercial winery in Victoria. Rather incredibly, some of its Shiraz vines are still alive today thanks to the outcropping sandy soils which have held phylloxera at bay.

1870

No-one quite knows why, but the fledgling Tasmanian wine industry simply ceases to exist. One theory is that cheap labour has rushed away to take advantage of the mainland's Gold Fever. Meanwhile, over on the mainland, New South Wales, South Australia and Victoria produce 8.7 million litres (1.9 million gallons) of wine between them in this year.

1875

Phylloxera is first discovered near Geelong and, in spite of the fact that it is known that the problem of dying vines can be overcome via grafting on to American rootstock, the government's reaction is to compel growers to rip out their vines which effectively shuts down the wine industry here for around 100 years.

1884

Another flutter of interest is witnessed in Tasmania when Italian silk merchant, Diego Bernacchi, plants vines on the rocky Maria Island, a former whaling station turned convict settlement off the east coast. The venture is soon abandoned, however, when he is declared bankrupt.

1889

Victoria passes the Planting Bonus Bill which offers £2.00 for every acre of vines planted in the state. Some 12,000 acres of vineyards are planted as a result, but the wine is so poor (because it is being made by people who have not the faintest idea about viticulture or vinification) that it almost irrevocably shatters the reputation of Australian wines in London.

1890

Coonawarra, the Aboriginal word for 'wild honeysuckle', is first planted to vines.

1900

Seppeltsfield, in the Barossa Valley, is now Australia's largest winery, producing two million litres (440,000 gallons) annually.

1901

Australia becomes a Federation and all tariffs on wines between states are abolished – in essence, only the fittest will survive from now on.

1912

The main irrigation channel of the Murrumbidgee Irrigation Scheme, designed by Walter Burley Griffin, and fed by the Burrinjuck Dam, reaches the town of Griffith.

1927–39

The United Kingdom imports more wine from Australia than it does even from France thanks to the Imperial Preference system. Most of this is fortified wine or table wine bearing the infamous Emu brand.

1930

South Australia is now producing over 75 per cent of Australian wine, though this is soon to become rather irrelevant in the face of the Depression, which will see domestic sales slump by 60 per cent, export volumes fade and many growers turn to the farming of cattle or sheep.

1939–45

The Second World War sees exports drop from 17 million litres to just 3.7 million (3.7 million to 800,000 gallons), a fall which is driven by U-boat activity and British embargoes on wine and spirit imports. However, domestic demand soars thanks to quota systems and the extra presence of United States servicemen, who are quite content to drink wine in place of their usual beer which is in short supply.

1944

Some 60 vine-free years have passed before a true – and lasting – renaissance in wine in Tasmania comes about with the founding of the Moorilla Estate on the River Derwent near Hobart by refugee textile magnate Claudio Alcorso.

1950s

Cold fermentation techniques in stainless steel are introduced by Orlando, which is to revolutionize the quality of Australia's white wines. Coonawarra also attracts the interest of the bigger wine companies.

1951

Following a visit to Europe, Penfolds' Max Schubert produces the first experimental vintage of Grange Hermitage, the legendary Shiraz-based red wine inspired by the magnificent, long-lived Cabernet Sauvignon-based red wines of Bordeaux. Today, it is considered as Australia's only 'First Growth'.

1960s

New technology in the winery and the simultaneous development of the bag-in-box industry inspires a boom in wine-drinking. The famous wine cask has been born.

1964

Seppelt pioneers cool climate viticulture at Drumborg and at Keppoch.

1974

Quite definitely the most influential winemaker in Tasmania, the pioneering Dr Andrew Pirie of Pipers Brook Vineyard, begins planting vines in the Pipers Brook-Pipers River district of the Tamar Valley.

1978

Margaret River establishes Australia's first state-approved Appellation of Origin system.

1979

Mudgee unilaterally declares itself as an appellation, though this is not officially backed by state legislation.

1994

As part of a trade agreement with the European Union, Australia agrees to introduce an appellation system. While one of Australia's traditional strengths has been the freedom to blend wines between regions (and, indeed, states), it is forcing producers to think more about individual sites and terroirs.

1995–96

For the first time ever, annual per capita consumption of soft drinks (115.2 litres/25 gallons) exceeds that of beer and wine combined (113.6 litres/24.5 gallons), owed in all probability to a combination of economic recession and stringent drink-driving laws.

1996

Strategy 2025 is launched by the Winemakers Federation of Australia.

Geographic Indications

One of the most dramatic changes to the Australian wine industry is being brought about by the introduction of a legally defined 'Geographic Indication' system – in reality, a hierarchy of viticultural superzones, zones, regions and sub-regions – which is tortuously being mapped in order to satisfy European Union and United States trade agreements (hugely important given the export dependency on the UK and the US).

No doubt the whole concept is causing angst to those members of the industry who are opposed to any kind of appellation system (though one assumes that they have quite happily adhered to the guidelines of the Label Integrity Programme up until now) and, initially, there was much head-scratching over the problem of how to accommodate the practice of cross-state and inter-regional blending. Despite all the deliberation, this has already proved irrelevant, with the definition of the South Eastern Australia zone which incorporates the whole of New South Wales, Victoria and Tasmania, and parts of Queensland and South Australia ... covering 95 per cent of Australia's vineyards, in fact! Another similar zone is Big Rivers, which encompasses the large irrigated regions of the Murray and the Darling Rivers.

In any case, the industry is adept at brand management. Grange sets the prime example: the label tells us virtually nothing about the source of the grapes – and, even if you ask, Penfolds will not reveal their source – yet it is Australia's equivalent of a First Growth Bordeaux. It is also open to debate whether the average consumer, however discerning, cares one jot about the precise origin of, say, Jacob's Creek (the top selling Australian brand in the United Kingdom); it is quality and value which will remain the crucial factors.

Whilst one can sympathize with the objectives of the protectionist European Union, Australia has never found it necessary to rely upon the prop of bureaucracy to make, market or, indeed, sell its wines.

New South Wales

'In a climate so favourable, the cultivation of the vine may doubtless be carried to any degree of perfection ... the wines of New South Wales may perhaps hereafter be sought with avidity and become an indispensable part of the luxury of European tables....'

So wrote Captain Arthur Phillip in 1788, thus demonstrating remarkable prescience, for today New South Wales fashions some very classy wines across the full range of styles in a climate which can actually be tricky in places, even with cutting edge technology at hand to iron out potential problems. A strong vitivinicultural tradition runs deep in this state, but it is by no means buried in history and neither is it merely standing still ... as the opening up and development of new regions clearly confirms.

Hastings River

This hilly, northerly area is eclipsed by just one winery, Cassegrain, though there were no less than 33 during the 1860s. As was common throughout many wine regions, however, the industry vanished in the early 1930s and was not resurrected until 1980. The extremely wet (1,280mm/50in annually), very warm and very humid maritime climate poses a real challenge to viticulture here, yet Cassegrain's example of meticulous canopy management and critical choice of picking dates has inspired the development of other vineyards along the northern coast of the state.

Inert gas plays its role when wine is being transported in bulk, when all the valves and seals and empty spaces have to be blanketed from potential oxygen damage.

Hunter Valley

A friend who lives here describes how she climbs into woolly jumpers first thing in the morning, but has stripped off to a bikini by lunchtime – the searing heat of the day then plunges dramatically again come nightfall. This kind of ding-dong climate provides a haven for grapes and, without doubt, the Hunter Valley is the source of Australia's finest Semillon and Shiraz.

From its renaissance in the early 1960s, the workhorse Upper Hunter Valley has established a reputation for white wines. It is slightly hotter, drier and less humid here compared with the Lower Hunter Valley and the irrigated vineyards on well drained and moderately fertile, black silty loams yield relatively high crop levels, so the wines tend to be light in style. This can sometimes be exacerbated by rainfall during

January and February – the peak harvest months – which dilutes the grapes. Yet producers such as Rosemount (at their Giant's Creek and Roxburgh vineyards) nevertheless craft soft, buttery, creamy Chardonnays and early-maturing (peaking at two to four years of age), fleshy Semillons, the two principal varieties of the Upper Hunter Valley. Look out, too, for Cabernet Sauvignon-Merlot blends and Pinot Noir which are showing signs of future promise.

Current statistics for the Lower Hunter Valley reveal that plantings of Chardonnay, Semillon and Shiraz are roughly equal (at about 450 hectares apiece), but just for once it is not Chardonnay which takes the limelight; the life blood of this district is its magical Semillon and Shiraz which have the propensity to age for decades. Cabernet Sauvignon, which was reintroduced to the Hunter Valley by Dr Max Lake in 1963, is also ubiquitous within the district, though it gives protean results. Of the plethora of other wines made, either as straight varietals or as blends, it is Verdelho which is arguably the most interesting.

Roxburgh vineyard of Rosemount Estate covers an area of 150 hectares at an altitude of around 250m (820ft) in the Upper Hunter Valley. In fact, it is a miracle that wine is made here at all; this is one of the hottest spots in Australia, and if it were not for the cooling effect of high rainfall (750mm/30in per annum), high humidity, cloud cover, thunderstorms and sea breezes, viticulture would be virtually out of the question. The heat wave experienced in 1998, for instance, when growers had to race to bring in their grapes before they became overripe, demonstrated how fragile the balance can be.

Mudgee

The 'nest in the hills' (to translate the Aboriginal) lies over to the western side of the Great Dividing Range, just across from the Hunter Valley, yet it could not be more different – indeed, growers such as Botolobar, Huntington, Miramar, Montrose, Rosemount and Thistle Hill believe the region to be so unique that they established their own appellation in 1979.

Principal Grape Varieties

Approximately 75 different grapes are grown commercially in Australia, and in 1998 white varieties comprised 51.6 per cent of the total area under vine. This represented a drop of nearly six per cent on the previous year as recently planted (and desperately needed) red varieties are beginning to bear fruit.

Cabernet Sauvignon

When made well from grapes of optimum ripeness, Australian Cabernet Sauvignon can be breathtaking; indifferent winemaking using overripe grapes, however, renders a liquid which invariably tastes more like a wishy-washy blackcurrant jam than wine. Having said that, if I was forced into a position where I had no choice but to buy an inexpensive Cabernet, then I would always opt for an Aussie version – at least it would always taste fruity. Give me fruit, however jammy, over the thin, dusty taste of cheap Claret any day.

While the variety is grown in all wine regions (contributing 97,800 tonnes of fruit in 1998), it is climate which dictates the detail of individual character. In cool areas, the wines lean towards taut, herbaceous and grassy styles, but give the maturing grapes plenty of warmth and sunshine, and the wines become more solid in structure, flaunting riper aromas and tucker-bags full of rich blackcurrant, mulberry, chocolate and redcurrant flavours – at times perhaps rather too much so, but arguably too much is better than too little. Then, of course, there are the wines which fall between both stools.

Cabernet Sauvignon very often turns up in blends, too – it has a particular affinity to Shiraz in Australia, but is also good teamed with Cabernet Franc and/or Merlot.

Chardonnay

There was a time when the phrase 'judicious use of oak' would not have been a familiar part of the vocabulary of most Australian winemakers, but this is not so true anymore. While some wines remain at the syrupy, hot toast and melted butter end of the taste spectrum, a far greater number are now being made to a more restrained style – the fruit is still exuberantly evident, but they have acquired a sophistication, structure and complexity hitherto untasted. This is slightly unfair to the cooler regions, which have always created wines to this style, most especially Margaret River, arguably the source of Australia's finest Chardonnay.

It is hard to believe in some respects that a grape variety which Australia has almost single-handedly popularized worldwide was hardly planted here 30 years ago; 173,000 tonnes of grapes were harvested in 1998, however, and it is currently the most widely planted premium grape in Australia.

Grenache

For many years this was a bedrock variety of very basic, inexpensive table wines and fortified wines – mainly because over-cropping turned out pretty mediocre stuff and no-one knew better. A growing understanding of this variety, however, alongside the discovery of some ancient vines, has turned the ugly duckling into a swan. Some terrific varietal wines are now being made from this grape, which is often blended with Mourvèdre and Shiraz to make Rhône-style wines.

Muscat

Vineyards along the Murray-Darling River churn out copious quantities of bag-in-box Muscat of Alexandria (often described as Gordo Blanco) which is just about acceptable if you favour sweetish gluggers. By far the best wines, though, are charmed from the Brown Muscat, a strain of Muscat à Petits Grains, which is turned into heavenly, to-die-for liqueur wines. These are the kind of strawberry, honey, raisin-styled wines which you can almost spoon into a glass. Orange Muscat is another one to watch.

Pinot Noir

The general consensus is that Australia makes lousy Pinot Noir and I am inclined to agree – it is generally too hot. However, the cooler pockets of Adelaide Hills, Eden Valley, Geelong, Hunter Valley, Margaret River, Mornington Peninsula, Tasmania and Yarra Valley are capable of creating superlative incarnations on a reasonably consistent scale – Pinot Noir is also an extremely important component in the many top class, bottle-fermented bubblies.

Riesling

The best Australian Riesling originates in its coolest wine region – Tasmania. But there are plenty of other spots where it performs well, especially the Clare and Eden Valleys. Styles vary according to the whim of the winemaker, but one can say that they all share a wonderful limey perfume. Many need years and years of bottle age to reach perfection while others can be drunk when they are young, fresh and crisp.

Sauvignon Blanc

This is a difficult grape to grow in Australia owing to the heat, though it can prove its worth in cooler spots – Adelaide Hills, Margaret River and Pyrenees leap to mind here. As producers become even more clever in the vineyard and in the winery, however, we may see more plantings of this variety, though one questions why they would go to the bother in light of the competition from other New World countries who, quite frankly, will always do it better.

Sémillon (written as Semillon)

If there is one place in the world which expresses the ultimate epitome of Semillon, then it simply has to be the Hunter Valley. Wines from the Granite Belt echo this style, but worthy as the effort is, it will never truly emulate the Hunter Valley quality. The traditional unoaked styles possess a racy acidity and newly picked greengage character when young, metamorphosing into a crescendo of honey-tinged opulence given decades of bottle age. The trouble is, of course, that everyone wants wines which can be drunk immediately nowadays, so this style has fallen somewhat out of fashion. This is a great pity, as these wines really are worth the wait. Some producers now use oak to create greater appeal, but there is no argument that the unoaked wines are superior. There are also copious brands of Semillon-Chardonnay and Semillon-Sauvignon Blanc blends to supply the commodity end of the market.

Testing for soil humidity among irrigated Chardonnay vines at Brookland Valley, Willyabrup, Margaret River, Western Australia. The results of these tests determine the precise amount of water which is to be fed to each vine, a hugely important factor influencing yields and grape quality.

Shiraz (Australian name for Syrah)

A consistently fine performer, regardless of where it is planted in Australia, though once again, the exact nature of the climate determines the individual style of the wine. Planted in the cooler areas, it gives deeply coloured, full-bodied, earthy, almost leathery beasts, bursting with spice, liquorice and pepper when young, but developing soft, sweet, velvety fruit with time in bottle (especially those created from old bush vines). Wines from warmer climes are generally less complex, but nevertheless sport a host of sweet ripe berry flavours. Shiraz is the most widely planted red variety and the second most important premium grape overall.

Grapes to Watch ... Barbera, Gewürztraminer, Marsanne, Mourvèdre (also known as Mataro), Nebbiolo, Sangiovese, Verdelho, Viognier.

Perhaps the best thing about Mudgee wines is their excellent value. Cabernet Sauvignon (usually made as a 100 per cent varietal, but sometimes blended with Merlot or Shiraz) and Shiraz are the tastiest wines of the region, all sharing a big, ripe and rich style.

Orange

Centred around the 1,396m (4,580ft) high Mount Canobolas, this pretty stretch of undulating land has always been fine orchard country, so it is surprising that vines were not planted here commercially until 1983. There are now 25 wineries (including Bloodwood, Canobolas-Smith, Highland Heritage, Horseshoe, Rosemount and Tamberlaine), though much of the fruit (made up of Cabernet Franc, Cabernet Sauvignon, Chardonnay, Merlot, Pinot Noir, Riesling, Sauvignon Blanc and Shiraz) is processed at wineries outside the region.

Cowra

Sometimes described as the Central West district, Cowra is a relatively new region dating back to 1973. Since then, it has expanded at breakneck speed, and it is estimated that it will be crushing some 20,000 tonnes of fruit by 2005. While Cowra Estate remains the dominant force locally, Arrowfield, Brokenwood, Hungerford Hill, Petaluma, Richmond Grove and Rothbury also source fruit from here.

Hilltops

Another small region situated high on the western, volcanic-soiled slopes of the Great Dividing Range, which is exploited in particular by McWilliams at their 100-hectare Barwang vineyard. Chardonnay is good, but Cabernet Sauvignon, Semillon and Shiraz exhibit a greater individual style. A region to watch.

Forbes-Wellington

Also known as Central North-West, this historical area west of Sydney was the site of Australia's original vineyards. Today, however, they are of curiosity value only.

Riverina

This naturally arid, bakingly hot and sunny region also goes under the more meaningful name of Murrumbidgee Irrigation Area (MIA). As this suggests, there is a heavy reliance on irrigation and almost 11 per cent of all Australian grapes are grown in 9,000 hectares of vineyards. As one might expect, this region is the fount of inexpensive cask wines, in spite of modern technology. However, some of Australia's most sublime (and, ironically, most pricey) botrytized wines are made from MIA Semillon. Some critics continue to knock the quality of MIA grapes and their wines, but one wonders where Australia would be without them.

Canberra District

Populated by 17 small boutique wineries, this tiny region supports a mere 75 hectares of vineyards in which Cabernet Sauvignon, Chardonnay, Gewürztraminer, Merlot, Pinot Noir, Riesling, Semillon and Shiraz can do well given enough attention. Arguably the best producer is Doonkuna, though Brindabella, Clonakilla, Helms, Kyeema, Lark Hill and Pankhurst come close seconds.

Tumbarumba

Way up in the Snowy Mountains, New South Wales' fastest-growing region is beginning to realize its potential for high quality sparkling wines made from Chardonnay and Pinot Noir. Altitude keeps temperatures low enough to preserve every ounce of acidity in the grapes, a vital element in the production of successful bubblies.

Corowa

The state's most southerly wine area with a rather passé reputation for dessert wines ... and losing popularity by the second.

Victoria

It was gold which brought the people to Victoria in the 1850s. Thousands upon thousands of prospectors flocked into the region in the short-lived hope of wealth – and with them came the vine. The canny planted vineyards with fervour to meet the demands of thirsty miners and a thriving wine industry ensued, producing half the wine made in Australia.

When the gold was exhausted, however, many of the wineries were forced to close owing to lack of business, nudged along by the disastrous consequences of the introduction of the 1889 Planting Bonus Bill, and in some parts the industry was to lie dormant for many decades to come. Once the domestic taste for wine started to swing away from beer and the heavy fortified wine styles to the gentler table wines – coupled, of course, with a rapidly expanding export market – interest in this neglected state was reawakened. After all, on a pro rata basis, Victoria has always had relatively more land potentially suited to the cultivation of premium grapes than any other state – Victoria is currently the second largest state with 26,072 hectares under vine and is projected to have the largest growth in specialist wine grape production over the next five years. Furthermore, the wonderful variation in topography and range of mesoclimates permits the growth of the whole spectrum of grapes and, in turn, a glorious array of different wine styles is made.

Murray Darling

In geographical terms, this is an extension of South Australia's Riverland region and the two regions between them churn out no less than 40 per cent of Australia's total wine production. Most of the vast expanse of the vineyards falls on the Victoria side of the border, but there are some important plantings in New South Wales too. Owing to the searing heat (they say that a baby left out in the sun will die within an hour) and the negligible amount of rain during the growing season, the vineyards are flood irrigated by water pumped straight from the Murray River which they straddle, and as a result yields from grapes such as Cabernet Sauvignon, Chardonnay, Chenin Blanc, Colombard, Grenache, Merlot, Muscat, Pinot Noir, Sauvignon Blanc, Semillon and Shiraz are high.

While most of the fruit is destined for inexpensive cask wines, Chardonnay and Sauvignon Blanc sometimes battle their way into bottle and both variety and source are often acknowledged. Occasionally, the name of one of the two proposed subregions appears on labels – Sunraysia (comprising Irymple, Karadoc, Merbein, Mildura and Robinvale) and Mid-Murray (which includes the districts of Lake Boga and Mystic Park). The subregion of Swan Hill has already been declared.

Rutherglen

This historic viticultural region lies in the North East Zone and is most famous for memorable fortified wines. While the quality of its solera-method sherries, vintage ports and Muscadelle-based Tokays is very high, the most celebrated Rutherglen wine is the unctuously sweet, oak-aged-for-ever, liqueur Brown Muscat. However, Rutherglen also produces its fair share of interesting table wines, and as the region expands into the hills we are likely to see more of these.

The traditional red wine of the region is made from Shiraz, fashioned to an unbelievably beefy style. Other regional specialities include Cabernet Sauvignon, Carignan, Durif and Mondeuse, either as single varieties or sometimes blended with Shiraz. These are also characterized by fearsomely high alcohol and fullness of body.

A profusion of sun-filled white wines is made from all the usual classic grapes – Chardonnay, Chenin Blanc, Gewürztraminer, Riesling, Sauvignon Blanc and Semillon – especially when they are planted in the cooler, higher foothills of the Australian Alps, though growers have to pay close attention to site selection because the climate is distinctly continental, which means that spring frosts are common (and can be devastating) and the growing season fairly short.

Milawa

Otherwise described as Glenrowan, there is a close resemblance in the style of Milawa's wines to those of Rutherglen – so close, in fact, that some people group the two regions together.

Stainless steel rotary vinificators at Milawa, Victoria. Until the introduction of stainless steel, runaway fermentation temperatures precluded the production of top quality wine.

King Valley

Encompassing the watershed of the King River, this region of the northeast is emerging as an important supplier of premium grapes to a number of leading wineries across New South Wales, South Australia and Victoria. Owing to its physical diversity, the full spectrum of classic varieties can be grown as long as they are planted in suitable sites. At its northern end, for instance, (where it merges into the Milawa region) the Valley slopes only ascend to 110m (360ft) above sea level; at its southern extremity, however, the Whitlands Plateau (known rather unimaginatively as the 'High Country') stands 800m (2,620ft), well, high.

As the region develops, we can probably expect more producers to follow Brown Brothers and Miranda's example of bottling 100 per cent King Valley wines – currently, the vast majority of the grapes are used in cross-regional blends.

Goulburn Valley

This region represents the foreigner's idea of quintessential Australia – a veritable maze of billabongs, with stands of tall, white-barked gum trees lining the edge of a meandering river filled with chattering exotic birds.

In this kind of landscape, it is soil type which dictates which grapes can be grown where. Climb up into the Strathbogie Ranges, however, and site selection will depend primarily on slope, aspect and altitude. Indeed, many voices within the industry argue that the contrast between the two locations is so absolute that they should be classed as separate regions.

Be that as it may, the heart of the industry is based on the valley floor and the wines (made from the whole gamut of classic varieties) are well known for their intensity of flavour and sound structure. Marsanne, the flagship speciality, is anchored here and Chateau Tahbilk and Mitchelton make prime examples. Complex, mouthfilling Shiraz is also made and another star turn is weighty, tropical fruit accented Riesling, arguably Victoria's best, which is capable of long life in the bottle.

Up in the cooler Strathbogie Ranges, delicate, taut Chardonnay and Pinot Noir is produced, much of it destined for sparkling wine. Cabernet Sauvignon can also be successful, sporting a firmer structure and finer fruit flavours compared with the dense, chocolate-licked versions which spring from the valley floor, though it is often blended with Shiraz.

Brown Brothers' Whitlands vineyard is set high up in the cool climate of the Great Dividing Range in northeast Victoria.

Bendigo

When Gold Fever struck this Central Victoria region in 1851, the vine soon followed in the footsteps of the new settlers. Early enterprise, however, was dashed by an outbreak of phylloxera in 1893, and the wine industry was not to be revived until 1969. Since then, Bendigo and its subdistrict, Heathcote, have forged a reputation as terrific producers of concentrated, inky, long-lived red wines based on Cabernet Sauvignon and Shiraz. Furthermore, companies such as Yellowglen have more than proved the viability of the higher, much cooler Ballarat subdistrict for the creation of world-class sparkling wines made from Chardonnay and Pinot Noir.

Labels to look for include Balgownie, Blackjack, Chateau Leamon, Jasper Hill, Passing Clouds, Water Wheel and Yellowglen.

Macedon Ranges

It is difficult to identify the beginning and the end of this ever-advancing Central Victoria winemaking area, though it certainly embraces Knights Hill, Kyneton, Lancefield, Mount Macedon, Romsey and Sunbury (this latter has now been declared as a region in its own right, much to the disgust of the growers of Kyneton, incidentally, who feel that they also deserve their own appellation). Either way, there is such an immense variation in topography, soils and mesoclimates that generalizations are made awkward.

The Goulburn Valley boasts the oldest and largest plantings of Marsanne in the world.

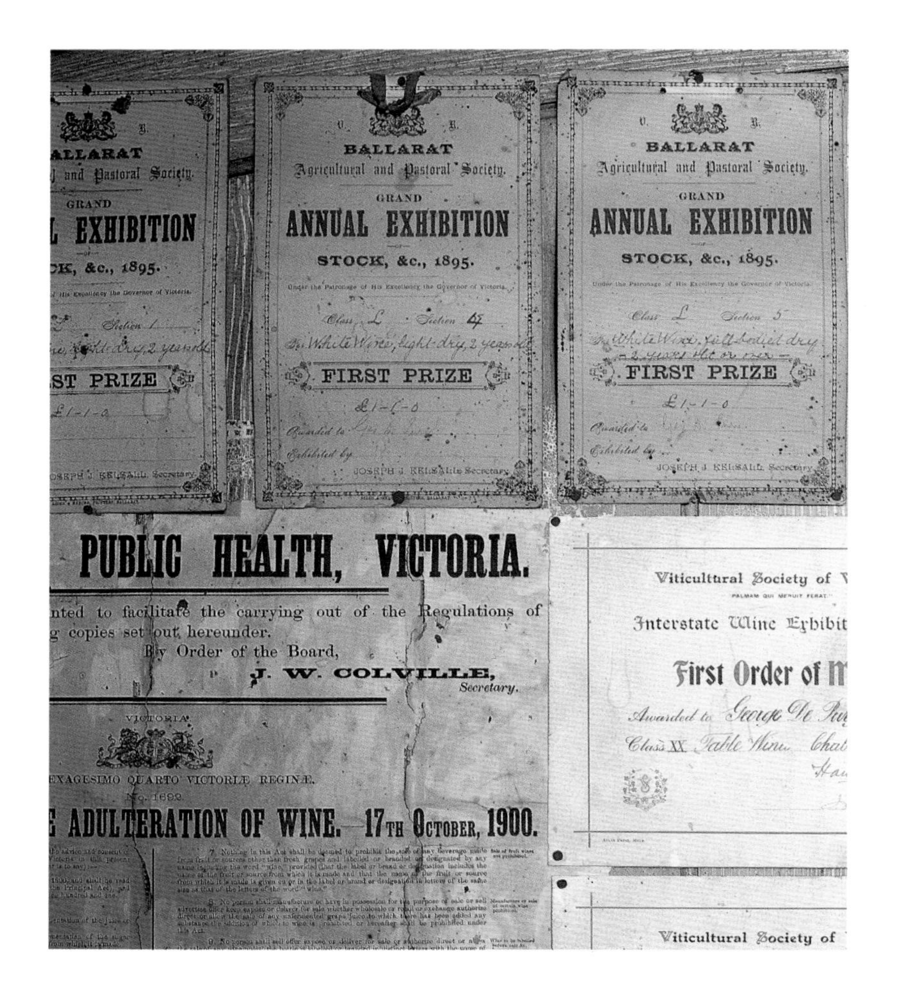

Prizes awarded to Yeringberg wines, dating back to 1895. The Yeringberg vineyards were the first to be established in the Yarra Valley, way back in 1862.

One uniting factor is clear, however: Macedon Ranges is one of the three coolest grape-growing regions on the Australian mainland. Altitude is the fundamental key in determining exactly how cool is cool at any given site – for example, Mount Macedon ascends to a striking 1,000m (3,280ft), significantly higher than the low plains of Sunbury. But it is not altitude alone which has a cooling effect. High or low, the whole region is plagued by strong winds – indeed, this is probably a good point at which to reinforce the importance of the deleterious impact which fierce winds can have on vines. Quite simply, apart from the obvious physical damage which can be inflicted upon the tender parts of the vine, the infamous wind chill factor causes the vine to shut down physiologically, a natural defence to hostile conditions, and the vine simply ceases to function as a result.

For these reasons, the choice of site selection is critical for grapes such as Cabernet Sauvignon and Shiraz (which are often blended together), though Chardonnay and Pinot Noir are much easier to cultivate, and are turned into table wines and sparkling wines with equal success. Names to look out for include Bindi, Cobaw Ridge, Craiglee, Hanging Rock and Virgin Hills who create somewhat avant garde wines for such a challenging region.

Pyrenees

Centred around the towns of Avoca (after which the region used to be called), Moonambel and Redbank, this region has traditionally been an important producer of palate-shocking red wines based on Cabernet Sauvignon and Shiraz, though improved vineyard site selection brought about something of a revolution with the white wines, and rich, elegant Chardonnay, stylish Riesling and vividly fruity Sauvignon Blanc are increasingly being made.

Grampians

Formerly known as Great Western, this region first shot to prominence during the Gold Fever years and the area positively teemed with small wineries. When the miners moved on, however, the number of vineyards began to dwindle and, today, only ten are in operation (and of these, eight are fairly newly established). The memory of some of the early vineyards lives on, however, in the names used on Seppelt labels – Chalambar, Moyston, Rhymney and Salinger – and one legacy of the gold rush period is the 1.6km (1m) of underground 'drives', or cellars, at Seppelt's Great Western winery, which were hand-excavated by redundant miners after the gold had run out.

While the region is best known for its top class sparkling wines (including delicious sparkling Shiraz), most of the grapes used to make these are trucked in from elsewhere. Regional specialities are crafted from varieties such as Cabernet Sauvignon and Shiraz, which make wines of great distinction and with an exceptional capacity to age. Chardonnay and Riesling are the top whites, and there are some promising new plantings of Pinot Gris and Sangiovese. Apart from Seppelt, names to watch include Best's (whose Nursery Block, planted in 1867, includes grape varieties so rare that they have defied all attempts at identification), Cathcart Ridge, Garden Gully, Montara, Mount Chalambar and Mount Langi Ghiran.

The Yarra Valley region has gained eminence as one of Australia's foremost producers of fine wines.

Geelong

This once-thriving and celebrated region was destroyed by phylloxera in the 19th century and its renaissance did not come about until the mid-1960s. Today, 16 wineries (including top names such as Bannockburn, Idyll, Innisfail, Prince Albert and Scotchman's Hill) create interesting wines of good varietal character from a plethora of grapes, though Cabernet Sauvignon, Chardonnay, Pinot Noir and Shiraz are the most important in commercial terms.

Yarra Valley

Since its phoenix-like rise from the ashes of a burnt-out wine industry only two decades ago, the Yarra Valley region has gained eminence as one of Australia's foremost producers of fine wines. More than a handful of the country's most talented winemakers are based here, charming first class wines from grapes such as Cabernet Sauvignon, Chardonnay, Merlot, Pinot Noir, Riesling, Sauvignon Blanc and Shiraz.

It takes more than magical winemaking and marketing wizardry alone to attain superstar status, however. The region's cool climate and first-class soils, which are in tip-top condition thanks to the many years where it was jumbucks which dominated the landscape, combine to give an ideal environment for the cultivation of premium grapes.

The topography is highly varied, ranging from flat river terraces to steep-sided slopes (some of the steepest in Australia, in fact) where aspect is critical to grape performance. The soils can be divided into two basic types: infertile, rock-sprinkled, grey to grey-brown loams over clay subsoil, found on the northern side of the Valley, and to the south a deep, fertile, red volcanic soil.

Vines adore these soils, but they also enjoy the range of microclimates offered by the different levels of altitude. Some prefer the high hillsides where it is

Sunset over Delatite Estate, on the northern slopes of the Great Dividing range at Mansfield, Victoria.

distinctly cool, while others favour the warmer, lower sites. Even here, though, it is still pretty cool by Australian standards (indeed, it is even cooler than Bordeaux or Burgundy).

Not surprisingly, therefore, the Yarra Valley has achieved great success with the capricious Pinot Noir – indeed, some would argue that Yarra makes Australia's finest examples. It certainly has the Burgundy stamp to its style and in some cases seems more Burgundian than the real thing! It follows that the quality of Chardonnay is also very high, though the wines bear enough of a tropical twang to their flavour to put them beyond comparison with Burgundy, except to say that they, too, can be long-lived. In fact, there is tremendous diversity in the Yarra Chardonnay style, which owes as much to the philosophy of the individual winemaker as it does to natural vintage variation.

Another wine which varies wildly in style is Cabernet Sauvignon. Usually blended with Cabernet Franc and Merlot, it can be light or it can be heavy, though they are invariably sophisticated and share a certain silkiness on the tongue. This characteristic is also a hallmark of Yarra Valley Shiraz, though these wines are much weightier and carry all of the usual Australian Shiraz bruising flavours – as long as the vines are planted in suitable, sun-trapped sites.

Harvest time at Coldstream Hills, Coldstream, Victoria, in the Yarra Valley. This estate was established by renowned wine critic, James Halliday. In 1996 he sold to industry giant Southcorp, who have maintained high standards.

The Yarra Valley seems set to expand beyond its current 45 wineries as more and more of the top winemaking names move in to grab their share of this exciting, buoyant region. Coldstream Hills, De Bortoli, Diamond Valley, Domaine Chandon, Eyton, Lillydale, Mount Mary, Seville, Tarrawarra, Yarra Ridge, Yarra Station, Yarra Valley Hills, Yarra Yering and Yeringberg are the names to buy, though very often demand simply exceeds supply.

A huge variety of red grapes are being cultivated and vinified in Victoria with some thrilling results.

Mornington Peninsula

One receives the strong impression that winemaking is a bit of a middle class hobby in these parts. This may have something to do with the large number of doctors, lawyers and accountants *et al* who have turned themselves into weekend winemakers. However, this is not the easiest place to grow vines owing to the profoundly maritime-influenced climate. Even the big producers have recognized the limits of cool climate viticulture and have not bought land here ... yet. In spite of difficult prevailing conditions, an array of exciting, delicate and gently flavoured wines is made (though there can be wild variations between vintages) from Cabernet Franc, Cabernet Sauvignon, Chardonnay, Merlot, Pinot Gris, Pinot Noir, Riesling, Sauvignon Blanc, Shiraz and Viognier, the majority being sold at the cellar door. Of the 36 commercial producers, Craigavon, Dromana, King's Creek, Main Ridge, Massoni, Merricks, Moorooduc, Paringa, Port Philip, Stoniers, T'Gallant and Turramurra take pride of place.

Gippsland

A sprawling, catch-all zone some 500km (310m) long and 150km (93m) wide which mops up around 50 disparate and very tiny grape-growing and winemaking operations along the coast to the east of Melbourne. To put this into perspective, only 150 hectares of vines are planted in total. Generalizations are dangerous, but it is fair to say that South Gippsland is the coolest area and, as a result, some promising Burgundian-style Chardonnay and Pinot Noir is being made by Bass Philip, McAlister and Nicholson River.

Drumborg

This remote area in the southwest of the state was pioneered by Seppelt in 1964 for the express purpose of supplying the company with cool climate fruit. Chardonnay, Pinot Meunier and Pinot Noir are planted to provide base grapes for their sparkling wines, but Cabernet Sauvignon (surprisingly – one would expect it to be too cool here to ripen this variety), Gewürztraminer and Riesling are also cultivated. Costs are high, but so is quality.

South Australia

If you like the notion of 43,916 hectares of vineyards and refinery-sized wineries, then this is fine, as long as the grapes which are being fed in at one end of the process are of reasonable quality and the wine being churned out at the other is drinkable....

In fact, it is projected that South Australia alone will account for an astonishing 57 per cent of all Australian wine by the year 2000. Much of the production is of everyday-drinking, bag-in-box standard, yet this state is also capable of creating some of the country's finest wines.

South Australia can also claim the nation's oldest, richest and most continuous winemaking legacy. Not only did the state suffer less from the ravages of phylloxera which took tenacious hold across the rest of the winemaking regions, but owing to its generally agreeable climate, which can support a wide range of grape varieties, a very proactive winemaking attitude has meant that producers have always been willing and able to adapt to market forces.

Riverland

This immense irrigation project on the Murray River is bargain bag-in-box territory and is hugely important to the Australian wine industry. Do not be deceived into thinking that the wines are poor as a result, however; Cabernet Sauvignon, Chardonnay, Chenin Blanc, Colombard, Malbec, Riesling, Sauvignon Blanc and Shiraz are of a consistently reliable quality.

The industry is dwarfed by three companies, Angove's, Kingston and the Berri-Renmano-Loxton group (the BRL component of BRL Hardy) who churn out copious quantities of wine under their own brands, but are also an important source of supermarket own-label wines in the United Kingdom. Many of the grapes are also destined for processing by large concerns based in the Barossa Valley and elsewhere.

Fizz giant Seppelt also has its Qualco Vineyard here. To maintain the quality of their fruit, the grapes are machine-harvested at night and crushing, draining and pressing are carried out immediately. The chilled juice is then sent to the Barossa Valley for fermentation. As chief winemaker Ian McKenzie says, 'What we expect – and get – from Qualco Vineyard is consistency of quality and style, particularly for Seppelt's very successful range of commercial wines.'

Berri-Renmano co-operative winery at Berri in South Australia – now part of BRL Hardy, Australia's second largest wine company.

Sunrise over Mountadam Estate vineyards, up on the high Eden Ridge in the Mount Lofty Ranges.

Clare Valley

Riesling is the grape of the strikingly beautiful and tranquil Clare Valley and its Auburn, Hill River, Polish Hill, Sevenhill and Watervale sub-districts. It achieves an exemplary structure bearing intense lime and peach blossom flavours and benchmark longevity, which cannot be matched anywhere else in Australia. Study the climatic statistics, however, and one would quite rightly wonder how this is attainable because the region looks very hot and dry on paper.

Provided the grapes are planted in optimum sites, some 400–500m (1,310–1640ft) up on the slopes of the series of sub-valleys which litter the region, then the cloud cover, cool afternoon breezes and chilly nights will slow down the ripening of the grapes during the growing season. Furthermore, while irrigation would appear essential, many growers choose to limit the amount of water fed to the vines (or, indeed, eliminate it altogether) which keeps yields down, a critical factor to quality.

Riesling accounts for the highest volume of the annual crush, but Shiraz is not far behind and produces voluptuous, sturdy, deep-flavoured wines. Cabernet Sauvignon and Semillon are also hugely important, with Cabernet Franc, Grenache, Malbec, Merlot, Pinot Noir and Sauvignon Blanc bringing up the rear. Unusually, Chardonnay appears to be the poor relation here, though there is no reason why it should not shine.

Of the 35 wineries Crabtree, Grosset, Jim Barry, Knappstein, Leasingham, Mitchell, Mount Horrocks, Paulett, Pikes, Quelltaler, Sevenhill, Skillogalee, Tim Adams and Wendouree are the best.

The cooper's art is often under-appreciated. Here, at Penfolds' Nuriootpa winery in the Barossa Valley, he is using fire to bend the staves of wood into shape. Fire is also used to char the inside of the barrel, the degree of which makes all the difference to the toastiness of the finished wine.

Adelaide Hills

The foothills of the Mount Lofty Ranges as they begin their northeasterly ascent from the city of Adelaide offer an ideal habitat for grapes and some very exciting premium wines, both still and sparkling, are emerging from this rapidly developing region. Indeed, if it were not for the limitations imposed by the lack of water for irrigation and the demand for land for other uses, its potential would be exploited even further.

While the 400-m (1,310-ft) contour line marks the region's southern, eastern and western boundaries, the vines are actually planted at higher altitudes – usually 500 to 600m (1,640 to 1,970ft) above sea level – where temperatures are lower. There is plenty of welcome sunshine, however, and though the amount of rain varies throughout the region, it falls mainly during the winter months (hence the need for irrigation).

I am generalizing wildly here, however. There is a host of different mesoclimates and microclimates depending on exact altitude, aspect and slope, and it is this, along with the varying soil types, which determines which grapes will grow best where. Early-ripening varieties such as Chardonnay, Pinot Noir and Sauvignon Blanc do well in the Lenswood subregion, for instance, while the northern extremities offer a terrain and mesoclimate better suited to grapes such as Cabernet Sauvignon which require a longer growing season. Shiraz can also be stunning if it ripens properly. Some of the best examples hail from Springton, a small area on the edge of the Adelaide Hills region. Riesling also responds according to where it is grown – versions from cooler sites are elegant and delicate.

As ever, styles of Chardonnay much depend on winemaking decisions, though owing to naturally high levels of acidity, it is very often used as the partner to Pinot Noir in bottle-fermented sparkling wines.

Pinot Noir is also now being turned into marvellous table wines which arguably best express the character of the region – Hillstowe makes an archetypal version. Indeed, there is no doubt that Adelaide Hills is South Australia's leading producer of this grape, and the new clones which are being phased in can only enhance quality even further. Definitely a grape to watch.

Adelaide Plains

In contrast to the cool Adelaide Hills, the utterly flat Adelaide Plains region is dramatically hotter and is best known as a source of low-cost grapes from high-yielding, highly mechanized, irrigated vineyards. The majority of the crop is trucked to the Barossa Valley for processing into cask wines, though Primo Estate charms astonishingly good Cabernet Sauvignon-Merlot blends, Colombard, Riesling and Shiraz from this region, which just goes to prove what can be achieved with double pruning (which delays the harvest), controlled yields and skilled winemaking.

Barossa Valley

This richly historic region forms the true heart of the Australian wine industry, where the potent fumes of fermenting wine are breathed as deeply as air. It is by far and away the leading source of premium wines within South Australia and is home to no less than 7,600 hectares of vines, 44 wineries and 540 growers. Impressive statistics. It is important to bear in mind, however, that much of the wine made here (or even just bottled or matured here) hails from grapes grown outside the region – the giant Penfolds offers a prime example of a Barossa-based operation which trucks in grapes from seemingly everywhere for its winemaking activities.

But it is also Penfolds who proved beyond all doubt that the Barossa Valley is capable of greatness in itself, with its most famous Shiraz creation, Grange, which was born here. Penfolds is by no means the sole producer of top-quality Shiraz, however, and almost every winery has a Shiraz or Shiraz blend in their portfolio – Barossa Valley Estate, Charles Burge, Peter Lehmann, Rockford, Saltram and St Hallett are among the best. While all share the quintessential Barossa style (long-lived, full-bodied and leathery yet velvety wines packed with dark fruit flavours, pepper and hints of chocolate), there are subtle differences in them depending entirely upon the siting of the vineyard. Indeed, there is a very sound argument for dividing the Barossa into smaller appellations such as Keyneton and Springton.

Barossa Valley produces long-lived, full-bodied and leathery yet velvety wines, packed with dark fruit flavours, pepper and hints of chocolate.

Max Schubert – Creator of the Legendary Grange

'I'd like to believe that the wines with which I have been associated are descended from one old ancestor vineyard established many years ago, marrying with another, and another, and even another if you like, thus creating and establishing a dynasty of wines.'

These words from the late Max Schubert, arguably the most influential figure in the modern Australian wine industry. From messenger boy in 1931, Schubert worked his way up through the ranks of Penfolds and was finally appointed Chief Winemaker in 1948. During a study trip to Europe two years later, he was introduced to mature Claret. Utterly inspired, he returned to Australia with the vision of producing an Australian red wine which would be comparable to the finest which Bordeaux could offer, and in 1951 Grange was born. The road to fame was not easy, however. On their release, the first Granges were almost universally condemned, drawing many scathing comments from industry sources. 'A concoction of wild fruits and sundry berries with crushed ants predominating' was one such example!

The costs of making Grange were high and Schubert was ordered to cease production before the 1957 vintage. However, he continued to make the wine in secret until production resumed officially with the 1960 vintage. A winning entry of one of his older, maturing wines in a tasting competition in 1962 was to change everything for Grange and, indeed, Penfolds was to lead the way during the 1970s in establishing an international reputation for Australian wines.

Of course Shiraz is not the only grape to triumph in the Barossa Valley. Charles Burge and Elderton, for example, make wonderfully rich Cabernet Sauvignon, though it is often best blended with grapes from other regions such as Coonawarra, Eden Valley or McLaren Vale. Grenache and Mourvèdre from ancient vines (some 100 years old) are also hugely in demand, and there is intense competition for these grapes between the fortified and table winemakers. Of the latter, Charles Melton and Rockford offer fine examples.

While the climate suggests that it should be too warm for white grapes to perform well, production is split more or less 50/50 between reds and whites. This is due in part to the region's Germanic heritage, but in fact, some very delicate, fresh and razor sharp white wines can be made as long as the grapes are planted off the flat, sandy loams of the Valley floor.

Eden Valley

This region has a history of viticulture as long as that of the Barossa Valley, and it also happens to grow the same mix of grape varieties. Indeed, there are so many similarities between the Eden Valley and the Barossa Valley that the two regions are often considered as one.

The principal, and all-important, difference between Eden and Barossa is its topography. Whereas most Barossa Valley vineyards are planted on the flat valley floor, here the vines cling to the fairly steep gradients of rolling, exposed hills. It is therefore cooler compared with the Barossa Valley so the growing season is longer, though it is altitude, aspect, slope and the strength of the wind which determine its precise nature.

Of all the various grapes grown, the region has justifiably become world famous for its intensely flavoured, long-lasting Riesling. However, the Eden Valley is also home to such renowned Shiraz vineyards as Henschke's 120-year-old Hill of Grace.

Chapel Hill Winery, McLaren Vale. Owing to a consistency of quality year in, year out, McLaren Vale grapes have always been a significant component in anonymous inter-regional blends, but the region has now become popular in its own right.

McLaren Vale

McLaren Vale seems to offer something for everybody. The hugely varied landscape of intermingling olive groves, orchards, forests, undulating hills and rivers (notably the Onkaparinga and its tributaries) offers a complex range of soils and mesoclimates, and as a result just about every popular variety of grape can be grown and every kind of wine style made.

The most widely cultivated variety is Semillon, followed in importance by Chenin Blanc, Cabernet Franc, Chambourcin, Cabernet Sauvignon and Mourvèdre, though there are also substantial plantings of Chardonnay, Merlot, Pinot Noir, Riesling and Sauvignon Blanc. The quality backbone of the industry, however, is formed by

Strategy 2025 – The Australian Wine Industry Looks Ahead

Back in 1966, fortified ports and sherries made up 78 per cent of domestic consumption, while premium varietal table wines barely ranked in the statistics. Indeed, astonishing as this may appear in hindsight, Chardonnay was not grown at all at this time!

Today, the position is almost the reverse, as table wines now account for 80 per cent of the Australian wine diet and Cabernet Sauvignon and Chardonnay alone contribute around 20 per cent of total production (which, in itself, has more than tripled since 1966). Furthermore, Australian wine has attained a significant presence in world markets and 36.4 per cent of production is now exported without any subsidies or trade protection measures.

The wine industry is not merely content to pat itself on the back in self-congratulation, however. There is no complacency about the future and the drive to push the industry to even higher goals is ever strong. Vision 2025, introduced in 1996 by the Winemakers Federation of Australia, forecasts that the Australian wine industry will achieve $4.5 billion in annual sales by being the world's most influential and profitable supplier of branded wines which will offer the consumer good flavour per dollar from an extensive range of wines with a diversity of styles. New markets will be pursued, most especially in Asia, while existing markets at home, and in Europe and North America, will be penetrated further.

Australia will need to double the current volume of wine if it is to meet the 2025 target. Productivity gains from existing vineyards will be required, therefore, in addition to the establishment of 40,000 hectares of new vineyards by 2022. Nevertheless, Australia may well continue to suffer from a shortage of red grapes in the medium term, which is ironic in light of the fact that it simultaneously has to deal with the problem of surplus Chardonnay....

juicy-sweet Grenache and richly textured, bold Shiraz, most especially those from older, low yielding vines which have miraculously defied the march of Adelaide suburbia. Chardonnay and Sauvignon Blanc create wines to impress among the whites.

Langhorne Creek

A mild climate and a flat terrain with deep, fertile, alluvial soils irrigated almost unlimitlessly from Lake Alexandrina combine to promote vine vigour and abundant cropping levels across 300 hectares of vineyards – so why all the fuss about Langhorne Creek? Well, Jacob's Creek, Orlando's most celebrated and successful of large-volume brands, is the cause. Orlando is just one of the big companies to have invested millions of dollars in new, computer-controlled vineyard projects, purpose-designed to supply component fruit for their top-selling wines. Grapes such as Cabernet Sauvignon, Chardonnay and Shiraz, which are planted in optimum soils types (of course!), are drip-fed from no less than 13km (8m) of pipeline, and each variety receives not a drop less, and certainly not a drop more, of water than they need to grow and ripen into top quality grapes – indeed, Langhorne Creek looks set to become one of the country's largest suppliers of premium grapes in the years to come.

Padthaway

Synonymous with Keppoch, this relatively newly developed region (1963) is dominated by major companies such as Hardys,

Red wine fermenting in new oak barrels in Wolf Blass cellars at Barossa Valley.

Lindemans, Seppelt and Wynns (Orlando and Penfolds also buy grapes from here), and only one small winery (Padthaway Estate) and one small grower (Browns of Padthaway) are to be found. In some respects, the lack of interest in Padthaway by smaller concerns is a mystery because the region has proved itself to be excellent for white wines and – as long as yields are controlled – equally successful for reds.

Which brings us neatly to another conundrum. Given the warmth of the climate, one would expect the bias to be more towards the production of red wines. In fact, it is Chardonnay which is the most celebrated grape of the region, giving flavours of fig, grapefruit, melon and peach.

Coonawarra

This low, 15km (9m) by 1.5km (1m) ridge of land in an otherwise completely flat and sky-filled terrain is composed of one of the world's most famous soils – the terra rossa. Along with its most celebrated progeny, Cabernet Sauvignon (which is universally considered as Australia's finest by a long chalk), this vividly red, porous, limestone-based veneer of earth has firmly placed Coonawarra on the global quality wine map – no wonder that it is one of the most expensive pieces of viticultural real estate in Australia. Balnaves, Bowen, Brand, Hollick, Katnook, Leconfield, Lindemans, Majella, Mildara, Orlando, Parker, Penfolds, Penley, Redman, Rosemount, Rymill, Wynns and Zema (the names to hunt down) are lucky enough either to be able to afford the land or to buy Coonawarra grapes.

It takes more than a very special soil to create illustrious wines, however. Situated only 100km (62m) inland, Coonawarra's maritime climate also sets the region apart: potentially high summer temperatures are tempered by extensive cloud cover giving conditions in which most of the classic grape varieties can ripen to utter perfection.

Take Cabernet Sauvignon, for example. The nature of the growing season allows the development of a full spectrum of refined, luscious, concentrated blackcurrant, plum, mulberry, red cherry and prune flavours. Yet the wines are not over-tannic, thanks to the fact that they are fully mature (do not forget that Cabernet Sauvignon is a thick-skinned variety and because the tannins are part of the skin's structure, the grapes need to be picked at optimum ripeness if tannic astringency is to be avoided). The fact that a lot of tannin is put back into the wine via oak-ageing is quite a separate matter; they create a different effect and, furthermore, their 'addition' can be controlled.

Limestone Coast

I have only recently seen this appellation on a label (a Chardonnay from Lindemans), but setting aside the somewhat salient fact that this zone technically encompasses Coonawarra and Padthaway, it does also embrace the rapidly expanding Mount Benson subregion

and the districts of Bordertown, Mount Gambier, Robe and Wrattonbully (which used to be called Koppamurra – do either of them sound better with an Australian accent, I ask myself?), of which we will hear more in times to come I am sure.

In particular, Mount Benson, Robe and Wrattonbully may turn out to be the spots to watch. The large companies are already planting....

Southcorp's Hungerford Hill sales room at Penola in Coonawarra. For all its modern-day fame, Cabernet Sauvignon was hardly cultivated in this region before 1950. It was Shiraz which created Coonawarra's reputation, cast into the shadow of Cabernet's limelight until the advent of Wynns Coonawarra Estate Shiraz. Likewise, Coonawarra's white wines have been completely obscured by the reputation of its reds, yet the quality and intensity of Chardonnay and Riesling is extremely high, owing to the cool climate.

Eyre Peninsula

Two wineries were established here in 1984, both close to Port Lincoln at the southern end of the Peninsula. The longer growing season here is favourable for late-ripening varieties such as Cabernet Sauvignon, though it is very often softened by the addition of Merlot, which is rather a waste of the latter because it makes stunning mint and berry-flavoured wines by itself. Riesling makes the best white wine.

Kangaroo Island

Across the other side of the Spencer Gulf, Australia's third largest island is planted with roughly 30 hectares of Grenache, Merlot, Pinot Noir, Riesling and Shiraz vines. These are sited on north and northeast facing slopes where they benefit from protection from the prevailing winds which are the chief downside to the Island's maritime climate. One to watch.

Western Australia

If you look at a map of Australia and draw an imaginary line between Perth and Albany, the triangle of land which is trapped appears diminutive against the rest of Western Australia. Nevertheless, this plot is where the whole of the Western Australia wine industry is concentrated and, in fact, it covers hundreds of square kilometres. This is not one unbroken expanse of vines, however; the 4,490 hectares of vineyards are focused in discrete regions which can be a long way apart and, in consequence, the state's contribution to the national wine pool is minuscule at just two per cent.

Do not dismiss Western Australia, however. Its grapes and wines are highly prized for their intrinsic quality – indeed, it is not unusual for grapes to be trucked across to eastern states for use in blends (no small distance), which is ironic in light of the fact that some eastern producers refuse to accept that Western Australian wines are worth even acknowledging.

It speaks volumes that Margaret River was the first Australian wine region to establish its own appellation. That it did not catch on at first is by the by; more to the point is that there exist producers who recognize the importance of regional styles, terroir and individual site selection. The stick-in-the-mud traditionalists would do well to look and learn.

Swan District

Chenin Blanc dominates production here, contributing approximately 25 per cent of the annual crush. This grape is not normally famed for its inherent quality in Australia, but the dry, sunny and hot climate (one of the hottest in the world) gives a delicious fruit salad richness to the wines. Plantings of Chardonnay are increasing, and Verdelho can offer a lovely honeysuckle flavour.

Perth Hills

A short drive to the east of Perth brings you into the Darling Ranges, a picturesque landscape of rivulets, dry creek beds, gentle hills and valleys which travel in every direction. A wide choice of aspect, slope, soil and microclimate (not unlike the Douro Valley in Portugal, in fact) provides good viticultural potential and it is a surprise that this area has not been commercially exploited long ago.

Geographe

Also known as the Southwest Coastal Plain, this narrow strip of land – just 2 km (1¼m) wide in parts – runs from Yanchep in the north to

Busselton in the south, a stretch of some 300km (186m). In spite of its large size, however, there are only 60 hectares under vine and the seven wineries produce wines which share similar characteristics thanks to the fine, grey tuart sands found in all of the vineyards.

Margaret River

It takes three and half hours to drive from Margaret River to Perth, and it takes three days to drive from Perth to Sydney, which gives you an idea of the isolation of this region. Nevertheless, it is one of the most vibrant and popular of Australian wine areas, rocketing to importance as a fine producer of powerful yet elegant Cabernet Sauvignons, Pinot Noir, Shiraz and Zinfandel.

But the region has also forged a reputation for the sheer poise of its white wines. Chardonnay, initially pioneered by Leeuwin Estate, is considered by many as one of Australia's greatest and most voluptuous examples of this variety. Sauvignon and Semillon do well, too, either on their own or as a blend, and have a unique intensity of herbaceous, grassy flavours.

Wines of this calibre must obviously be crafted from high-quality fruit, and it is the influence of the sea which brings this about. It creates a climate best described as Mediterranean – there are no huge swings in seasonal or diurnal temperature (which gives an unusually even growing season in terms of warmth), spring frosts are very rare and most of the 1,160mm (46in) of annual rainfall occurs during winter which keeps disease levels low. However, the lack of precipitation over the summer months can cause problems, exacerbated by the drying effect of salty onshore winds, though they can be countered by irrigation and windbreaks.

There are many luminary producers within Margaret River (46 in total), but my votes are cast to Arlewood, Brookland Valley, Cape Mentelle, Chateau Xanadu, Cullens, Devil's Lair, Evans & Tate, Leeuwin, Lenton Brae, Moss Wood, Pierro and Vasse Felix. They are currently farming around 1,500 hectares of low-yielding vines, though this is expected to double over the next five years.

Pemberton

This karri-forested region situated southeast of Margaret River was first planted experimentally in 1977 and is now home to 670 hectares of vines. The cool climate of southern parts is very akin to that of Burgundy, so it is not surprising to find that Chardonnay and Pinot Noir are planted here. Further north towards Manjimup, though,

A mobile crushing and refrigeration plant at Gingin, Western Australia. The grapes are being harvested during the cool of the night to help preserve their freshness.

the Bordeaux-style climate better suits Cabernet Franc, Cabernet Sauvignon, Merlot and Sauvignon Blanc.

The jury is still out on the consistency of wine quality – though there have been some exciting results from wineries such as Bronzewig, Chestnut Grove, Picardy, Salitage and Smithbrook, particularly with sparkling wines from Chardonnay and Pinot Noir, and tropical fruit styled Verdelho.

Great Southern

Extending 150km (93m) north to south and 100km (62m) east to west, this is a big wine-producing area. While the vineyards are well and truly scattered throughout the region, and just about every style of wine is made, there is nevertheless a remarkable uniformity to them despite a marked diversity of climate, ranging from coastal maritime to interior continental.

Production is dominated by austere, powerful, long-lived Cabernet Sauvignon, elegant, lime and grapefruit-flavoured Chardonnay and fragrant, ageworthy Riesling, though Cabernet Franc, Chenin Blanc, Malbec, Merlot, Pinot Noir, Sauvignon Blanc and Shiraz are also cultivated with some exciting results. Of the 25 wineries, Alkoomi, Chatsfield, Frankland Estate, Galafrey, Goundrey, Harewood, Houghton (Frankland River vineyard), Howard Park, Jingalla Porongurup, Karrivale, Pattersons, Plantagenet and Wignalls stand out.

Queensland

Surprisingly on the face of it, Queensland produces less than a quarter of the volume of wine of even tiny Tasmania. I say this because it has three times as much land under vine compared with Tasmania, and the state occupies roughly a quarter of the whole of Australia.

This is easily explained, however, by the fact that most of the grapes grown here end up being eaten. The majority of the state is very hot and dry, after all, particularly as one moves towards the interior from the coast, and the vineyards have to be planted high up in the hills if they are to produce grapes of winemaking quality. While there are signs that the region is beginning to expand its winemaking activities, growth is being slowed by the strict quarantine laws governing rootstock imports ... Queensland is phylloxera-free and wishes to stay that way.

Granite Belt

Though some wine is available internationally, the chances are that you will probably never taste Granite Belt wines outside the area itself, yet 19 producers, including Bald Mountain, Ballandean, Granite Cellars, Kominos, Mountview, Robinson Family, Rumbalara and Stone Ridge, are now making more than palatable Cabernet Sauvignon, Riesling and Shiraz varietals alongside Semillon-Chardonnay blends, liqueur Muscat and, somewhat astonishingly, late harvest Sylvaner.

Roma

The one winery, 25 hectare plot situated roughly halfway between Brisbane and Charleville has very little going for it, quite honestly. It is simply too hot and too dry here, where the locals dodge the sun in the way the British duck out of the rain, and even Bassett's Romavilla Winery's fortified wines (which one might anticipate as passable, even in this climate) do not live up to one's expectations.

South Burnett

Queensland's newest and very picturesque wine-producing region was first planted with commercial grapes as recently as 1994. Most of the wineries are small, nestled in the rolling hills of the 1,100-m (3,600-ft) high Bunya Mountains (part of the Great Dividing Range) where the soils vary from rich red volcanic to grey loams.

Although this sub-tropical area has long, hot summers and mild winters, its elevation does pose the risk of the occasional spring frost, though this is offset by cool summer nights which help to preserve acidity in ripening grapes.

Northern Territory

Who would dream that the Northern Territory could be home to a winery? Yet Chateau Hornsby defies the searing outback heat and chronic aridity (not to forget the crocodiles!) and, with a lot of help from an extensive drip irrigation system, cultivates three hectares of various grape varieties at Alice Springs.

Anyone looking for a truly funky way to bring in the new millenium should volunteer to be a grape-picker here – Shiraz grapes for Chateau Hornsby's Early Red are always harvested at one minute past midnight on 1 January!

Tasmania

There is more to Tasmania than the atlas might suggest. The geography is complex, giving a huge diversity of scenery – from the lush, green, fertile valleys of the Huon and Tamar Rivers, the unspoiled beaches of the east coast, alpine heathlands and tall, often impenetrable, eucalypt forests in the mountains.

Indeed, in some respects the island seems more Scottish than Australian – and it is true to say that Tasmanian wines are not at all like their mainland cousins, either. It would be romantic to think that the natural home of the legendary Tasmanian Tiger could also be host to some obscure, indigenous grape varieties, but unfortunately this is not the case. Setting aside the plastic grapes which Diego Bernacchi hung from vines to attract investors (circa 1884), Tasmanian wines are made from the familiar classics – Cabernet Sauvignon, Chardonnay, Gewürztraminer, Pinot Noir and Riesling, with some Merlot, Pinot Gris, Sauvignon Blanc and Sémillon. What distinguishes them, however, is their unique style: Tasmanian wines are subtle and delicate, with elusive aromas and complex, finely balanced structures and restrained fruit – far more 'European' in character, in fact, than other Australian wines.

The cool climate is the key, of course. In real terms, this means mild, temperate and maritime, divided into four distinct seasons, with a summer (December to February) average maximum of 21°C (70°F) and a 4–12°C (39–54°F) range in winter (June to August). Rainfall – 62cm (24in) in Hobart to 240cm (94in) on the west coast – is evenly distributed year-round. In a nutshell, the climate is like Bordeaux, Burgundy and Champagne rolled into one and, lying at sunshine-filled latitudes equivalent to those of central Spain, Tasmania offers a grape-growing elysium impossible to find anywhere else in Australia.

Climate is one thing but 'weather' is quite another and, as always, average statistics do not paint the whole picture. The east side of the island is generally much warmer and drier compared with the west and there are also distinct variations between coastal areas and the highlands.

For these reasons, the island's 535 hectares of vineyards are sited in the eastern half of the island at low altitudes, but it is the special microclimate which determines precisely what grapes are grown where. Although it is true to say that all Tasmanian grapes benefit from a slow ripening period, a high number of sunshine hours is needed to ripen grapes of all kinds, and impeccable canopy control is required to allow every second of sunlight through to help the ripening process. Aspect, clonal selection and cropping levels are also critical.

Half of the island's vineyards are located in the Pipers Brook-

Pipers River Region, dominated by Tasmania's premier winery, Pipers Brook Vineyard. Some remarkably fine wines are crafted here, most especially Chardonnay, Gewürztraminer, Pinot Gris, Pinot Noir and Riesling, and excellent sparkling wines are also of growing importance. Cabernet Sauvignon, however, does better in the Tamar and Coal River Valleys.

A Pinot Noir vineyard in early autumn at Moorilla Estate, Berriedale, Tasmania. At this time of year, the weather tends to be extremely changeable – indeed, there is a lovely Tasmanian saying: 'If you don't like the weather, come back in half an hour!'

New Zealand

The most southerly and one of the smallest wine-producing countries in the world, New Zealand holds a pre-eminent position with its supremely varied range of reds, whites and sparkling wines.

Small is Beautiful

Variety to match any other country in the New World

Tiny and distant in relation to most of the rest of the world, New Zealand nevertheless has a burgeoning wine industry with probably the fastest rate of growth of all. With her recent establishment as a net exporter of wines, the revolution continues....

Even today, sheep outnumber people by fifteen to one in New Zealand. But looking at the fantastic rate of development of the world's most southerly wine industry in recent years, one wonders if 'sheep may safely graze' for much longer, now that so much pasture is being turned over to vines.

New Zealand currently represents a droplet in the global wine spittoon, producing just one per cent of world output. However, this is set to rise as demand grows – indeed, New Zealand became a net exporter of wines in 1998 and exports are confidently expected to exceed $100 million before the close of 1998, two years ahead of projections. Since the late 1980s, exports (of which the UK, the major export market, takes 52 per cent by value) have increased almost eight-fold, the domestic market now drinks ten per cent more Kiwi wine each year, and the number of wineries has doubled. Indeed, it is estimated that 20 new wineries will open every year.

Each of New Zealand's regions provides quite different wine styles, shaped by variations in climate, topography and geology. The country may be small, but it spans a length of 1,600km (1,000m) north to south, which roughly equates to the distance between New Zealand and its nearest neighbour, Australia. No-one expects Kiwi wines to taste like Aussie wines owing to the difference in latitude, and exactly the same principle applies to New Zealand itself. To put it another way, if New Zealand was transposed to European latitudes, it would stretch from Germany's Rhine Valley right down into southern Spain – and what a contrast one finds between their wines!

Naturally, to a northern hemisphere dweller like me, everything is upside down and back to front. North Island is therefore warmer than South Island, though both share a cool maritime climate, strongly influenced by rain-bearing westerly winds. The southerly latitude gives an average of 2,200 concentrated sunshine hours each year, however, which is ideal for the growing of premium quality grapes across a wide range of varieties, though mesoclimates and microclimates are critical.

Principal Grape Varieties

White varieties tend to fare better in New Zealand's cool climate, though some reds (particularly in Northland-Matakana, Waiheke Island, Hawkes Bay and Martinborough) are proving hugely successful, thanks to microclimate and improved vineyard management techniques.

The high-cropping Müller-Thurgau used to proliferate as a cheap source for blends and boxed wine, but was overtaken by Chardonnay as the most-planted variety in 1992. Today, Chardonnay and Sauvignon Blanc account for nearly a quarter of total vineyard plantings between them.

For such a small country, New Zealand produces an amazing array of wines. It is the variety of its topography and climate which allows such diversity.

Cabernet Sauvignon

New Zealand's most-planted red grape, which can give long-lived wines of terrific fruit and texture if grown in the right spot. As a thick-skinned variety, its chief disadvantage is the time it needs to ripen properly ... and quite often this simply runs out. It is often bottled as a single varietal, but is also partnered with Merlot and Cabernet Franc to make Bordeaux-style blends.

Chardonnay

A relative newcomer in importance, gaining popularity in the early 1990s when Marlborough Chardonnay shot to fame. To put this into perspective, 350 hectares of plantings in the late 1980s has grown to 1,400 hectares today. Styles vary considerably from north to south, though Chardonnay performs particularly well in Gisborne and Hawkes Bay. It is also an important component in many fine sparkling wines.

Pinot Noir

Many producers regard the enigmatic Pinot Noir as the future of New Zealand's red wine industry, and plantings are expected to rise to 800 hectares by the millennium. An incredibly fussy variety, it is exceedingly challenging to handle, but the results can be thrilling, rivalling the best that the world can conjure up. Martinborough and parts of South Island are top sources. Much Pinot Noir is also used in New Zealand fizz.

Sauvignon Blanc

New Zealand's most famous grape, making wine with a vivid, zingy, intensity of aroma and flavour that cannot be matched anywhere else in the world. Marlborough Sauvignon Blanc is the defining standard against which all others are judged, though New Zealand also produces good examples from Hawkes Bay, Auckland and Gisborne, though they are usually more mellow in style.

Grapes to watch ... Gewürztraminer, Pinot Gris, Merlot, Riesling.

Pinot Noir is an incredibly fussy variety, but the results can be thrilling, rivalling the best that the world can conjure up.

As England's March daffodils begin to bloom, New Zealand is picking the first of its grapes, Müller-Thurgau (Cabernet Sauvignon is the last to be harvested, usually in April/May).

In line with the global enthusiasm for varietal bottlings, most New Zealand grapes destined for the export market are not turned into nameless blends (though blending is not necessarily to be frowned upon as it can give wines of greater complexity and flavour). If a label states a specific variety, however, then 85 per cent of the wine must be made from that variety (reduced to 75 per cent for domestic sales), and this rule also applies to any claim to origin.

It is also important to appreciate that many wineries use grapes bought in from dedicated grape-growers. This can work well under arrangements whereby payment is awarded for quality rather than quantity, but the best wines come from wineries who own their own vineyards, as they have control over every step of the grape-growing process.

While it is clear that nature will dictate to a great degree the individual characteristics of each region, it is equally obvious that wine quality depends as much on sound viticultural practice, and on the technological expertise of those who craft the wine. Today's breed of winemakers are usually Australian-trained, and often have invaluable experience of producing wine in other countries. They grasp the importance of getting things right in the vineyard, especially in an environment where climate and soils promote vine vigour which, in turn, discourages full grape-ripening. Increased vine density, new trellising methods (generally Scott Henry) and the planting of companion crops help to rectify this. Ongoing replanting schemes offer opportunities to move vineyards to better sites, using virus-indexed vines, superior clones (such as Riparai Gloire, 101-14 and 3309C) and new phylloxera-resistant rootstocks.

Thanks to a combination of superb weather giving nearly ideal growing and ripening conditions, and an extra 550 hectares of vines coming on stream, 1998 recorded New Zealand's largest-ever crop at 78,300 tonnes from 7,940 hectares of active vineyards (from a total of 8,720 hectares planted), a whopping 30.5 per cent increase in quantity on 1997. If the beneficial effects of 'El Niño' continue in the years ahead (as is suggested in some quarters), the new 2002 export target of $150 million could be attainable provided growers continue to learn how to maximize their natural advantages. And, as closer attention is paid to site selection, we are likely to be treated to more bottlings of individual estate wines of high quality and greater longevity.

Owing to the imagination, dedication and energy of its grape-growers and winemakers, New Zealand has come a long way in a short time and the future is full of new opportunities and challenges ... more change is in the air!

Expatriate New Zealand film producer Michael Seresin, at his Seresin Estate in Marlborough.

Highlights of History

1819

The Reverend Samuel Marsden, Chaplain to the Government of New South Wales in Australia, plants the first vines at Kerikeri in the Bay of Islands.

1835

James Busby (father of Aussie viticulture) plants cuttings of French and Spanish vines, also in the Bay of Islands. Charles Darwin calls here during his voyage on the *Beagle* and witnesses well-established vineyards.

1840

Busby produces the first-known wine, which he sells to British troops.

1851

The Marist religious order also brings vines to New Zealand, finally settling at Taradale in Hawkes Bay. Indeed, the Mission Vineyard is regarded as the country's oldest vineyard – and it is still around today.

1860s

The first of many temperance societies is founded, and restrictions cripple the development of the wine industry.

1876

Oidium (powdery mildew) begins to take hold, wiping out many vineyards in its path.

1890s

Dalmatian immigrants begin to plant vineyards, though most of the grapes are turned into pretty awful fortified wines, which became known as 'Dally Plonk'.

1894

The services of Italian viticulturalist Romeo Bragato are secured to assess potential. He also identifies phylloxera and recommends the grafting of vines onto phylloxera-resistant, American hybrid rootstock. Unfortunately, many growers simply plant the rootstocks and a whole new wave of inferior wine is born.

1901

Bragato is appointed as the first government viticulturalist and a research station is established at Te Kauwhata.

1908

Prohibitionists re-commence their campaign to ban the production and consumption of alcohol.

1920s and 1930s

In spite of post-war economic depression and the threat of Prohibition, the wine industry gradually expands.

1945–58

Soldiers returning from European battlefields with a taste for wine create a boom. However, a Royal Commission finds that much New Zealand wine is 'unfit for human consumption'. This condemnation leads to a flood of cheap imports, which threatens the domestic wine industry.

1958

Rises in duty on imported wines turn the nation's attention to domestic wines and sales are given a boost.

1950s and 1960s

George Mazuran, winemaking president of the Viticultural Association, successfully lobbies against fresh calls for national Prohibition. New licensing laws allowing the sale of wine in restaurants (1960) and taverns (1961) encourage foreign investment and, between 1965 and 1970, the area under vine trebles, spreading south to Hawkes Bay and Gisborne. Some producers take advice from the Rhine Valley's Dr Helmut Becker, who suggests that New Zealand's climate is suitable for Germanic styles and, consequently, much Müller-Thurgau is planted,

The Richmond Ranges, viewed from a vineyard in the Wairau River Valley and as depicted on the world-famous Cloudy Bay wine label.

though the American hybrid Albany Surprise is still the most widely planted variety in 1960.

1970s

South Island begins to be developed.

1975

The Wine Institute of New Zealand is founded.

1976

Customers are permitted to bring their own wine to restaurants.

1979

New Zealand's first wine bar is opened.

1980

Wine dilution is banned (and it is incredible that this practice was allowed to continue for as long as it did).

1983

A large harvest, following a very rapid expansion of vineyards, brings about a surplus of wine.

1986

A vine pull scheme is initiated which sees a reduction of 25 per cent in total vineyard area. However, growers are offered NZ$2,500 an acre to replant and French grape varieties begin to make an appearance.

1989

The 1989 Sale of Liquor Act deregulates much of the drinks industry.

1990

Supermarkets are licensed to sell wines and Marlborough gains its position as New Zealand's largest wine region.

North Island

It is impossible to make generalizations here because every five degrees or so of latitude makes subtle, but noticeable, differences to the mesoclimate ... and hence to the wines. It is safe to say, however, that North Island wines are riper, more full-bodied and softer in style compared with those of South Island, owing to the generally warmer weather.

Auckland

Chances are that the next New Zealand wine you will drink will have been bottled in Auckland ... though the odds also dictate that it is unlikely to have been made from Auckland grapes. While over 90 per cent of New Zealand's wine production is bottled here, Auckland can boast less than four per cent of the country's area under vine.

But this was not always the case. Thanks to the wine-thirsty Dalmatian and Lebanese immigrants who worked the kauri gum forests in the early twentieth century, Auckland was home to more than half of New Zealand's vineyards right up until the early 1970s. The very heart and soul of the wine industry was centred here, which is why a large number of producers – including the great wine giant Montana, New Zealand's biggest producer – continue to house wineries in the region, trucking in grapes or juice from other areas for processing, bottling and distribution.

The planting and development of other vineyard areas to meet the growing demand for wines has now reduced the amount of true Auckland wine to a bare trickle, but do not let this put you off hunting them down! What the region lacks in size is more than made up for in strength: Auckland makes some of New Zealand's finest and most fabulous of wines – especially some impressive Cabernet and Merlot-based reds, stuffed with warm, ripe flavours, capable of ageing for a decade in favourable vintages.

The rolling hills of Northland-Matakana, which hosts New Zealand's northernmost winery (Monty Knight's Okahu Estate), is wonderful red wine country, thanks to plenty of rainfall, hot, humid summers and mild winters. Merlot and Shiraz are grown, but it is Cabernet Sauvignon that is particularly successful (especially from Heron's Flight Vineyards and Providence Vineyards). It tends to suffer from excessive vigour thanks to

French oak barrels in the barrel room of Delegat's, Henderson, near Auckland.

Pruning vines in winter (June), at Kumeu River Wines, Kumeu-Huapia, Auckland. In many parts of the New World, especially in large-scale vineyards, this task would be carried out by machine.

the climate, but this is being controlled by better canopy-thinning techniques. It certainly does not appear to have discouraged growers from beavering away at planting even more.

Another exciting (and most fashionable) source of elegant, long-lived Cabernet and Bordeaux-style blends is Waiheke Island, located a half-hour ferry ride away from Auckland in the Hauraki Gulf. This sub-region may be relatively young (Goldwater Estate was the pioneering force here; their first vintage was in 1982), but it has already forged a reputation out of all proportion to its diminutive size. In spite of salty Pacific sea breezes, it is much drier and less humid than mainland Auckland, with lower summer rainfall and a higher number of sunshine hours. The mesoclimate is so good, in fact, that no other viticultural area in New Zealand can harvest Cabernet Sauvignon so early and so ripe. Producers are able to craft wines of world-class quality, though the volumes made are so minute that prices are (unfortunately for us) very high – indeed, Stephen White's

The vineyard and winery of Nobilo Vintners, Huapai, near Auckland. New Zealand's fourth largest winery is most famous internationally for its Müller-Thurgau based white wine, 'White Cloud'.

flagship Stonyridge Larose is one of New Zealand's most sought after and most expensive red wines.

The equally tiny district of Kumeu-Huapia is also known for premium wines (reds and whites), though there are only ten wineries. Of note is the family-owned, adventurous Kumeu River Wines who create wonderful fruit-driven Sauvignon Blanc, a soft Sauvignon Blanc-Sémillon blend and a gorgeously jammy Cabernet Sauvignon-Merlot. As with the other wineries, much of their fruit has to be sourced from other wine regions, though, because the area simply is not big enough to supply enough grapes to support them.

In complete contrast, Henderson, which nestles in the foothills of the Waitekere Ranges, is one of the most prolific grape-growing areas in New Zealand, despite heavily-leached clay soils and lashings of rain. Stylish blends are put together from Cabernet Sauvignon, Cabernet Franc and Merlot (or bottled as single varietals); there is a drop of Pinotage from Soljans Wines, and some sophisticated Chardonnay and Sauvignon Blanc, particularly from Collards Brothers' Rothesay Vineyard.

Waikato and Bay of Plenty

The Te Kauwhata Government Viticultural Research Station, established under the supervision of Italian viticulturist Romeo Bragato, was the first to put this region on the wine map. Today, the Rongopai winery occupies the old site, though it supplements its grapes from Marlborough and Hawkes Bay.

While this inland region produces dry wines from Sauvignon Blanc, Chardonnay and Sémillon (plus dollops of Cabernet Sauvignon and Pinot Noir), its hallmark wine is gorgeously luscious and sweet botrytized Riesling. High morning humidity, promoted by the proximity of Lake Waikere, is chased by hot, dry, sunny days – the perfect conditions for the development of the infamous 'noble rot', though there is no guarantee that it will happen every year.

East of Waikato, Morton Estate and Mills Reef Winery are the only two wineries to inhabit the Bay of Plenty, but even they have to bring in grapes from Hawkes Bay. Galatea has one solitary winery – Covell Estate – which makes intensely-flavoured, ageworthy Pinot Noir, Chardonnay, Riesling and a Cabernet Sauvignon-Merlot blend.

A whole raft of quality white wines has come on stream from Gewürztraminer, Riesling, Sémillon, Sauvignon Blanc, Chenin Blanc and Chardonnay.

Gisborne

Accepted wine wisdom preaches that a flat valley floor, fertile soils, a high water table and hot, sticky weather with heavy autumnal rain are not ideal conditions for vines. Yes, plenty of grapes will be produced, but they will not amount to much in terms of quality. Yet top Gisborne growers have proved that it is possible to obtain premium fruit, in spite of these natural disadvantages.

It was not always like this, though. The prime reason for developing Gisborne was to meet the demand of the cask and bag-in-box wine industry; the vineyards could yield over twice the volume of those in Auckland or Waikato, especially when planted with a high-cropping variety like Müller-Thurgau. When it became cheaper (half the price!) to import bulk wine, growers soon recognized the need to switch to 'fine wine' grapes – that is if they wanted to stay in business.

New varieties have been planted in carefully selected sites, and, with assiduous vineyard management, a whole raft of quality white wines has come on stream from Chardonnay, Chenin Blanc, Gewürztraminer, Riesling, Sauvignon Blanc and Sémillon. Indeed, Gisborne has been christened locally as 'The Chardonnay Capital of New Zealand'. There is no doubt that Gisborne Chardonnay is good wine, with a lovely, soft, peach-and-melon, tropical-styled weight which is not found elsewhere, but I would venture that it is second-in-line to the quality of Hawkes Bay Chardonnay.

Reds have fared less well and standards vary enormously, though Merlot is drinkable, and there has been a promising start to Pinot Noir from Matawhero Wines and Millton Vineyard, which is grown mainly to augment supply for the country's sparkling wine industry. And this sums up neatly the Gisborne paradox: the region is New Zealand's third largest wine grape producer, yet even though the fruit is much improved, most

New Zealand whites are characterized by an unequalled zestiness and freshness, owing to a combination of climatic conditions and New World winemaking techniques.

of the crop is still being dispatched to wineries elsewhere to be turned into anonymous blends.

The old name for Gisborne used to be Poverty Bay. Well, far from it, I say, as long as more producers are willing to capitalize on the potential of bottling unblended Gisborne wines.

Hawkes Bay

This prestigious region has it all! A perfect climate, some excellent soils, a solid, proud history of commercial winemaking and, most important of all, an unfettered enthusiasm to make the very best of its natural assets. No wonder that Hawkes Bay not only makes premium wines of its own, but is also a popular source of grapes for wineries outside the region.

Consider the geography. The mountains of the heartland Kaweka and Ruahine Ranges soak up most of the rain borne by the prevailing west winds, leaving Hawkes Bay fairly dry. The summers are warm, with low humidity; the autumns are dry; and there is sunshine in abundance. Indeed, full advantage is taken of the ripening influence of the sun, thanks to new trellising systems and judicious leaf-plucking. All good news for a late-maturing variety like Cabernet Sauvignon.

Growers also increasingly understand the significance of maintaining low yields in a complex geological terrain. Traditionally, vineyards were planted on the wide expanse of the river flats of the Heretaunga Plain, but the soils (mainly alluvial loams over gravel) are very fertile here. This encourages vines to grow vigorously, and they produce masses of grapes of dubious and unreliable quality. Since the 1980s, however, there has been a growing recognition of the advantages offered by the lower slopes of the limestone hills further inland: the deeply bedded, gravelly soils are well-drained and less fertile, and because the vines are stressed more as a result, vigour is reduced. Grapes are riper and better balanced, resulting in wines of far superior quality. Interestingly, while dry conditions are beneficial on the whole, around ten per cent of Hawkes Bay's vineyards need to be irrigated. Good water management helps to control yield and grape acid levels, however, so it is not as disastrous as it might sound.

While Hawkes Bay offers a diverse range of wines, its reputation (or, at least, its modern-day reputation) rests on high-quality, berry-flavoured, Claret-style blends made from Cabernet Sauvignon and Merlot (and the high volumes produced make them very competitive) – Brookfields Vineyards, C.J. Pask Winery and Esk Valley Estate are amongst the top producers. Chardonnay is also highly prized and can certainly challenge Gisborne's claim to being the Chardonnay capital of New Zealand (and if you do not believe me, just try Te Mata Estate's delicious example). The character of Hawkes Bay

Maori Legend

The small town of Martinborough lies in the mountainous shadow of the Nga-Waka-A-Kupe, which translates as 'the three canoes of Kupe'. Kupe was the first Maori to discover New Zealand, and legend has it that a mighty earthquake shook the land when Kupe reached shore, which caused the land to rise and carry his canoes inland. To this day, the outlines of Kupe's three canoes can still be seen as three kinks etched into the hills.

Chardonnay sits neatly between the powerful ripeness of the north and the delicate freshness of the south: they're rich, weighty, hearty wines, but they also shout 'Grapefruit!' and all the welcome acidity this suggests.

Of the other wines, Sauvignon Blanc flaunts a distinctively mellow and tropical style, which has a tendency to lack crispness, and there is tart, stylish, sometimes arrestingly good Riesling (especially from Coopers Creek). Babich has recently released an inspiring Chenin Blanc. There is a sprinkling of bottle-fermented sparkling wines, and minute quantities of drinkable Cabernet Franc, Pinot Noir, Syrah and Gewürztraminer (Kemblefield Estate's is excellent).

Hawkes Bay is second only to Marlborough in terms of size and rate of expansion, and its future looks good. A number of sub-regions have been identified as great sites for the production of premium wines and I have no doubt that these will continue to be developed.

Gimblett Road, for example, has emerged as one of the most fashionable 'new' wine areas for red wines thanks to top growers such as Stonecroft Wines and Villa Maria Estate who have planted vineyards here. Its free-draining, shingle soils and slightly warmer temperatures are ideal; vine vigour is kept at bay and the grapes ripen properly. Te Mata/Havelock North, Taradale/Meeanee/Brook-

The Stables Winery of the top quality, boutique Ngatarawa Wines, near Hastings, Hawkes Bay.

fields, Haumoana/Te Awanga, Fernhill/Ngatarawa/Ohiti, Mangatahi/Maraekakaho, Esk Valley/Bayview and Dartmoor/Puketapu are also districts which should be watched.

Wellington

Pinot Noir, the grape of Wellington. Or perhaps I should say the grape of Martinborough, one hour's drive away from the city across the Rimutaka Ranges, in the Wairarapa sub-region. With a 15-year career in making fine Pinot Noir, no other winemaking region in New Zealand can charm such expression of fruit and flavour from this most capricious of grapes, offering wines which approach the subtlety and complexity of that most famous of benchmarks – red Burgundy.

Well, that is one view. Some critics say that Martinborough Pinot is not consistent enough to rival Burgundy (but when was Burgundy ever consistent, I ask?); others comment that it is even better. I would say that it all depends on which style of Pinot Noir you favour, though even this argument is weakened by the fact that Martinborough produces everything from big, seductive, super-concentrated wines (like Larry McKenna's at Martinborough Vineyard), to lighter, more ethereal, quasi-Burgundian interpretations (such as Ata Rangi Vineyard's style).

What is not in doubt is Martinborough's eminent geographical suitability for the cultivation of Pinot Noir. It has the driest mesoclimate in North Island, with plenty of sunshine, dry autumns and moderately cool temperatures – remarkably similar to the climate of Burgundy, as it happens. The vines are grown in free-draining, infertile soil, many on terraced vineyards carved out by the same river action which left its bed of pebbles and gravel stranded as topsoil. The vines are not over-stressed, but they have to work hard, and this has a beneficial effect on grape quality.

Even under such ideal growing conditions, clonal selection is critical and cropping has to be controlled. As Chris Buring of Te Kairanga Wines says: 'If you don't keep the yields down, you end up making rosé.' And good Pinot is also tricky to actually make; the thin-skinned grapes need to be handled delicately, so foot-crushing or whole bunch pressing is common practice in order to avoid high tannin levels. All in all, this adds up to expensive wine.

Pinot Noir may be Martinborough's most distinguished grape variety, but the area also produces New Zealand's top Pinot Gris and Gewürztraminer from Dry River Wines. Notable success has also been achieved with Cabernet Sauvignon, Chardonnay, Chenin Blanc, Merlot, Riesling, Sauvignon Blanc and Syrah.

While most of Wellington's vineyards are clustered around Martinborough, the coastal vineyards of Te Horo are showing some promise, with varieties such as Montepulciano, Pinotage, Sangiovese and Zinfandel.

Dirty Wellingtons

Ata Rangi Vineyard uses the 'Able' clone of Pinot Noir, which they originally attempted to smuggle into New Zealand in a pair of Wellington boots (how apt!). Needless to say, they did not get away with it and the clone was quarantined. Happily, this clone is now on general release.

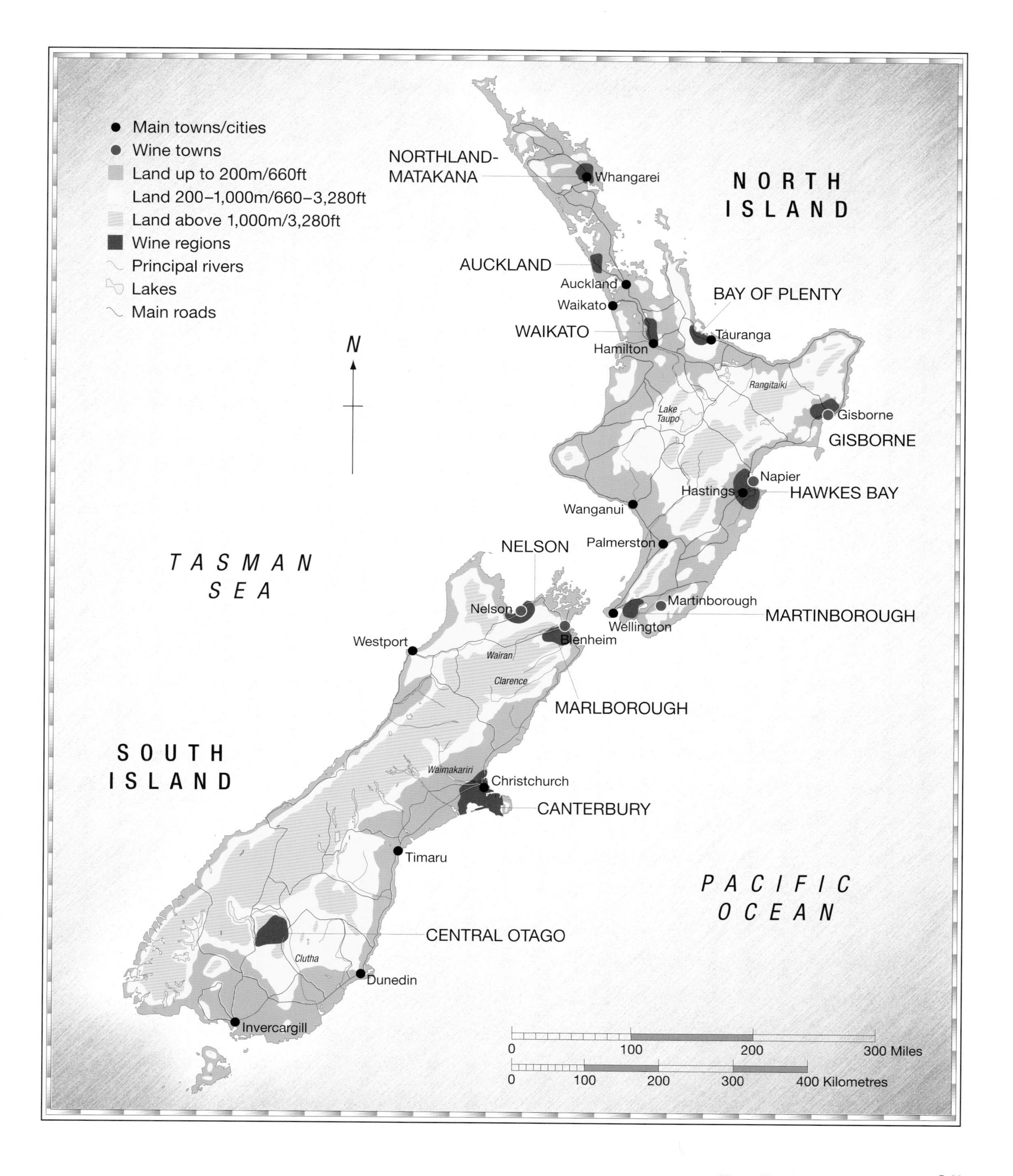

Main towns/cities
Wine towns
Land up to 200m/660ft
Land 200–1,000m/660–3,280ft
Land above 1,000m/3,280ft
Wine regions
Principal rivers
Lakes
Main roads
N
NORTH ISLAND
NORTHLAND-MATAKANA
Whangarei
AUCKLAND
Auckland
Waikato
BAY OF PLENTY
WAIKATO
Tauranga
Hamilton
Rangitaiki
Lake Taupo
Gisborne
GISBORNE
Napier
Hastings
HAWKES BAY
Wanganui
Palmerston
NELSON
TASMAN SEA
Nelson
Martinborough
MARTINBOROUGH
Wellington
Blenheim
Westport
Wairau
Clarence
MARLBOROUGH
SOUTH ISLAND
Waimakariri
Christchurch
CANTERBURY
Timaru
PACIFIC OCEAN
CENTRAL OTAGO
Clutha
Dunedin
Invercargill
0
100
200
300 Miles
0
100
200
300
400 Kilometres

South Island

This part of New Zealand developed well behind North Island in every economic sense, so it comes as no surprise to learn that the wine industry did not really evolve until 1973. Once improved lines of communication opened, South Island rushed to catch up, and today the island is proving its potential for fine wines, especially with cool climate grapes.

Marlborough

It is rather depressing to realize that I was already well into my teens when modern-day Marlborough sprang to life in 1973! Even more astonishing is the fact that it has taken only 26 years for the region to establish its position as New Zealand's most prominent and most important wine area; I simply cannot think of any other place where the rise to stardom has been so meteoric.

While Meadowbank Farm was founded as Marlborough's first commercial vineyard in 1873 – and others soon followed – the 1960s witnessed the shutdown of the wine industry owing to lack of demand. Montana Wines was the first company thereafter to consider the region viable for growing good quality grapes at a time when new sources were being sought. One century after Meadowbank's historic move, Montana took the plunge by purchasing options to buy around 1600 hectares of Marlborough land, a pioneering but risky venture.

And, indeed, things did not go well at first. Seventy to 80 per cent of the first vines died, simply because the area was too arid. Some prompt attention to irrigation soon conquered this problem, however, and by 1975 nearly 400 hectares had been planted successfully. Marlborough has since grown to become New Zealand's largest wine region with more than 3,000 hectares of vineyards (nearly 40 per cent of the country's total).

Two-thirds of the vines are concentrated in the flat, lowland flood plain of the Wairau Valley, though vine cultivation is now slowly spreading south into the Awatere Valley. Flanked on three sides by the towering Southern Alps, the Wairau Valley is a suntrap – indeed, Blenheim is said to be New Zealand's sunniest town with an average of 2,395 sunny hours each year. At this southerly latitude, however, sunshine doesn't necessarily equal heat; temperatures rarely exceed 24°C (75°F), and frost can be troublesome at certain times of year.

Marlborough's Cloudy Bay Winery also creates a super traditional-method sparkling wine called 'Pelorus'.

The sun-filled vineyards of Seton Vineyard at Woodbourne in Marlborough, with the dramatic backdrop of the lofty Southern Alps.

Nature's compensation for this comes in the form of large pebbles and rocks (abandoned by the river when it shifted course) which line patches of the valley floor. These reflect sunlight during the day, but also absorb and store heat which is radiated at night, helping to keep the vines warm. Ironically, in spite of the cool climate, there is a chronic lack of water owing to desiccating winds, so trickle irrigation systems are common. The flip side is that water shortage forces the vine roots to dig deeper for water, which reduces vine vigour.

The vine also has to struggle for water in the Awatere Valley, where many vineyards have been terraced from flinty, shallow, less fertile soils. This, coupled with a slightly warmer mesoclimate, has created a sub-regional style: the wines are more concentrated, with a mineral edge to their flavour.

What Marlborough is really famous for, however, is Sauvignon Blanc. It is amazing how such a relatively humble white grape variety, which had previously attracted little attention outside France's Pouilly Fumé and Sancerre, has been responsible for launching Marlborough into wine orbit. Yet Marlborough Sauvignon Blanc has touched the vinous hearts and souls (not to forget tastebuds!) of

Sunset over a vineyard at Marlborough, South Island.

millions of oenophiles in an incredibly short period of time.

Nowhere else in the world can coax such a unique and unbeatable array of exhilarating aromas and tastes from this grape. It is quintessential stuff ... pungent flavours of gooseberries, green peppers, freshly-cut grass and, sometimes, tropical fruits, all rounded off by a sharp snap of lime zest acidity.

This is not necessarily easy to achieve, however. Marlborough soil (mainly alluvial loams over deep deposits of gravel) is fairly fertile, particularly towards the north of the region, and Sauvignon Blanc grows like a weed if it is put in the wrong place. Vigorous growth does nothing for grapes – they simply will not reach full maturity, which gives an unattractive 'green' flavour to the wine. Many producers attempt to overcome this by picking Sauvignon Blanc at different levels of ripeness in order to lend complexity to the finished wine – indeed, the wines are not as one-dimensional as they once were. Leaf-plucking can also tone down grassy flavours and add tropical notes. Better clones can also help. And some wineries, including the legendary Cloudy Bay Vineyards, often add some Sémillon to temper their Sauvignon. Which leads to another startling date-fact: Marlborough's rise to fame only really kicked off with the production of this benchmark wine ... in 1985! Today's top Sauvignon producers include Hunter's Wines, Jackson Estate, Lawson's Dry Hills Wines and Wairau River Wines.

Sauvignon Blanc may be the jewel in Marlborough's crown, but the region can also celebrate resounding success with opulent botrytized wines, some outstanding Champagne-method sparkling wines (originally inspired by Daniel le Brun), Riesling (particularly at Cairnbrae Wines and Grove Mill Wine Company), Sémillon, Gewürztraminer and, of course, the ubiquitous Chardonnay.

Chardonnay was overtaken by Sauvignon Blanc as the most-planted variety in Marlborough as recently as 1994, but it remains one of the region's top grapes. Owing far more to winemaking intervention than terroir, it comes in an enormous range of styles without any distinctive regional signature. When handled well, though, it is one of the most rich and complex wines that New Zealand can offer.

Success has been more limited with red wines – the region is not really hot enough. It seems quite literally a waste of space for producers to be attempting to grow Cabernet Sauvignon when it only ripens one year in six here. Merlot is showing some promise, though, and Pinot Noir does well at Fromm Winery. In fact, the latter can produce some stunning wines in good years from top producers, and, of course, it is an essential ingredient in many fizz blends.

As for Marlborough's future, more emphasis will be placed on producing wines exclusively from individual vineyards, and the growing sub-regional divide between the Wairau and Awatere Valleys seems set to expand further, so that marked differences in style will continue to emerge.

Nelson

It takes just two hours to drive across the mountains that separate Nelson from its closest wine neighbour, Marlborough, yet the topography of the two regions could not be more different. While Marlborough comprises little more than the flat flood plain of the Wairau River, the breathtakingly beautiful Nelson landscape is a mass of rolling hills and valleys which sweep down to meet the Tasman Bay by way of the verdant, silty-soiled Waimea Plains.

Vines thrive in this kind of terrain. But they also love Nelson's climate of long warm summers, cool autumn nights and lots and lots of sunshine – this is one of the sunniest spots in the country. However, while a wide range of varieties can perform well here, vineyard site selection is critical. The best wines come from the warm, clay and gravel soils of the Upper Moutere hills in pockets that offer shelter from heavy autumn downpours that can all too frequently ruin a crop, the one downside to the climate.

The region's strength lies in its white wines, especially those made from Chardonnay, Riesling and Sauvignon Blanc. Chardonnay, in particular, gives some wonderfully delicate, fragrant wines that retain a fresh, lime-edged bite – indeed, Neudorf makes one of New Zealand's top examples with flavours which often approach the complexity of Puligny-Montrachet.

Reds are less consistent, although Pinot Noir from producers such as Glover's Vineyard is now starting to realize its potential. Merlot is also showing promise – an early-ripener, it is more reliable than the later-cropping Cabernet Sauvignon.

Nelson is home to some of New Zealand's most exciting small boutique wineries, led by Seifried (the first to plant vines in the Upper Moutere hills, back in 1973). As other parts of the region are developed – the stony-soiled Rabbit Island, for example – we are bound to hear more from this tiny region.

Canterbury

References to French peasants do not pop up too often in Kiwi history, so it is a treat to learn that they were the first to make drinkable wines in Canterbury – at Akaroa on Banks Peninsula to the east of Christchurch, in 1840 to be precise. It was not until 1973,

The breathtakingly beautiful Nelson landscape is a mass of rolling hills and valleys which sweep down to meet the Tasman Bay.

Cloudy Bay

No, Cloudy Bay is not named after the wine! The Wairau River spits so much silt into the sea that the bay is decidedly murky. Captain Cook observed this phenomenon, and thus named these waters 'Cloudy Bay'.

Rippon Vineyard on the shore of Lake Wanaka, Central Otago, South Island. The large expanse of water, which has warmed up during the hot summer months, helps to keep the vines warm and snug thoughout the cold of winter.

however, that local wines began to be taken seriously, sparked off by viticultural research carried out by Dr David Jackson of Lincoln University.

Canterbury's climate is pretty cool by South Island standards and frost can be a problem in October and April (though a low annual rainfall of just 620mm (24in) and a long, slow ripening season are its saving graces). Furthermore, the region suffers from strong, warm, vine-dehydrating nor'-westers, though they help to keep humidity levels down. Dr Jackson therefore set out to establish the most suitable locations for grape-growing – and the most appropriate grapes to grow there – under the prevailing climatic conditions.

The white varieties of Chardonnay, Riesling (especially when turned into a sweet botrytized style by producers such as Giesen Wine Estate), Sauvignon Blanc, Sémillon, Pinot Blanc and Pinot Gris were identified as the grapes most likely to do consistently well, whether grown on the flat, exposed plains around Christchurch or the gently rolling terrain 40km (25m) to the north at Waipara. Incidentally, this proved wrong the previously held hypothesis that Germanic grapes would be best for the region!

Some wines are made from Cabernet Sauvignon, though they tend to be too herbaceous as the grapes do not ripen well. Pinot Noir, however, is developing a growing reputation for producing wines with an unusually rich and smooth character which can rarely be matched elsewhere in the country. Mark Rattray Vineyards, Pegasus Bay Winery and Waipara West handle Pinot best.

Since 1978, when the first commercial vineyard (Saint Helena) was established in Belfast (north of Christchurch), there has been no looking back and, today, Canterbury is New Zealand's fourth largest wine region, supporting over 25 wine companies, and further growth is predicted.

Central Otago

'I would rate Central Otago as being pre-eminently suitable for premium wine production.' These words from Romeo Bragato in 1895 – and how right he was: New Zealand's newest wine region is rapidly building a reputation for excellent wines bursting with stunning, mouth-wateringly fruity flavours and a fine, slowly-evolving concentration.

Not only is this region the latest to hit the Kiwi wine headlines, but it is also the fastest-growing. In just ten years, a lowly seven hectares of vineyard area has grown to 250. Still pretty tiny, but impressive enough, nevertheless, and set to expand even further – there are currently 13 wineries and many more are planned. Isolated it may be, but the land is relatively cheap compared with higher profile regions.

On some levels it is hard to see why everyone is getting so excited about Otago. Owing to its southerly latitude (the region's Black Ridge Vineyard can claim the title as the most southerly vineyard and winery in the world) and high altitude (250–350m/ 820–1,150ft above sea level), the climate is distinctly marginal for growing vines – indeed, this is the only winemaking region in New Zealand with a continental rather than maritime climate, which means long, hot, dry summers, cold winters and a significant risk of frost damage at all the wrong times of year. Under these conditions, consistency of quality can vary enormously from vintage to vintage.

These kinds of problems do not worry Old World producers, however, and, similarly, Otago grape-growers have recognized the necessity of tailoring viticultural practice to suit the prevailing conditions. For example, vineyard sites are selected carefully in order to maximize available warmth. Small vineyards are carved out from rocky, steep-sided gorges (preferably north-facing to catch the most of the sun). Others are clustered around Lakes Wakatipu and Wanaka where the climate is moderated by the influence of the water.

All is not doom and gloom, though, as Otago's mountainous terrain and unique climate offer many benefits. Grapes can be left to ripen on the vine for longer than usual thanks to dry, sunshine-filled autumn days; low summer humidity checks fungal infection (and therefore rot); severe winter temperatures kill off any latent bugs and disease, and also gives the vine buds a much-desired period of dormancy. All good news.

Chardonnay, Gewürztraminer, Pinot Gris, Riesling and Sauvignon Blanc all shine, though Pinot Noir is swiftly becoming the most popular and distinguished variety.

Hollywood Wine

New Zealand-born, Hollywood actor Sam Neill (of *Jurassic Park* fame) owns the Two Paddocks Vineyard in Central Otago and makes some jolly good Pinot Noir which sells quickly. The Central Otago Wine Company is hoping to be able to offer it for sale on-line soon.

North America

The richest and most powerful country in the world boasts a wine industry to match, exploiting superlative natural resources to the full in several different states.

God's Own Country

The land of milk and honey also makes some very fine wines

National statistics reveal that 18.64 million hectolitres of wine were made in 1996 (the latest figure available), making the United States the fourth largest producer of wine in the world. A further 491,000 hectolitres of bulk wine was shipped into the country for eventual bottling.

A pretty hefty set of numbers.... California alone is responsible for some 90 per cent of all wine made in the country, so it is clear that the balance is spread rather thinly across the remaining 49 states – and even more so if you take the burgeoning Pacific Northwest region and New York state out of the equation.

Perhaps surprisingly, there are very few states which do not produce wine on some scale – I can find no evidence of commercial winemaking (and please note the commercial tag here) in Alaska, North and South Dakota or Wyoming. Many states, however (Alabama, Delaware, Florida, Hawaii, Illinois, Iowa, Kansas, Kentucky, Louisiana, Maine, Minnesota, Mississippi, Montana, Nebraska, Nevada, New Hampshire, North and South Carolina, Philadelphia, Rhode Island, Tennessee, Utah, Vermont, West Virginia and Wisconsin), have so few wineries between them that their contribution to the national wine pool is no more than a negligible trickle.

One would naturally assume that it is an unsuitable climate which rules out commercial viticulture in these areas and, in many cases, this is absolutely true. But the influence of a deeply rooted cultural and religious aversion to alcohol which continues to reign in some parts of the United States should never be underestimated. The citizens of Maine, for instance, voted to go dry in 1846, some 74 years ahead of the Volstead Act, and Kansas followed in 1880, in spite of the fact that the state was a considerable producer of wine at the time. In fact, some 30 states were already dry by the time of Prohibition.

After California, the greatest concentration of vitivinicultural efforts can be found in the eastern states and the Pacific Northwest, but there are some enterprising winemaking ventures taking place in pockets elsewhere. Many producers remain faithful to native varieties and hybrids rather than vinifera (though many producers grow both, of course, or buy in grapes from other states). In certain areas, however, growers have no choice, thanks to the vinifera-destroying Pierce's Disease, and this is proving to be the biggest brake to expansion of vinifera plantings throughout the United States.

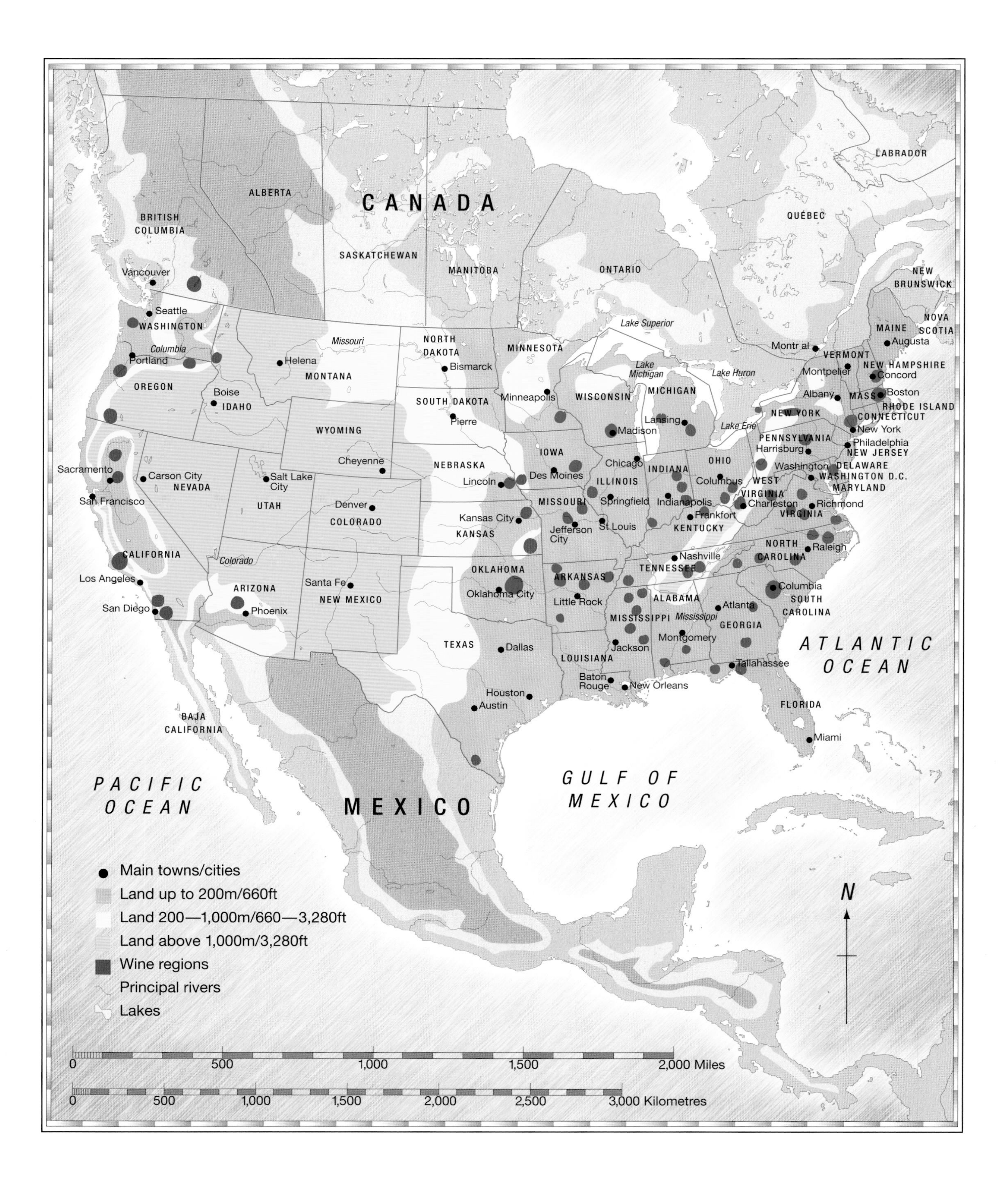
CANADA
ALBERTA
BRITISH COLUMBIA
SASKATCHEWAN
MANITOBA
ONTARIO
QUÉBEC
LABRADOR
NEW BRUNSWICK
NOVA SCOTIA
Vancouver
Seattle
WASHINGTON
Columbia
Portland
OREGON
Boise
IDAHO
Missouri
Helena
MONTANA
NORTH DAKOTA
Bismarck
SOUTH DAKOTA
Pierre
MINNESOTA
Minneapolis
WISCONSIN
Madison
Lake Superior
Lake Michigan
Lake Huron
Lake Erie
MICHIGAN
Lansing
Montr al
MAINE
Augusta
VERMONT
Montpelier
NEW HAMPSHIRE
Concord
Albany
MASS
Boston
RHODE ISLAND
CONNECTICUT
NEW YORK
New York
PENNSYLVANIA
Harrisburg
Philadelphia
NEW JERSEY
DELAWARE
Washington
WASHINGTON D.C.
MARYLAND
WYOMING
Cheyenne
NEBRASKA
Lincoln
IOWA
Des Moines
Chicago
ILLINOIS
INDIANA
OHIO
Columbus
WEST VIRGINIA
Charleston
Richmond
VIRGINIA
Sacramento
Carson City
NEVADA
Salt Lake City
UTAH
San Francisco
Denver
COLORADO
Kansas City
KANSAS
MISSOURI
Springfield
Indianapolis
Frankfort
Jefferson City
St Louis
KENTUCKY
NORTH CAROLINA
Raleigh
CALIFORNIA
Colorado
Nashville
TENNESSEE
OKLAHOMA
ARKANSAS
Los Angeles
ARIZONA
Santa Fe
NEW MEXICO
Oklahoma City
Little Rock
ALABAMA
Columbia
SOUTH CAROLINA
San Diego
Phoenix
Atlanta
MISSISSIPPI
Mississippi
GEORGIA
TEXAS
Dallas
Montgomery
Jackson
LOUISIANA
ATLANTIC OCEAN
Tallahassee
Baton Rouge
New Orleans
Houston
Austin
FLORIDA
BAJA CALIFORNIA
Miami
PACIFIC OCEAN
MEXICO
GULF OF MEXICO
Main towns/cities
Land up to 200m/660ft
Land 200—1,000m/660—3,280ft
Land above 1,000m/3,280ft
Wine regions
Principal rivers
Lakes
N
0
500
1,000
1,500
2,000 Miles
0
500
1,000
1,500
2,000
2,500
3,000 Kilometres

California

When one thinks of Californian wine, does an enigmatic, entrepreneurial Hungarian exile leap to mind? I suspect not. Nevertheless, Agostón Harászthy is generally credited with being the father of modern Californian winemaking. He put the classic European vines – Cabernet Sauvignon, Chardonnay *et al* – on the Golden State's viticultural map, back in 1857.

Early enterprise was soon dashed by the spread of phylloxera, Prohibition, the Depression and the Second World War. But this did not stop California emerging as the leading force in introducing to the world 'varietal' wines – those made from single grape varieties. The giddy wine boom of the 1970s was not fostered by revolutionary marketing wizardry alone, however. Equally important was the ability of her pioneers to challenge France's hegemony as the world's greatest quality wine nation by turning traditional winemaking practices on their head ... with huge success.

But bust has always had the knack of following boom in California, and in the early 1990s this came in the form of another crippling attack of phylloxera: biotype B finally succeeded in gnawing away at low-resistant AxR#1 vine roots. The North Coast vineyards were particularly hard hit and many of the older plantings had to be replaced at huge cost, both in terms of money and time (a vine takes a few years to yield its first crop of fruit, after all). Estimates suggest that well over half of the vineyards will have been replanted by 2000 in this region alone.

The good thing to come out of this sorry state of affairs has been the opportunity to address a few key viticultural issues. The vineyards have been replanted at higher densities with more suitable vines; improved rootstocks have been adopted that are better allied to a cocktail of superior clones (which, in turn, can be matched to soil types); the vines have been retrained on vertical trellis systems which open up the canopy to more sunshine and ventilation; and so on.

A change in winemaking techniques was prompted, too – practices such as cold soaking the must before fermentation, utilizing different yeast strains, using malolactic fermentation to better effect, blending lots from selected vineyards and shortening barrel-ageing time have

Dusk over vineyards at Rutherford in the Napa Valley, with Mt St Helena beyond.

all brought about improvements. While the market has not ceased to crave the 'fighting varietals' – Cabernet Sauvignon (the top red variety), Chardonnay (the leading white grape), Merlot, Sauvignon Blanc and Zinfandel – there has at least been an elevation in quality. Today's wines are more subtle, elegant and complex in flavour and have moved away from the big, bold, over-oaky monsters of the past.

There is one dark cloud looming on the horizon, however. No sooner has the industry picked itself up and dusted itself down in the wake of phylloxera, when a new disease appears to threaten the vineyards – the incurable, vine killing Pierce's Disease, which has already surfaced in the North Coast regions of Napa, Santa Cruz and Sonoma. Indeed, the possibility of an epidemic of this disease is the greatest and most justified fear of all Californian vine-growers ... they would have to uproot all of their vines in order to eradicate it. This scourge is caused by bacteria spread by the Blue-Green Sharpshooter. Unfortunately, this insect enjoys warm, damp conditions and many of the new, post-phylloxera plantings have been sited closer to the rivers. Furthermore, young vines are especially vulnerable, of which California now has plenty. Let us hope it stays that way.

Mendocino County

Mendocino's early wines remained relatively unknown because the region was isolated from the larger city markets to the south. Indeed, by the time the railroad and highways had pushed north to reach the county, the Napa and Sonoma wineries were already well-established in the burgeoning, key, San Francisco market. Mendocino wines did not make their mark, therefore, and the final nail in the coffin came in the form of Prohibition, which virtually put a complete stop to the nascent wine industry.

Hygiene in the winery is critical to wine quality. It is essential that barrels are washed out before the new vintage arrives.

While grapes were grown once again in the post-Prohibition years, most were shipped south to generic wine producers in Sonoma County. A revival came about in the 1960s, however, and with new vineyard locations, different varietals, improved viticultural techniques, a strong regional emphasis on organic grape-growing, and skilled winemaking, wineries such as Parducci and Fetzer (by far the largest winery in the county) had gained worldwide distribution by the 1980s, and there are now five separate AVAs.

The most talked-about AVA is Anderson Valley where the wine industry has gradually evolved since the mid-1800s, when fledgling vineyards were planted by Swiss and Italian settlers. Exceptionally, even Prohibition did little to halt its development, thanks to the demands of thirsty local loggers, the chief market at that time.

Spring mustard flowering in the vineyards of Alexander Valley, Sonoma County, California. Approximately 83 per cent of total plantings is devoted to the cultivation of Cabernet Sauvignon, Chardonnay, Merlot, Sauvignon Blanc and Zinfandel, though some Nebbiolo, Pinot Noir, Sangiovese, Syrah and Tempranillo is also grown.

Lake County

Cut off from the influence of the Pacific Ocean by the coastal mountains, this land-locked county is good Cabernet Sauvignon, Chardonnay and Sauvignon Blanc territory, owing to its relative warmth. Most of the vineyards are concentrated in Clear Lake AVA, (the eponymous lake is California's largest), and companies like Konocti and Louis M. Martini grow vines here.

Sonoma County

The AVA structure in this county is unusually complicated. While there is no county-wide appellation, Northern Sonoma AVA encompasses all other AVAs except Sonoma Valley AVA. A complicated region, therefore, but one which produces some fantastic wines from its 14,500 hectares of vines.

Highlights of US History

1565

British Admiral Sir John Hawkins finds 20 hogsheads full of wine which have been made from wild Scuppernong Muscadine vines – and so the first American wine is born.

1609

Franciscan missionary monks plant vineyards in the sunny, fertile Rio Grande Valley of what is now New Mexico, and then move on to the Ysleta Mission near El Paso in what is to become Texas.

1647–64

Grapes are planted on Manhattan Island in New York by order of the governor, Peter Stuyvesant, who decrees that sailors are to have a daily ration of wine. While efforts are made to produce wine from imported European vinifera varieties, these prove futile, and so native grapes found growing wild are used.

1683

William Penn imports cuttings from France and Spain and plants them in the Colony of Pennsylvania, but the vines soon die. Some 50 years later, however, James Alexander, gardener to the son of William Penn, creates the 'Alexander' grape.

1733

General James E. Oglethorpe orders the settlers of Georgia to grow grapes to make wine which is destined to be drunk in England.

1767

The Royal Society of Arts in England awards two New Jersey vintners with recognition as the first Colonists to produce quality wines.

1769

Captain Gaspar de Portola, the Spanish governor of Baja California in Mexico, leads an expedition to California and forts are established at San Diego and Monterey. Franciscan monk, Father Junípero Serra, founds the Mission San Diego de Alcala, the first in a chain of 21 missions stretching from here to Sonoma. Nearly all of them end up producing wine for sacramental purposes, made from the Mission grape which Serra has brought with him.

1774

Thomas Jefferson persuades Italian Filippo Mazzei to plant European vinifera vines at Monticello, Virginia.

1793

The Pennsylvania Vine Company is formed in Philadelphia, the very first commercial grape-growing venture to be established in the United States.

1815

Napoleonic soldiers, fresh from their whipping at Waterloo, emigrate to Alabama bearing Bordeaux vine varieties. Most of the cuttings die, however, and it takes until the 1830s for wine to be produced on any commercial scale.

1825

Traders working for the Hudson's Bay Company plant vines at Fort Vancouver in Washington state, though it is not known whether wine is actually produced at this time.

1830s

The first wines are made in Missouri and the level of production eventually becomes second only to that of California. However, disease, over-production and a burgeoning local Prohibition movement forces the collapse of the industry, which is not revived until the creation of the Missouri Wine Board in 1978.

1833

California's first commercial vinifera winery is opened by Jean-Louis Vignes.

The story of North American wine is one of many highs and lows. However, the USA now has one of the greatest wine industries of all.

1838

George Calvert Yount, a trapper from North Carolina, recognizes the potential of the Napa Valley and acquires a few Mission vines from General Mariano Vallejo's Sonoma vineyard – the Napa wine industry is born.

1839

Brotherhood Winery in the Hudson River Region of New York state is established by Jean Jacques and Thomas Lake Harris and remains the nation's oldest continuously operating winery.

1848

On 2 February, California is annexed by the Americans. Just a few days earlier, however, on 24 January, James Wilson Marshall discovers gold at Sutter's Sawmill in Coloma Valley, near Sacramento. The promise of wealth brings thousands of 'forty-niners' to stake claims in northern California, and the state's white population trebles by 1850, making the California Gold Rush one of the largest migrations of people in world history. As the promise of gold vanishes, many newcomers turn their hand to viticulture, which transforms the nascent wine industry, and in just two years, the number of vines planted doubles, rising to nearly four million. By 1859, California is producing half a million gallons (two and a quarter million litres) of wine from over 100 European vinifera varieties.

1849

Hungarian *bon viveur* Agostón Harászthy moves to San Diego from Wisconsin to set up a fruit farm. He imports cuttings of 165 different vine varieties from Europe and purchases 230 hectares of land near the town of Sonoma in which to plant them, an estate which he christens Buena Vista. Only seven years later, his land holdings have expanded to 2,430 hectares. He is considered to be the true founding father of the California wine industry, thanks to his pioneering and far-reaching viticultural research.

1854

Oregon's Rogue River Valley becomes home to the state's first vinifera vines.

1860s

Italian immigrant Pasquale Saturno pioneers grape-growing and winemaking in the city of Walla Walla in Washington state, using Cinsault (which he calls 'Black Prince') and Zinfandel (brought up from California). In the meantime, Roberts establishes one of Washington's first vine nurseries from 80 different grapes imported from France.

1861

John Patchett plants the first commercial vineyard in Napa Valley, and Charles Krug opens the first commercial winery – by 1889, there are 140 of them.

1864

Tariff protection for American wines against imports is introduced, in spite of French opposition.

1867

California experiences a glut of grapes – the first 'bust' in a 'boom and bust' cycle which is to last for many years to come.

1869

The railroad linking east and west is completed. For the first time, Californian wines can compete properly with the 'domestic' wines of the midwest and eastern states. A year later, California becomes the leading wine-producing state of America.

1870

The fresh grape juice industry is founded by Drs Thomas and Charles Welch of New Jersey ... not to be underestimated in importance, even today.

1873

The deadly enemy, phylloxera, is identified in Sonoma, and it is to spread throughout California; by the year 1900, 7,200 hectares of vineyards will have been reduced to just 1,200 hectares.

1880

A national census of grape-growing is carried out and reports a flourishing industry in Alabama, Arkansas, California, Georgia, Illinois, Indiana, Iowa, Kansas, Kentucky, Mississippi, New Jersey, New Mexico, New York, North Carolina, Oregon, Pennsylvania, Tennessee, Utah and Virginia.

1883

Grapes are planted by a family of German immigrants, the Reuters, at Laurel Ridge Winery in Oregon, which is considered as the state's first truly commercial winery.

1903

A subsidiary of the Northern Pacific Railroad brings large-scale irrigation to eastern Washington, unlocking the dormant potential of the rich volcanic soils and warm, sunny, desert-like climate.

1920–33

The Volstead Act is brought into force and America embarks on the dry years of Prohibition. In theory, only 100 wineries are permitted to continue production, strictly for sacramental, medicinal and salted cooking wines.

1934

Federal wine quality and wine labelling standards are brought into force.

1938

A post-Prohibition boom leads to the production of one million gallons of wine in Oregon. Even at this stage, however, the California wine industry has regained its dominance.

1939

Frank Schoonmaker is the first to label wines by the variety from which they are made.

1945

Though Philip Wagner has imported French hybrid varieties into Maryland in 1935, Boordy Vineyards is the first to actually grow them on any commercial scale and goes on to introduce them to other parts of the northeast of the United States.

1950s

Trial studies for vinifera grapes are conducted by Dr Walter Clore, known as 'Grandpa Grape', at Washington State University. However, the first commercial plantings are delayed until the 1960s when, under the guidance of André Tchelistcheff, vineyards are established in the Yakima Valley by the predecessors of companies which have now become Chateau Ste

Michelle and Columbia Winery. At around this time, an intensive programme of research is embarked upon by the University of California at Davis, and its findings both in the vineyard and in the winery will consequently revolutionize winemaking practices at home and abroad.

1957

The first successful vinifera vines are cultivated by Dr Konstantin Frank (a Ukrainian-born professor of plant science) and Charles Fournier (former winemaker at Veuve Clicquot Ponsardin) in New York state.

1959

The Oregon wine industry is revived by Richard Sommer, a graduate in agronomy and viticulture at the University of California at Davis, who plants Riesling in his Hillcrest Vineyards at Roseburg in the Umpqua Valley.

1966

Robert Mondavi sets out to make wines in the French style from classic French grape varieties at his Napa Valley winery, and also popularizes the use of varietal labelling. He is set to lead California into the New World revolution.

1969

Washington state becomes a free market, ending years of the state monopoly governing wine sales. This is the stimulus which effectively launches the state's modern wine industry.

1972

Sutter Home Winery in California's Napa Valley creates the first blush Zinfandel, thus reviving interest in this grape variety.

1976

A blind tasting is organized by Englishman Steven Spurrier in Paris, which sets six Chardonnays and six Cabernet Sauvignons from California against illustrious French wines such as Puligny Montrachet Premier Cru Les Pucelles 1972 from Burgundy and Château Mouton-Rothschild 1970 from Bordeaux. Much to the shock of the judging panel (comprising French experts, incidentally), California's Chateau Montelena Chardonnay 1973 and Stag's Leap Wine Cellars Cabernet Sauvignon 1973 beat the French wines hands down. This preludes a veritable rush to California by the French to determine how and why this country's wines triumphed so unexpectedly. The Old World is suddenly awakened to the potential of the New.

1979

Oregon's Eyrie Pinot Noir 1975 is entered in the Gault Millau blind wine-tasting competition in Paris organized by Robert Drouhin and takes second prize to Joseph Drouhin's 1959 Chambolle Musigny (much to Drouhin's dismay !) ... Oregon Pinot Noir is launched to international acclaim. Meanwhile, in California's Napa Valley, Robert Mondavi collaborates with Château Mouton-Rothschild to create Opus One, the first great Franco-California joint venture wine. Down in Texas, meanwhile, commercial plantings of vinifera vines are made on High Plains.

1986

Following research by Professor Gordon Dutt and Robert Webb, the first winery is opened in Arizona.

1991

Almost overnight, red wine (most especially Merlot) becomes fashionable following a 12-minute feature entitled *The French Paradox* during a nationwide television programme which links red wine consumption to reduced levels of heart disease in France. By 1997, sales of red wine in the United States will have soared by 151 per cent from 23.2 million cases to 58.2 million cases, against a mere 12 per cent rise in sales of white wine.

1995

Phylloxera devastates the vineyards of California.

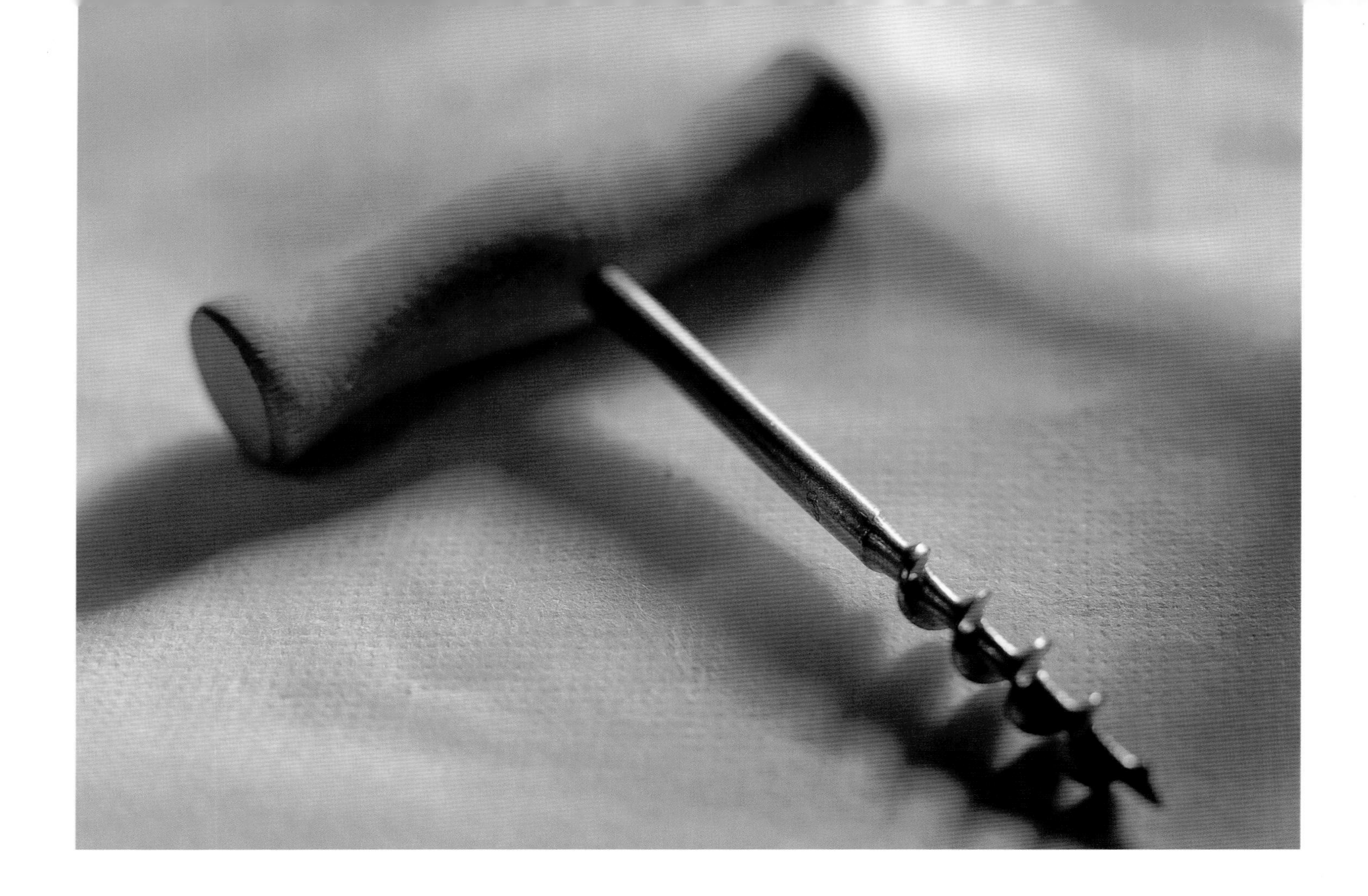

It is impossible to generalize about a county which possesses more appellations and sub-appellations than anywhere else in the state, except to say that they all share the characteristic of low-yielding vines (the lowest yielding region of California, in fact) which tends to create powerfully structured wines with complex, concentrated flavours.

As is common throughout California, many wineries source grapes from more than one area. At Chateau Souverain, for example, winemaker Tom Peterson adopts a 'best of the best' approach, first identifying the growing regions in Sonoma County for which each grape variety is best suited, and then selecting superior fruit from within each of these areas: Alexander Valley is home to the winery and provides the grapes for Cabernet Sauvignon, Merlot and Sauvignon Blanc; his Chardonnay and Pinot Noir is sourced from Los Carneros and Russian River Valley; and Zinfandel comes from old vines in Dry Creek Valley.

Alexander Valley AVA is the largest and most densely planted of Sonoma County's vineyard valleys. Its complex mosaic of soils and terrain, ranging from steep rocky hillsides (where the best vineyards are sited), to loamy benchlands, to a gravelly valley floor (though the composition of this changes every few years when the Valley floods), and temperate, fog-free microclimates, enables the Valley to produce exceptional grapes, both red and white.

The rolling Russian River Valley AVA, named for a Russian trading post which was centred here in the past, is designated as a cool area because of the fog which pushes its way up the Valley and

Sebastiani is the largest winery in the Sonoma Valley, though Matanzas Creek stands out as a brilliant producer of ultra-premium Sauvignon

its tributaries during the late spring and summer. It is also the wettest appellation within the county. The lower temperatures allow for a slow, even ripening of the fruit without sacrificing natural acidity. Refined, polished, tight-knit wines from Chardonnay and Pinot Noir are exceptional in their own right (try Davis Bynum, Dehlinger, De Loach, Gary Farrell, Iron Horse, Kistler, Lynmar, Martinelli, Pellegrini, Rochioli, Rutz, Sonoma-Cutrer and Williams Selyem) – indeed, some say that Russian River Valley is challenging Carneros as the Pinot Noir capital of California. But this is also sparkling wine country, and more traditional-method sparkling wine is created here than anywhere else in the state.

It is not surprising to find that the orchard-filled, 400-hectare Sonoma County Green Valley AVA shares many of the characteristics of Russian River Valley, as it is a sub-appellation of the latter. Its geographical position, however, means that the Pacific exercises a greater influence, so the area is marginally cooler on the whole. This creates a favourable environment for the predominant Chardonnay and Pinot Noir, and gives a greater intensity of flavour in the finished wine.

South of the city of Santa Rosa is the incredibly diverse, steep-sided Sonoma Valley AVA, described as the 'Valley of the Moon', which can sustain the growth of a wide range of grapes. Cabernet Sauvignon, Chardonnay, Gewürztraminer, Merlot, Pinot Noir, Sauvignon Blanc and Zinfandel all thrive here, though some depend on being planted in the warmer northern half of the Valley, notably Cabernet Sauvignon and Zinfandel, in the high, scenic Sonoma

Vínland

Leif Eriksson, the Norse explorer also known as Leif the Lucky, is reputed to have reached North America in about AD1000, according to the Viking Grenlinga ('Greenlander') and Eirik (after Eirik the Red) Sagas of the late 12th and early 13th centuries. One saga suggests that his ship was blown off course on his journey to Greenland (where he was sent by King Olaf I of Norway to convert the Greenlanders to Christianity) and reached North America instead. Another version of the tale is that he went to explore the islands which had been sighted west of Greenland, which may well have been Baffin Island, Labrador and Newfoundland. The latter was christened 'Vínland' – 'Wine Land' – owing to the number of wild grapes reported to have been growing there.

In 1004 Thorfinn Karlsefni, Leif's brother-in-law, apparently returned to settle Vínland at L'Anse aux Meadows on the northernmost tip of Newfoundland, but it is believed that he abandoned it soon afterwards thanks to opposition from the Maritime Archaic Indians and, possibly, the Dorset Eskimos. The site has been well excavated and the evidence does seem to support this theory. So, who knows, perhaps another European beat Christopher Columbus to it, after all?

Mountain AVA where Benziger, Jack London Ranch, Laurel Glen (which is dedicated to Cabernet Sauvignon) and McCrea make particularly complex wines.

Sebastiani is the largest winery in the Sonoma Valley, though Matanzas Creek stands out as a brilliant producer of ultra-premium Sauvignon Blanc (arguably California's finest) and lush, top-notch Merlot. Arrowood, Cohn, Carmenet, Chateau St Jean, Gundlach-Bundschu, Hanzell, Kenwood, Kunde, Kunkee, Ravenswood, St Francis and Wellington also make good wines and are set to continue with their success, providing they can hold out to the tempting sums being offered by housing developers for their land.

Hugging the Pacific coastline is the huge Sonoma Coast AVA, covering some 1,940sq km (749sq m), and the 4,860 hectares of vines are scattered over a very wide area. Indeed, this is one reason why the AVA is so big; producers wanted to be able to draw fruit from any of their vineyards and still be able to claim the appellation. The irony of this, however, is that very few producers use this AVA on their labels these days.

Napa County

'Napa', the 'Land of Plenty', was how the Wappo Indians described this region when they first inhabited it. Well, they must have had some kind of prescience, for while it is not the largest in terms of size, and neither is it the one with the oldest winemaking history, Napa County is home to the greatest concentration of vineyards and wineries in the state, and there is no doubt that it has carved a reputation for creating California's most highly prized, prestigious, classic-styled wines from the noblest of grapes.

Napa is also famed for the many sparkling wine producers who have teamed up with Champagne and Cava houses to great acclaim. The Chardonnay and Pinot Noir used for many of these hail from Los Carneros AVA, a scrubby grassland area patchworked by the stark contrast of vineyard green, split between Sonoma and Napa Counties. As a cool area strongly affected by summer morning fogs and the winds which follow when they burn off, this is an important spot for these grapes. Very low rainfall and dense, shallow soils give naturally low yields and high natural acidity, so they are ideal for sparkling wines.

Carpenter Vineyard in the autumn with grass cover. St Helena, Napa County.

Of all of the county's AVAs, the one which has attained true worldwide fame is Napa Valley AVA. Generally considered to be the premier wine area of the United States, the Napa Valley presents the slick, neat, well-ordered side of the Californian wine industry. Here, the Land of Plenty could also be interpreted as the Land Of Big Bucks – some of the world's most expensive wines hail from here.

From San Pablo Bay to Mount St Helena, vines carpet a 40km (25m) long, scenic, narrow

The door and barrels of Atlas Peak Winery, Napa Valley, California. Wonderful Sangiovese-based wines are made here, the fruit hailing from vineyards owned by the celebrated Italian winemaker, Piero Antinori.

strip of land truncated by Route 29, which features over 14,000 hectares of vineyards and more than 240 wineries. Grape-growers and winemakers alike – and there are some very eminent names amongst them – combine cutting-edge technology with traditional techniques, and many of California's finest, most strapping Cabernet Sauvignons spring from here, wines which Robert Louis Stevenson, who honeymooned in the region, described as 'bottled poetry'.

But there is more to the Napa Valley than top-flight Bordeaux-style lookalikes (trademarked as Meritage in the United States). The Valley's unusual geological formation (which boasts no less than 32 different soil types) and maritime climate (characterized by warm, dry summers and cool, wet winters) yield a diversity of wine styles. The southern end of the Valley, which is obviously closer to the winds and convection fog banks of San Pablo Bay, is considerably cooler than the northern end, and this affects which grapes can be grown where. Furthermore, in three-dimensional terms, differences in taste are also created depending on whether the vines are planted on the Valley floor or on the mountain slopes above it (and above the fog line).

Owing to the complex geography of the Valley, a number of sub-appellations have been established in recognition of some very localized terroirs. Perhaps the most famous terroir of all is the gravelly Rutherford Bench, a sloping seam of alluvial land which runs along part of the west side of the Napa Valley. The boundaries

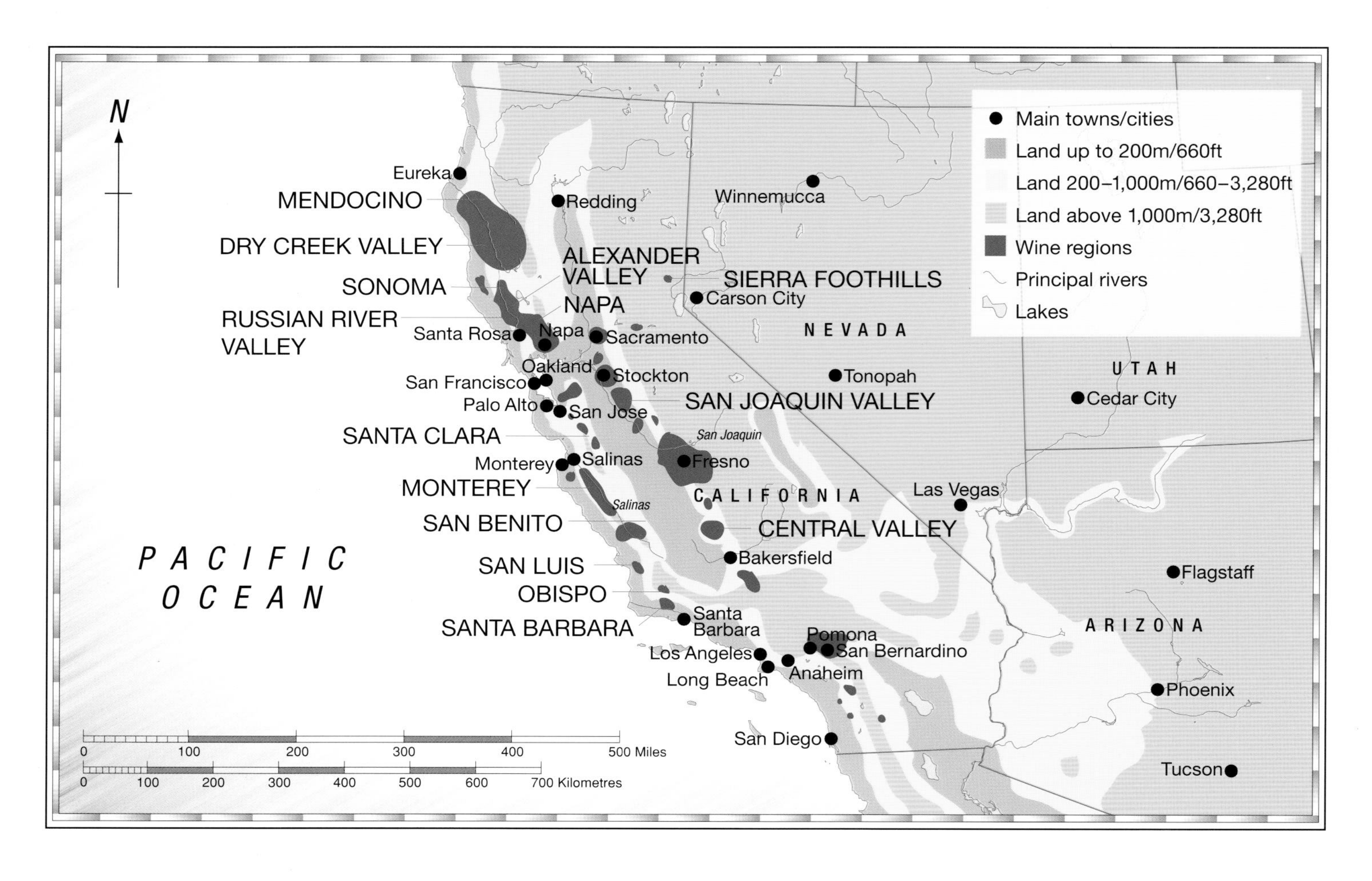

Napa County has carved a reputation for creating California's most highly prized, prestigious, classic-styled wines from the noblest of grapes.

of the original AVA petition were drawn to include benchland sites only, but in the final analysis, all of the land running down to the Valley floor was included and, in consequence, the new appellation was called Rutherford AVA. This was a controversial decision, but nevertheless, Rutherford is home to many classy estates which produce some of California's most luxurious, extraordinarily long-lived Cabernet Sauvignons. One characteristic shared by them all is a curious earthy, allspice taste known as 'Rutherford Dust'.

Rutherford, however, runs into another celebrated sub-appellation, Oakville AVA, which shares much of the same terroir – indeed, many consider the Oakville Bench, the most precious site within the AVA, to be a mere extension of the Rutherford Bench. Again, superlative mint and eucalyptus-styled wine is made from Cabernet Sauvignon and super-premium Meritage blends are also made in profusion here; however, the area is equally proud of the quality of its Chardonnay, Merlot and Sauvignon Blanc, with good cause. Sangiovese and Syrah are also beginning to make their mark.

The long list of producers who make the most of these environments include Beaulieu, Caymus, Dalla Valle, Franciscan, Grgich Hills, Groth, Joe Heitz (famous for Martha's Vineyard on the Oakville Bench), Niebaum-Coppola (known as 'movie wine' in our household as the estate is owned by film director Francis Ford Coppola), Opus One, Robert Mondavi, Screaming Eagle and

Swanson. In addition, producers such as Beringer, Flora Springs, Joseph Phelps and Sterling have extensive holdings here in the belief that Oakville and Rutherford will eventually be sub-divided into even smaller appellations.

Many pundits strongly believe that the wines of Stags Leap District AVA are even better than those of Rutherford or Oakville. Well, as ever, that is a matter of personal preference, but either way, no-one can refute the extraordinary quality of its wines – you only have to sip the seductively lush and supple Cabernet Sauvignon and silky-soft, berry-styled Merlot from producers such as Chimney Rock, Clos du Val, Pine Ridge, Shafer, Silverado and Stag's Leap Wine Cellars (and, yes, the apostrophe is included here) to confirm this.

The quality of Cabernet Sauvignon, Chardonnay, Merlot and some very old Zinfandel from Howell Mountain AVA is so good that it is much in demand, and the wines of Mount Veeder AVA are also praised for their pure, textured, concentrated flavours and their ability to age well. Good wines are also emerging from St Helena AVA. Cain and Spottswoode are perhaps the most fashionable producers here – it will be interesting to see how Cain's new plantings of Malbec shape up.

The Napa Valley may be packed full of famous names, but even Atlas Peak Vineyards of the tiny, one winery Atlas Peak AVA can boast advice from the famous Chianti maestro, Piero Antinori, when it came to pioneering their Sangiovese wines – indeed, they grow more than a quarter of the state's total plantings of this grape.

Alameda County

Home to just one AVA, Livermore Valley, which is tucked at the base of San Francisco Bay's Coast Range, this century-old wine region has long offered a host of wonderful wines, red and white, though it is the whites which stand out, and Sauvignon Blanc and Sémillon are its finest prodigies. Having said that, Cedar Mountain makes fabulous Cabernet Sauvignon, and fine Petite Sirah is produced by Concannon, both in vineyards which are screened from morning fogs and cooling Pacific breezes.

Groth Winery of Oakville, Napa Valley, California, producer of one of California's finest Cabernet Sauvignons and Sauvignon Blancs.

Santa Clara County

The most exciting wines of this county hail from Santa Cruz Mountains AVA. The vineyards may be scattered (and possibly shrinking in area), but producers such as Clos LaChance, Mount Eden, Ridge and Thomas Fogarty make beautifully long-lived Cabernet Sauvignon and sublime Chardonnay. Pinot Noir can be enticing, too, especially from David Bruce and Santa Cruz Mountain Winery.

Monterey County

The 'Salad Bowl of the World', Monterey is California's leading vegetable producer. But Monterey AVA (the broadest appellation covering the whole of the viticultural area and its sub-appellations, with the exception of Carmel Valley AVA and Chalone AVA) is also one of the state's largest premium winemaking regions and is expanding all the time – plantings are expected to have risen to 16,200 hectares by the turn of the century. The resurgence of wine interest was originally kicked off by jug wine giants Mirassou and Paul Masson, but the focus is now firmly placed on growing commercially popular grapes which will consistently produce world class wines of exceptional varietal integrity.

Nature lends a hand here in the form of a very favourable climate. Its primary attribute is the cooling fogs which shroud the long, wide valley of the Salinas River during the growing season – indeed, because bud break often occurs two weeks ahead of other California regions, and harvest typically begins two weeks later, the grapes benefit from a longer than average hang time, which helps to develop the hallmark intensity of varietal flavour and an ideal grape sugar-acid balance. The only inherent danger of such an extended growing season is that the fruit may not ripen evenly, but viticulturists overcome this by raising the canopy which covers the grape bunches.

Another important viticultural control is driven by the lack of rainfall. Irrigation is necessary, but this gives growers the advantage of being able to govern the timing and the amount of water which the vines receive. Withholding water achieves wonders in terms of concentrating grape flavours.

Chardonnay accounts for approximately 40 per cent of the county's total plantings and arguably epitomizes the 'California Chardonnay style' more than any other appellation. The wines exhibit a zippy, bracing acidity, yet this does nothing to stop the deep, rich, complex fruit flavours from shining through. As with other white varieties of the region (Gewürztraminer, Pinot Blanc and Riesling), alongside some Pinot Noir, most of the plantings are in the cooler northern areas of the county.

There has also been a dramatic viticultural shift over the past 20 years towards Cabernet Sauvignon (the county's second most heavily planted variety), Merlot and Zinfandel, particularly on the high, western, alluvial slopes of the southern half of the Salinas Valley. This district is only partially influenced by the maritime climate of Monterey Bay and the growing season is distinguished by warmer days and nights compared with the northern section of the Valley.

San Benito County

By comparison to Monterey, San Benito County is pretty small – in wine terms, at least. The flurry of activity which stirred up viticulture in the 1970s did not really lead to anything of great substance. For example, one hardly hears or sees anything of the wines from the AVAs of Cienega Valley, Lime Kiln Valley and Paicines.

There is always an exception to prove the rule, however, and Mount Harlan AVA is it. By strange coincidence, not only is it just along the San Benito Range from Monterey's Chalone AVA, but it also shares the characteristic of being a one winery AVA. In this case, Josh Jensen of the trailblazing Calera Wine Company can take full credit for exquisite Pinot Noir and fabulous Viognier which flourish on the 750-m (2,460-ft) high limestone-rich slopes of the Gavilan Mountains.

San Luis Obispo County

Well, the secret is out. The former 'no questions asked' outlaw country is being invaded by 'foreigners' from Napa Valley, Washington state, France and even Australia, who have spotted the untapped potential of this county. It seems certain that even more interest will be attracted from Napa and Sonoma producers who are busily searching for new vineyard sites as they run out of room for expansion at home. They certainly have a good choice of feasible locations.

With 2,450 hectares under vine, the rolling, gravelly, upland plains of Paso Robles AVA is by far the biggest viticultural area in the county and, owing to the fact that it is geographically positioned at the very limit of Pacific Ocean influence, it is crowned with the laurels as the hottest AVA in California. Cabernet Sauvignon, Chardonnay, Merlot, Sauvignon Blanc and Sémillon prefer the eastern section of the area where it is marginally cooler. Further inland, however, Zinfandel and Italian and Rhône varieties bask gloriously in the sweltering heat

Merlot grapes being tipped into the crusher/destemmer at Frog's Leap Winery, Rutherford, Napa Valley, California.

Fog clearing as the sun rises over Fairview Farm Vineyard, Paso Robles, San Luis Obispo County, California. In spite of its 'land of sunshine' reputation, many parts of California are distinctly chilly, owing to the pervasive fog which is funnelled up the valleys from the Humboldt Current-cooled Pacific Ocean.

and Adelaida, Creston, Eberle and Eos make tasty examples. York Mountain AVA, a sub-appellation of Paso Robles which nestles in the Santa Lucia Mountains, also supports Zinfandel by tradition, but I have never seen or tasted any wines which claim this provenance. Incidentally, a fiercely alcoholic Zinfandel was the local grog back in the 19th century, apparently.

Santa Barbara County

This county has suddenly become incredibly trendy in its own right. For years, Napa winemakers were buying grapes from here, but such is the demand by the growing band of local producers that less than 50 per cent of the grapes are sold on today. Indeed, a few of the top Napa producers – Beringer, Gallo, Kendall-Jackson and Robert Mondavi, for example – are moving in fast to snap up their own tracts of land.

In fact, Santa Barbara is a great case study in how quickly things can change in the California wine world. In 1970, only 81 hectares of vines were planted; this has now risen to 3,845 and there are more than 30 separate wineries, located primarily in the AVAs of Santa Ynez Valley and Santa Maria Valley, though there are plantings in the non-AVA Los Alamos Valley and Santa Rita Hills (the latter is seeking AVA status). All this is thanks to the efforts of producers such as Au Bon Climat, Fiddlehead, Firestone, Lane Tanner, Qupé, Sanford and Zaca Mesa, who remain powerful forces within the industry today.

While all of the classic grape varieties can be grown in Santa Barbara County owing to the many mesoclimates, there is one grape variety which has not only soared to spectacular heights of popularity and success, but is now beginning to challenge the supremacy of France's Burgundy region ... Pinot Noir. And, yes, this has taken a whole lot of people by surprise. This, perhaps, is linked to the popular image of Santa Barbara ... miles of sandy beaches, sub-tropical vegetation, no rain and lots of sunshine. It does not seem possible that the area is cool enough for the cultivation of such a capricious grape. But the unusual east–west traverse of shoreline from Point Conception to Rincon is particularly prone to foggy weather and provides a corridor for the inland flow of ocean breezes, so the area is actually one of the coolest viticultural areas in California during the late spring and summer months with a long growing season.

South Coast AVA

The stretch of coast running south from Los Angeles is not a producer of 'famous name' wines, but there are four AVAs. The most substantial vine plantings are housed in Temecula AVA, a small area halfway between San Diego and Riverside, known principally for phylloxera-free Chardonnay, Sauvignon Blanc and Sémillon, although some Cabernet Sauvignon, Pinot Noir and Zinfandel has been attempted. I use the word 'housed' deliberately: the vineyards quite literally run in between rows of housing. Callaway is the major winery. Cucamonga Valley AVA was one of California's original viticultural sites, but lost importance as the industry migrated northwards. San Pasqual Valley AVA offers a number of different mesoclimates, but is currently in disuse, and Malibu-Newton Canyon AVA has just one vineyard.

Central Valley

This vast, 805km (500m) long, very flat valley is California's bulk wine demesne and the state's most prolific grape-producing region churning out 60 per cent of California's grapes (and well over 50 per cent of California's total wine crush) which are destined as jug wines for domestic consumption, dessert and fortified wines, table grapes, fruit juice and dried fruits. Some thought.

The majority of the grapes are grown in the San Joaquin Valley where, in places, the vine has to compete with increasing urban sprawl, particularly around San Francisco. I am reminded here of Lex Luther, of *Superman* fame, who devised a Machiavellian plot to sink 'America's richest land' into the Pacific. His plan involved buying up huge tracts of the desert of the San Joaquin Valley, which would become highly prized following the demise of the West Coast! Well, perhaps E & J Gallo know something we don't, as their main winery, the largest in the world, is based in this wilderness.

The Santa Barbara wine industry is a good example of how quickly things can change in California. It has mushroomed spectacularly, producing ever better wines.

California Dreaming

Clichéd as it sounds, the Californian wine industry can boast some pretty bold and beautiful statistics. Wine grapes (as opposed to table grapes) are grown in 45 of California's 58 counties, covering over 163,416 hectares of land, and rank among the state's top ten agricultural products. Perhaps surprisingly, the majority of California's 820 wineries are small, family-owned businesses. Roughly half of them sell less than 5,000 cases a year in total (some as few as 300 cases) and only 20 can be considered as blockbusters (accounting for 90 per cent of all Californian wine). To put this into perspective, the giant E & J Gallo makes half as much wine again as the whole of Australia!

Nearly three out of every four bottles of wine sold in the United States comes from California, and the state accounts for 90 per cent of all US exports (which totalled 60 million gallons of wine worth $425 million in 1997) reaching some 160 countries and representing some eight per cent of California's production. Indeed, despite successive crop shortfalls in 1995 and 1996, and stiff international trade barriers, most California producers continued to supply their hard-won export customers. The UK remains the largest export market, with 1997 sales jumping 33 per cent to $108 million.

The region is a monument to stainless steel, which is pretty unromantic, but is testament to the application of modern winemaking methods – in other words, the wines are pure, fresh and clean. But the fertile soils, intense heat and cheap and plentiful flood irrigation (a prerequisite in the arid climate) promote high yields which dilute grape flavour, so the wines will never be more than simple, sweet-edged (because this is how the Americans like them), easy-drinking gluggers, though it must be said that their quality is admirably consistent. This is explained in part by the fact that the chief wine grape varieties grown are Chenin Blanc and Colombard, grapes which are able to preserve their acidity even under the hottest of conditions.

The most important district is the historical Lodi AVA. Responsible for a massive 15 per cent of California's annual crush in 1997, it is nevertheless making a name for itself; Mondavi's Woodbridge facility is based here (though watch out for their Merlot – it hails from southern France!), and some lovely warm, fleshy Zinfandel and juicy-fruit Ruby Cabernet emerges from the district. Of far more significance, however, is the fact that most Lodi grapes end up in the blends of other AVAs throughout the state – bear in mind that the AVA rules allow for 15 per cent of the wine to come from elsewhere, and Lodi is very often the 'elsewhere'. Indeed, the area is the most popular source of Cabernet Sauvignon, Chardonnay, Merlot and Sauvignon Blanc and the second largest supplier of Zinfandel to producers state-wide.

Even further north is the one-winery Dunnigan Hills AVA where R.H. Phillips makes everyday wines from a number of varieties. A more distinguished district, which lies at the heart

Sanford Vineyard and Winery, Buellton, in the Santa Ynez Valley, Santa Barbara County, California. Pinot Noir specialist Richard Sanford recognizes the importance of planting the right grape variety in the right site.

of San Joaquin Valley, is Madera AVA, famed for the high quality of its dessert and fortified wines. If you have not yet discovered Andrew Quady's top-notch Elysium and Essensia, then I urge you to try them.

Sierra Foothills AVA

Right up until Prohibition, the steep, rough, western slopes of the Sierra Nevada Mountains buzzed with winemaking enterprise. This was Gold Rush country, after all, and demand for wine was high. As was so common, however, the industry collapsed when the Volstead Act was enforced and it took until the 1970s for interest to be revived (Boeger Winery was the first to take up the challenge). Today, the region has established a reputation for top-quality Barbera (which eight out of ten growers make), Cabernet Sauvignon, Merlot, Riesling and Sauvignon Blanc, though it is Zinfandel which wins all the applause. Incidentally, though I have never seen it, I read that Late Harvest Zinfandel has been made here – highly unusual!

Just about all of the wine is made by an eclectic set of boutique wineries who appear quite happy to battle with a difficult climate, the result of sheer altitude – some of the tiny vineyards are carved into slopes 1,220m (4,000ft) high. The Sierra Foothills AVA is a blanket appellation covering the whole of the region, but there are four distinct sub-appellations: El Dorado, North Yuba, California Shenandoah Valley and Fiddletown.

Principal Grape Varieties

The list of grape variety names which have been approved by the Director of the Bureau of Alcohol, Tobacco and Firearms for use as type designations for American wines is exhaustive. These are just a few of the favourites.

Cabernet Franc

A very fashionable variety in both California and Washington, and also showing definite signs of growing popularity in New York state and Oregon. One reason that growers like this grape lies in its ability to survive freezing winter weather. Traditionally used with Cabernet Sauvignon and Merlot for Bordeaux-style blends, it is being bottled increasingly as a single varietal.

Cabernet Sauvignon

King of the red grapes in Washington (with 1,418 hectares planted), its wines are tasting better as the vines age. Down in California, however, it is only the second most widely planted variety of the vinifera reds with 44,991 hectares – there are more plantings of Zinfandel here. It is also showing much promise in New York state and Texas.

Chardonnay

The United States is enjoying tremendous success with this variety, thanks to strong consumer demand, and in California and Washington, for example, it is the most widely planted white vinifera variety (86,955 and 2,157 hectares respectively). It is also a star grape in Connecticut and New York state, and a mainstay variety of Oregon and Texas.

Chenin Blanc

The third most important white grape in California, its chief virtue is its ability to yield lots of grapes which manage to retain their acidity, even under hot climatic conditions such as those of the Central Valley.

Gewürztraminer

This is the kind of grape which actively enjoys cooler climates where it can best express its hallmark aromas and flavours of perfume, spice, roses, lychees and so on, and makes excellent wine in the Pacific Northwest. Planted in warmer climes, however, it yields oily flavours more akin to tropical fruit laced with sweet pea.

Merlot

A variety which thrives in the United States, especially in California, New York state, Oregon and Washington. Traditionally used in blends, Merlot gained popularity as a stand-alone wine in the early 1970s, and it is now renowned for its soft, sweet cherry and brambly flavours and complex, mint, cigar box and spice aromas.

Pinot Blanc

Almost by stealth, Oregon Pinot Blanc is gaining an international following, appealing to the ABC ('Anything But Chardonnay') drinker in particular. It is usually made to a delicate, unoaked, dry, steely style with a lick of citrus acidity, though some can be more herbaceous in character.

Pinot Gris

A speciality of Oregon giving light, crisp and spicy wines on the whole, though some have more of a ripe, peachy character somewhat redolent of Alsace versions.

Pinot Noir

Look no further than Oregon and California's Carneros region for the United States' top Pinot Noir wines. This mercurial variety creates wondrous wines here which can be compared to the finest red Burgundy. Other parts of California – Monterey, Russian River Valley and Santa Barbara, for example – are the places to watch in the future.

Riesling (or Johannisberg Riesling and White Riesling)

Popular in Oregon where the slightly warmer and more humid growing conditions produce grapes

with high sugar levels and balanced acidity. In Washington, where it is the second-most widely planted premium white grape, it gives delightfully fruity wines with an aroma of fresh peaches and apricots. Down in California, Riesling was one of the Big Four back in the 1960s, but it is diminishing in importance nowadays. In New York state, however, plantings are on the increase.

Sangiovese

This is arguably the cult grape of tomorrow for the United States, and it is growing like topsy in many parts of the country.

Sauvignon Blanc (also known as Fumé Blanc)

If your personal preference leans towards the bone-dry, lean and grassy style of Sauvignon Blanc, then you need to find a wine which has been made from grapes grown in the cooler parts of the country. Some memorable wines are made in California and Washington, but fine examples are also emerging from Texas.

Sémillon

A major variety which tastes good on its own or when blended with Chardonnay or Sauvignon Blanc. Young wines have a very fresh quality, with lots of zippy citrus notes and flavours of fig, pear and melon. Leave them to age, however, and they become rich, honeyed and nutty.

Syrah

Another grape which has come from absolutely nowhere to a position of relative prominence in many parts of the country.

Zinfandel

If the United States can glory in one quasi-indigenous vinifera variety, then this is it. Today, it is the leading red vinifera grape of California, very often turned into a blush wine.

Grapes to Watch ... Baco Noir, Barbera, Gamay, Grenache, Malbec, Maréchal Foch, Marsanne, Mourvèdre, Nebbiolo, Norton, Petite Sirah, Pinotage, Viognier.

The Pacific Northwest

In some respects, lumping the wine industries of Idaho, Oregon and Washington state together may seem strange, as each has its own discrete personality. However, they share so many common characteristics (small, innovative operations making wines of clean fruit and sound acid structures) that the term 'Pacific Northwest' has now passed into common parlance within the wine world, a position strengthened by the formation of the Pacific Northwest Wine Coalition in 1991 to promote the wines of the three states abroad.

As a young wine industry, the Pacific Northwest is definitely New World, yet owing to its northerly location, it shares one major feature with many countries of the Old World: significant vintage variation. In Washington, for example, 1998 proved to be a bumper year; but this contrasts sharply with 1996 when a big freeze wiped out 40 per cent of the crop. Oregon's most famous grape, Pinot Noir, has also suffered its ups and downs; 1994 and 1996 were fine vintages, yet 1995 proved disastrous.

Machine harvesting of Riesling grapes at Idaho's leading winery, Ste Chapelle. They also create export standard Chenin Blanc and Syrah, as well as hand-crafted sparking wines.

Idaho

Idaho's winter months are bitterly cold indeed, when temperatures can drop as low as a shivering minus 20°C (-4°F) – brutal enough to kill the more fragile vine varieties. During the summer, however, the days are decidedly hot. This is offset by two factors – drawn-out summer days expose grapes to extra sunlight during the critical ripening period, and an altitude of 762m (2,500ft) gives cold nights, even at the height of summer. This gives grapes high in acid and sugar, which if handled carefully can be turned into wine with vividly intense varietal flavours.

The area under vine is very small (just 243 hectares) and there are only 18 wineries, most of which are concentrated in the southwest along the Snake River, where the vineyards mingle with thousands of hectares of orchards and fertile farmland. The river draws off warm air in the summer and provides frost protection in the spring and autumn, and Cabernet Franc, Cabernet Sauvignon, Chardonnay, Gewürztraminer, Merlot, Pinot Noir, Riesling, Sauvignon Blanc and Sémillon can be grown as a result.

Oregon

Driving through the lush, rolling hills of the picturesque Beaver State, you cannot fail to stumble across at least one of Oregon's 125 wineries. Most are small (cultivating fewer than four hectares apiece) and most are winemaker-owned, but the sense of enthusiasm amongst them is almost tangible. This is a very exciting state, which is still learning how best to unlock its unquestionable potential.

If you have not yet had the opportunity to taste any of Oregon's wines, then you are not alone. For a start, only two per cent of production (18,500 tons in 1997) is exported from just 16 producers. Secondly, it is most likely that you would be wanting to try the wine for which Oregon has become renowned – Pinot Noir – and there really is not enough to go around. This is a variety which cannot deliver grapes of superlative quality with each vintage, thanks to the changeable nature of the prevailing maritime climate.

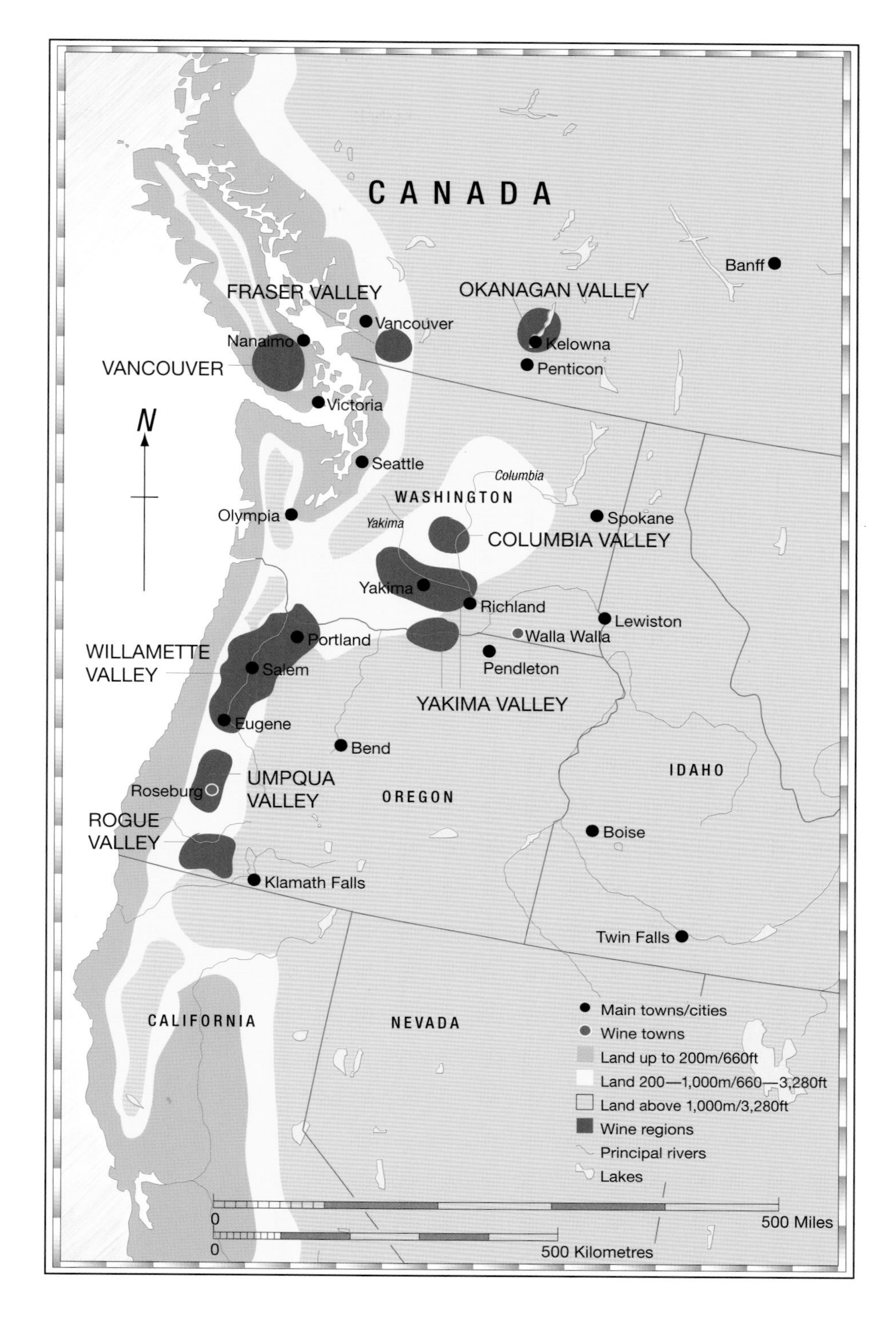

To a great extent, this is why Oregon has seemingly failed to live up to the expectations raised when an Oregon Pinot Noir beat all but one of a line-up of red Burgundies in a blind tasting competition held in France in 1979. Mind you, the fact that a wine industry developed here at all flies in the face of earlier advice; the first modern-day pioneers were thought foolhardy for even considering growing vines in such a cool, wet and marginal climate.

What they discovered, however, is that premium varieties can grow well given specific mesoclimates (of which there is an enormous variation), and since then, better canopy management, new clones and more sophisticated vinification procedures have done much to increase the chances of a more uniform success across a range of different grapes. Apart from Pinot Noir, the principal varieties grown include Cabernet Sauvignon, Chardonnay, Gewürztraminer, Merlot, Pinot Gris, Riesling, Sauvignon Blanc and Zinfandel, with production split roughly half and half between red and white wines.

The majority of Oregon's vineyards lie in the coolest and most temperate appellation, the Willamette Valley AVA, famed particularly for the beguiling quality of its signature variety, Pinot Noir, considered by many to be second only in quality to Burgundy. Pinot Gris can also be thrilling in the hands of sensitive winemakers.

Just south of Willamette Valley lies Umpqua Valley AVA, which is drier and slightly warmer on the whole. The region is not described as 'the hundred valleys of the Umpqua' for nothing: the terrain is made up of a network of small mountain hillsides and river

Rex Hill's Maresh Red Hills vineyard in the sub-region of Red Hills of Dundee – so called for their uniquely coloured, well-drained, Jory loam soils – in Willamette Valley AVA.

valleys providing a geo-climatic diversity which can support the cultivation of a number of the classic grape varieties.

The most elevated appellation, and the one most strongly influenced by the Pacific Ocean, is the rocky Rogue Valley AVA in the south. A similarity in climate and growing conditions to France's Bordeaux region makes the vineyards especially well suited to varietals such as Cabernet Franc, Cabernet Sauvignon and Merlot.

Last but not least are the extensions of Washington state's Columbia Valley and Walla Walla appellations, where a wide variety of grapes are grown, though many end up in Washington wines.

Washington State

Washington is now affirmed as the second largest producer of vinifera grapes in the US (albeit a long way behind California), accounting for five per cent of the total national wine production, with wines exported to more than 40 countries. While many of the wineries are situated in or near Seattle, the majority of the vineyards lie to the east of the Cascades, which provide a natural barrier to the moist weather patterns of the Pacific. Three of the four AVAs are located here (the exception is the state's newest appellation, Puget Sound, which embraces the islands and land adjoining the Pacific, but there are currently only 14 hectares of vineyards) where the warm, dry, summertime conditions are welcomed by a wide range of classic grapes (providing they have managed to live through the deep cold of winter, that is), though viticulture would not be possible without irrigation.

The largest of these AVAs is Columbia Valley. Nearly 3,845 hectares are planted with vinifera grapes, making up more than 60 per cent of the state's total. The rain-shadow effect of the Cascade Mountains protects the region from the influence of the Pacific Ocean, so it receives less than 200mm (8in) of rain each year. Low humidity and cold winter temperatures minimize disease, and the gradual onset of winter can create favourable conditions for stunning Late Harvest and Icewine styles.

Lying within the Columbia Valley, the unirrigated 'place of many waters', Walla Walla AVA is home to a mere 81 hectares of vineyards and produces just one per cent of Washington's wines. However, it is the state's most exciting and progressive wine region. Yakima Valley AVA is also located within Columbia Valley, with most of the vineyards planted on the slopes of the fearsome-sounding Rattlesnake Hills in the foothills of the Cascade Mountains. Thanks to a strong (and essential) network of irrigation channels, this area is highly agricultural, growing everything from apricots to potatoes, and has the highest density of vineyard plantings in the state, representing 40 per cent of Washington's total.

One of the great natural advantages of the state is its latitude – 46° north – which, in summer, gives ripening grapes an average of 17.4 hours of sunlight per day, about two hours more than the prime growing districts of California. With 300 cloudless days per year, this adds up to quite a lot of extra sunshine. Furthermore, the hot days and cool nights during the critical maturation period help to preserve acidity in the grapes, and the nature of its soils discourages vegetative activity, thus intensifying fruit flavours. All in all, this gives some pretty interesting and enigmatic wines, of which the ratio of reds to whites is currently 42:58, though reds seem set to catch up with whites as producers continue to switch to world-class red varieties, to which the state is well-adapted topographically and climatically. As Gary Figgins of Leonetti so eloquently says: 'In Washington state, our future is so bright we have to wear shades!'

Pinot Noir is picked by hand in Washington state. The area available for future plantings is immense – of the 4.3 million hectares of the Columbia Valley, for example, only 4,763 are currently planted to wine grapes.

New York State

The New York wine industry is experiencing a dramatic and exciting renaissance. While the Empire State has been the nation's second largest producer of grapes and wine for many years, it is only in recent times that a reputation has been gained for its premium wines. Decades of scientific experimentation are now yielding a broader mix of grape varieties and improved winemaking techniques, and there is a renewed commitment to producing innovative wines of world-class quality.

New York has enjoyed a long history of winemaking, but the real boom did not commence until the Farm Winery Act was passed in 1976 – of the state's 125 wineries, no less than 106 have been established since this date. Most of these are small, family-operated farm wineries concentrating on production of varietal wines and, typically, their owners oversee the entire process from the planting of the vines to the marketing of the wines.

One of the most important factors to drive the industry forward has been the switch from the traditional, 'foxy', native American grapes, such as Concord, Delaware and Niagara (though they remain consumer favourites), to the less pungent French-American hybrids, such as Aurora, Baco Noir, Chancellor, DeChaunac, Maréchal Foch, Norton, Seyval, Vidal and Vignoles. In addition, the New York State Agricultural Experiment Station in Geneva (affiliated with Cornell University) has developed several new varieties such as Cayuga, Chardonnel, Melody and Traminette, which are attaining popularity. These hybrids not only taste superior, but are better able to cope with freezing winters, high humidity and short growing seasons, and are more resistant to pests and diseases. Incidentally, these wines, along with those made from native grapes, are banned from import under European Union law.

Of far more significance, however, was the pioneering work of Charles Fournier and Dr Konstantin Frank in the 1950s, who proved that vinifera vines could be cultivated in New York in spite of the punishing cold of the winter months. This 'second discovery of America', as Dr Frank's son, Willy, likes to describe it, has brought about a veritable sea change within the industry and plantings of vinifera varieties have increased by nearly 400 per cent since 1980. To keep this in perspective, however, vinifera covers just 1,416 hectares against 4,047 hectares of hybrids.

Another significant facet of the New York wine scene is the roaring trade in sparkling wines, and some of them are very good indeed. While Catawba, Delaware and Elvira grapes remain important to the traditional side of this industry, the best sparklers are created from the classic blend of Pinot Noir, Chardonnay and Pinot Meunier and are made by the traditional method. Flagship examples are being produced by Glenora and Chateau Frank (the sister winery to the trailblazing Dr Konstantin Frank's Vinifera Wine Cellars) in the suitably cool conditions of the Finger Lakes AVA. As owner Willy Frank says, 'Our climate is probably better for growing Champagne grapes than Champagne'.

It is also important to bear in mind that while New York harvests an average of 175,000 tons of grapes each year, only 45 per cent of the crop is turned into wine; the balance is used for grape juice, grape jelly or table grapes.

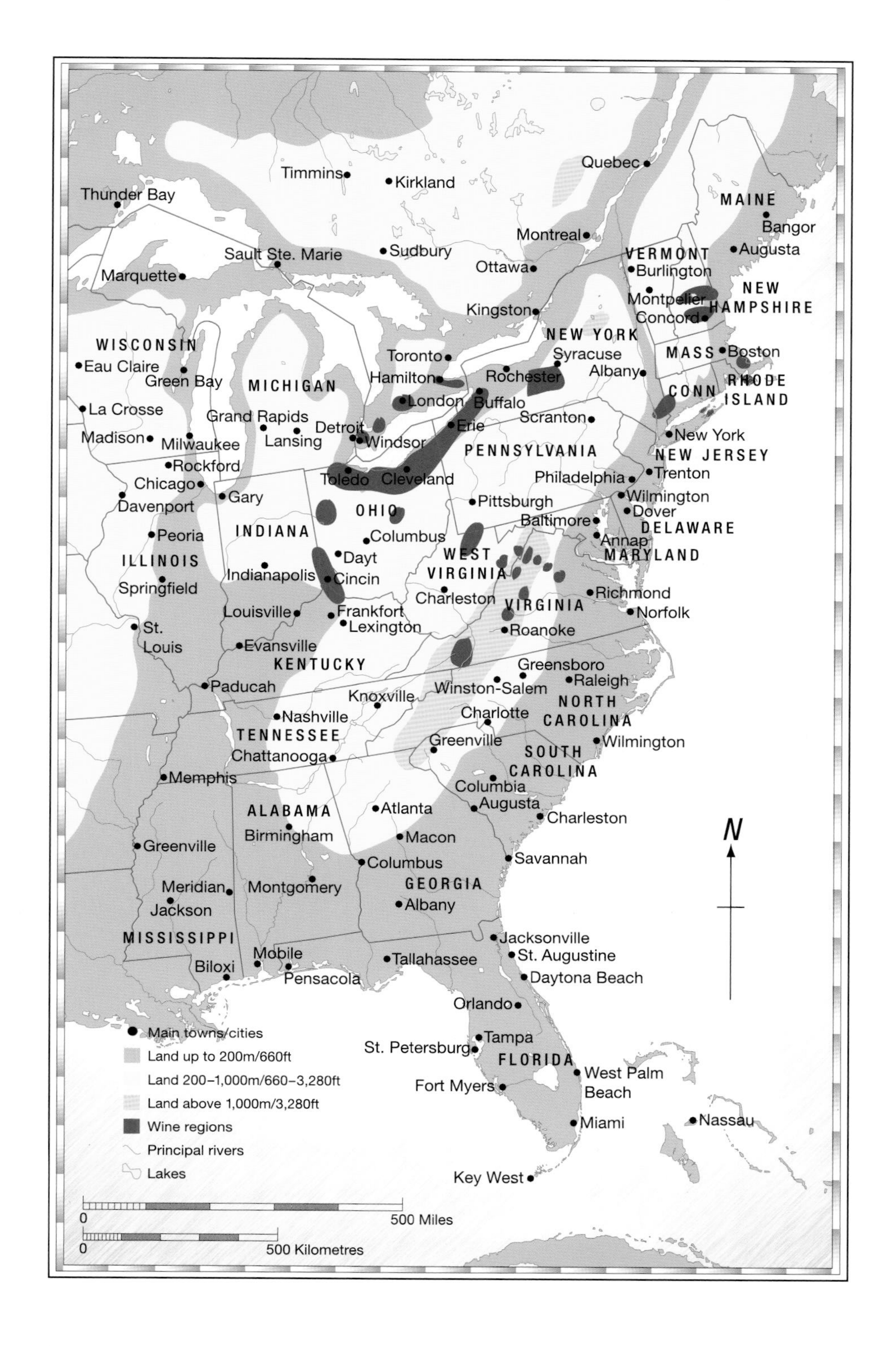

Lake Erie AVA

Though this appellation is shared with Ohio and Pennsylvania, the vast majority of the 8,094 hectares of vineyards lie within New York – indeed, this region is responsible for 59 per cent of New York's total grape production. Seven wineries are located on the high Allegheny Plateau, a fertile benchland site running parallel to Lake Erie which traps the water-warmed air and thus decreases the risk of late spring and early autumn frosts. The lacustrine climate also means that there is less hail and precipitation, and fewer convection thunderstorms. In spite of these natural climatic advantages, 90 per cent of the area is still planted to the native Concord variety, making Lake Erie the country's largest grape juice producer and processor. Aurora, Cascade, Catawba, Chancellor, Delaware, Ives, Niagara, Seyval and Vidal are also grown, though Chardonnay and Riesling are appearing in ever-greater quantities, so we may well hear more of this region in future.

Finger Lakes AVA

Here in the most beautiful of New York's wine regions, 61 bonded wineries produce 90 per cent of the state's wines from over 4,200 hectares of vines planted in the verdant hills overlooking Lakes Canandaigua, Cayuga, Keuka and Seneca. Indeed, it is the lakes themselves which make possible the cultivation of grapes. Sculpted out by ice age glaciers some 10,000 years ago, the deep waters warm up during the summer and the stored heat is then radiated back onto the vineyards in the autumn, providing protection against hazardous frosts. Furthermore, because the shale-soiled, rolling hills which surround the lakes slope all the way down to the water's edge, warm air is forced to rise by cold air draining down to the lakes, blanketing the vineyards in warmth during the winter months.

This is a gross over-generalization, of course, because the topography of each lake is different and a number of very crucial mesoclimates exist – indeed, Cayuga Lake has individual AVA status as a result. Interest was sparked here in the late 1970s when it was discovered that Cayuga's lower altitude created an exceptionally favourable microclimate for vinifera varieties. This is aided by the fact that the growing season can be a critical 15 to 30 days longer than in the rest of the Finger Lakes, especially in years when there is an Indian summer.

Anthony Road, Bully Hill, Chateau Frank, Dr Konstantin Frank's Vinifera Wine Cellars, Fox Run, Glenora, Hermann J. Wiemer, Hunt Country, Knapp, Lakewood, Lamoreaux Landing, McGregor, Prejean, Standing Stones and Wagner feature the classiest wines from the Finger Lakes region. But it is also the headquarters of the mammoth Canandaigua Wine Company, the United States' second largest winery, producing more than 28 million gallons of wine each year which is sold in all 50 states, Europe, Asia and Canada. Incidentally, Canandaigua is the parent company of the Finger Lakes' Widmer's Wine Cellars, famous for the Kosher Manischewitz brand.

While this region was the cradle of the vinifera revolution, the whole gamut of vine varieties continues to be cultivated – native labrusca, French-American hybrids and, of course, vinifera. The best wines are made from Chardonnay, and Riesling, though some Cabernet Franc, Cabernet Sauvignon, Gewürztraminer, Merlot, Pinot Blanc and Pinot Noir is grown, too. Sparkling wines and Icewines are also a regional speciality.

Rudolf Marchesi of Alba Vineyards in New Jersey, one of just 19 wineries state-wide.

Hudson River Region AVA

With just over 200 hectares of vines, the birthplace of the New York wine industry is now gathering fame for the high quality of its modern-day wines. There are 22 wineries producing a mix of hybrid and vinifera wines which, for the most part, are very tasty. Of these, Benmarl and Clinton are

generating some very exciting examples, though Millbrook is arguably the best producer of the region's Chardonnay and Pinot Noir.

The Royal Kedem Wine Company also rates a mention as an important producer of Kosher wines, the biggest in the world. But while I am not in the habit of knocking individual producers (especially when they are lovely people), I am compelled to say that this is the dirtiest, smelliest and most unhygienic winery which I have ever visited. The fact that their wines are pasteurized, however, does mitigate the risk of 'dirt damage' (to put it succinctly).

At 180 to 196 days, the Hudson River Region's growing season is shorter compared with New York's other winemaking areas (Long Island enjoys 215 to 233 days, for example), and though the river itself moderates temperatures to a degree, it is the steep palisades which create the greatest ameliorating effect by acting as a conduit to the maritime air generated by the Atlantic Ocean.

A number of grape varieties prosper in the complex admixture of shale, slate, schist and limestone soils which vary hugely in depth, rockiness and fertility from place to place, though the mainstays are the white French-American varietals, most particularly the popular Seyval Blanc.

Restaurant workers tasting wine at the Taylor Wine Company, Hammondsport, New York state.

Long Island

One can almost breathe the multi-millions of dollars which are being pumped into the wine industry in Long Island. Everything has a meticulously neat, slick and modern feel to it here, which is not

Vine Valley Vineyard above Canandaigua Lake in the Finger Lakes region of New York state.

surprising in light of the fact that the first modern-day vines were planted at a former potato farm only as recently as 1973. Moreover, in just over a quarter of a century, it has built up a loyal following for its high priced wines, which is the envy of the rest of the state.

Long Island is the warmest and mildest growing region of New York and, as a result, the viticultural area is almost exclusively planted to vinifera varieties – indeed, it is the most important region for vinifera in the state. It is without doubt the easiest region in which to grow varieties such as Cabernet Sauvignon,

American Viticultural Areas (AVAs)

Prior to 1978, the year in which the Bureau of Alcohol, Tobacco and Firearms (BATF) issued new regulations to control standards of wine labelling, there were no official rules governing the use of geographical names on US wine labels. The introduction of the concept of formally recognized American Viticultural Areas was therefore a substantive leap forward. The first AVAs were assigned in 1983 and, to date, 137 have been approved.

The first action which had to be taken by BATF, of course, was to actually identify and define the new AVAs. Absolutely anyone, anywhere could (and can still) petition BATF, but even in the areas where certain geographical terms had been in traditional use for a very long period of time, BATF demanded that strict criteria were met before awarding the AVA designation.

In spite of all of this, the regulations merely define a viticultural area as a 'delimited grape-growing area', and while provenance is guaranteed if an AVA is stated on the bottle (85 per cent of the wine must be made from grapes grown within the boundaries of the stated viticultural area), it does not promise anything about the quality of its contents.

for example, a grape which demands warmth and an extended growing period if it is to ripen properly, and the state's best renditions are made here – Long Island is not dubbed 'New York's Bordeaux' for nothing.

The moderating effect of the sea on three sides of each of the narrow forks of Long Island creates a unique set of maritime climatic conditions, giving an encouragingly long, warm and sunny growing season (the longest in the state). The ocean winds act as a buffer to the extremes of temperature, so the vineyards are warmed during the chilly winter months and cooled during the summer. Also, the fogs which roll in during the spring raise temperatures by just enough to prevent an early bud break – this is vital because young buds are highly vulnerable to frost damage, of which there is a high risk at this time of year. Furthermore, the onshore breezes reduce the humidity which can cause rot and everything which follows in its wake. The only other potential perils are tropical storms and hurricanes, and the havoc caused by flocks of birds which love to feast on ripening grapes during their migratory passage.

Production is firmly centred on varieties such as Cabernet Franc, Cabernet Sauvignon, Chardonnay, Chenin Blanc, Gewürztraminer, Merlot, Pinot Blanc, Pinot Gris, Pinot Noir, Riesling and Sauvignon Blanc. Many Bordeaux-style blends are also created to great acclaim.

The largest appellation of the region is North Fork of Long Island AVA, currently covering some 607 hectares of vineyards, though more plantings are planned. Of the 19 wineries in operation within the AVA, Bedell, Gristina, Hargrave, Lenz, Palmer Vineyards, Paumanok, Peconic, Pellegrini and Pindar stand out as the quality leaders, though it must be said that nobody makes poor wine here.

Comprising a lowly 40-odd hectares of land under vine, The Hamptons Long Island AVA on the Southern Fork of Long Island is certainly much smaller, but its two bonded wineries, Duck Walk and Sagpond make delicious wines. Soils here have a higher concentration of silt and loam (the product of the gradual erosion of glacial moraine), which means that the vineyards require far less irrigation than those of North Fork. This peninsula is less sheltered, however, which reduces the growing season by roughly one to three weeks compared with the North Fork of the Island.

In general, the differences in the kinds of wine being made throughout the region can be put down to individual winemaking styles, but as the industry matures, I have no doubt that producers will begin to look at the variations which exist between each vineyard, and even at the differences between various blocks of vines within each vineyard.

Vineyards and building of the Taylor Wine Company on the western side of Lake Keuka, New York state.

Other states

California, Oregon, Washington and New York might produce the lion's share and the best of North American wine, but a number of other states are offering increasingly acceptable fare.

Arizona Irrigation, altitudes of between 1,200 and 1,500m (3,900–4,920ft), and over 300 days of sunshine a year are the attributes which afford the Grand Canyon State the luxury of being able to grow grapes. Today, there are ten wineries focusing on Rhône varieties (with Callaghan, Dos Cabezas and Kokopelli making particularly interesting wines), though the Village of Elgin Winery creates a range from a number of grapes including Cabernet Sauvignon, Colombard, Merlot, Pinot Noir, and Sauvignon Blanc.

Arkansas There are currently seven wineries making wine in three mountainous AVAs (Altus, Arkansas Mountain and Ozark Mountain), the only surviving remnants of the 100 or more which thrived on the production of the Concord grape at the beginning of the century.

Colorado The winters of the Centennial State can be lethal and the growing season is short, but the Grand Valley AVA was identified as a good spot to grow vinifera varieties at the beginning of the 1970s. The mesoclimate is slightly more forgiving here, and Chardonnay, Gewürztraminer, Merlot, Riesling and Viognier were planted on an experimental basis. Today, there are 21 wineries in production (Plum Creek Cellars is the largest).

Connecticut Eleven wineries make the most of a climate which is ameliorated by coastal waters and stretches of rolling hills. Chardonnay does particularly well as a result (especially at the Chamard and Stinington wineries), but wines are also made from Cabernet Sauvignon, Merlot, Riesling and the hybrid Seyval Blanc.

Georgia The Empire State of the South has a long winemaking history dating back to 1733. Vinifera grapes have always been something of a rarity, however, owing to the short growing season. Of the state's eight wineries, Chateau Elan, a 16th-century French-style estate surrounded by 81 hectares of vineyards on softly rolling land, is the most important.

Indiana In the words of the Hoosier State's Wine Grape Council (established in 1989 by the Indiana General Assembly), 'Indiana wines are back!' While the first vineyards were planted by Swiss immigrants in 1802 (said by some sources to be the nation's first successful commercial vineyards), the industry failed to revive post-Prohibition. The last decade, however, has witnessed a rebirth and there are currently 19 wineries, with many more in the offing.

Maryland Maryland's wine industry was built on hybrid varieties. Since 1980, however, equipment and facilities have been modernized and there has been a shift in emphasis towards premium varietal wines, with good examples coming from Basignani, Elk Run and Woodhall. Indeed, the future of the Old Line State looks extremely promising and there is every chance that it could soon pose a threat to the likes of New York state in terms of quality.

Massachusetts This state is most famous for being home to the very chic island of Martha's Vineyard – and there is a Martha's Vineyard AVA, too. Surrounded by the sea, the ocean breezes give a long growing season, which is advantageous to vinifera grapes (introduced by Chicama Vineyards). The Bay State also forms part of the Southeastern New England AVA (shared with Connecticut and Rhode Island).

Michigan This state is proud to brag that it was the original source of 'Cold Duck', a curious blend of New York state 'Champagne' and Californian 'Burgundy' invented by a Detroit restaurateur at the turn of the century. Today's 21 wineries, centred in the Great Lake State's four AVAs (Fennville, Lake Michigan Shore, Leelanau Peninsula and Old Mission Peninsula), are producing more palatable fare.

Missouri In spite of a long winemaking history, hybrid grapes such as Chardonel, Cynthiana, Rayon d'Or, Seyval Blanc and Vidal Blanc remain dominant in the Show Me State, although some producers grow the classic Bordeaux and Burgundy varieties. There are 35 thriving producers, however, from which Augusta, Blumenhof, Hermannhof, Les Bourgeois, Montelle, Norton, Röbler, St James and Stone Hill stand out.

New Jersey The Garden State now has 19 wineries in operation, with vineyards located in part of the Central Delaware Valley AVA and in Warren Hills AVA. Frost and rot can be a problem here, so selecting the right site in the right mesoclimate is crucial.

New Mexico This state has a long history of winemaking, but as ever Prohibition put the proverbial spoke in the wheel of a healthy wine industry and it took until the 1980s before the industry showed any sign of revival. There are now 21 wineries, led by the French-owned Gruet (who make traditional-method fizz from Chardonnay and Pinot Noir), Anderson Valley, Balagna, Casa Rondeña, La Chiripada, La Viña, Las Nutrias and Mademoiselle de Santa Fe.

Ohio There are 49 wineries in Ohio today (Meier's is the oldest and largest in the state), with the best situated on the Bass Islands of Lake Erie. Vinifera varieties (such as Cabernet Sauvignon, Chardonnay, Gewürztraminer, Pinot Gris, Pinot Noir, Riesling and Zinfandel) grow successfully here because the warm water of the Lake acts as a kind of hot water bottle during the cold months, so the vines are protected from winter frost.

Pennsylvania In spite of the fact that one in four vintages is distinctly suspect owing to inclement weather, some 62 wineries are managing to carve a living from the vine. Chaddsford is the best-known producer, making wine from Barbera, Chardonnay, Pinot Gris and Riesling, in addition to a Bordeaux-style blend.

Texas Since 1978 (the year in which vineyards were allowed to be established in the counties which were formerly dry), the number of wineries in Texas has leap-frogged to 28, the amount of land under vine has increased to 1,225 hectares, there are over 450 growers, and Texas has become the fifth largest wine producer of the United States. A state to watch.

Virginia Thomas Jefferson's vision is now being realized as Virginia's wineries make their mark on the American wine scene. Old Dominion now boasts 50 wineries, offering a mix of native American, hybrid and vinifera wines, and of the latter, it is Cabernet Franc, Cabernet Sauvignon, Chardonnay, Gewürztraminer, Malbec, Merlot, Mourvèdre, Pinot Noir, Riesling, Sauvignon Blanc, Sémillon, Syrah, Viognier and Zinfandel which are the most important, though Barboursville Vineyards is carrying out trials with Barbera, Pinot Grigio, Malvasia, Nebbiolo and Sangiovese.

Top wineries include Barboursville, Chateau Morrisette, Horton, Jefferson Vineyards, Linden, Meredyth, Naked Mountain, Piedmont, Prince Michel, Rapidan River, Tarara and Williamsburg with the very best found on the eastern slopes of the Blue Ridge Mountains in Monticello AVA.

The USA is probably the most blessed country in the world in terms of topographical and climatic variety – much of it well-suited to vitiviniculture – so it is no wonder that so many states have flourishing winemaking industries of their own.

Canada

It may come as a surprise to some, but Canada is now home to a vibrant, forward-thinking and very exciting wine industry with a pencil-tip focus clearly sharpened on creating fine wines from the noblest of grapes which can compete in quality standards at every international level. And many producers are achieving just this – simply taste the new generation of wines and be stunned by the flavours.

Furthermore, the industry is progressing at such a rapid pace that 'the amazing stuff that is happening today is going to be the day after tomorrow's news'; these cogent words from Frank Baldock, one of Canada's leading wine journalists. Indeed, one of the most impressive achievements of Canadian wine producers has been the speed with which they have transformed an industry traditionally based on hybrid grapes into a forceful, modern enterprise which has embraced the superior vinifera varieties with gusto.

Even though vinifera vines were pioneered much earlier, the concept that Canada could be environmentally capable of creating premium wines was not really taken seriously until the 1980s. Canadian winters may be brutally cold, but I have burnished my tan in Montréal well into September – indeed, the sheer length of the summer means that the relatively delicate vinifera varieties will grow successfully as long as they are planted in areas where they can be protected from the worst effects of the Arctic-like temperatures of the winter months and the unpredictable weather which often occurs in spring and at harvest. Once this realization took hold, the more adventurous producers rushed to replant their vineyards and doubled their efforts in the wineries.

De Sousa Wine Cellars, Beamsville, Ontario Province, Canada. John de Sousa was the first Portuguese-born winemaker to open a winery in Canada.

Canada is most famous for its Icewine, described locally as 'winter's gift to wine'. This unctuously sweet white wine is made mainly from Riesling or the hybrid Vidal Blanc grapes which are picked in the depths of winter when they are dehydrated and frozen on the vine – the temperature must drop below minus 8°C (18°F) before the grapes can be picked, which is usually done by hand and is invariably done at night.

The water content of the grape has turned into a plug of ice so, when the fruit is pressed, only a syrupy juice of very high acidity and extract is expressed. It may be minuscule in quantity (yields are often as low as five per cent of the norm), but this treasured nectar is outstandingly rich in quality. It is then fermented very slowly for several months. Unfortunately, you will not find Canadian Icewine on sale in Europe owing to a frankly idiotic piece of European Union wine law.

While four of Canada's ten provinces have suitable conditions for the growing of vines, the majority of the vineyards are amassed in just two: the Niagara Peninsula in Ontario and the Okanagan Valley in British Columbia. Interestingly, while Ontario and British Columbia each have an almost equal number of operating wineries (38 and 35 respectively), most of Canada's vines can be found in the former: Ontario possesses nearly 6,500 hectares against just 1,966 in British Columbia. All regions are developing at a galloping gait, however, so it will be interesting to review the next set of statistics when they are released.

Harvesting Riesling grapes for Lakeview Cellars on the Niagara Peninsula, Ontario.

Ontario

The Iroquois certainly had a talent for description: 'Ontario' was their word for 'land of the shining waters' and this province, covering some one million square kilometres (386,100 square miles) in area, is without doubt the land of the lakes (there are literally thousands of them), and is wonderfully lush and green during the spring, summer and autumn months. Indeed, average monthly temperatures during these seasons can be compared to many fine wine regions of the world. To this end, Ontario produces 80 per cent of Canada's wines from some 520 vineyard sites. A wide range of styles is made, though 75 per cent of production (32,310 tonnes in 1997, of which approximately

Other Canadian Winemaking Areas

To the south of the Okanagan Valley, high up in desert cattle country, lies the Similkameen Valley. Led by the evocative-sounding Blue Mountain Vineyard, Burrowing Owl Vineyard, Crowsnest Vineyards, Hester Creek and Tinhorn Creek Vineyard, some promising Cabernet Franc, Cabernet Sauvignon, Chardonnay, Gamay, Gewürztraminer, Merlot, Pinot Blanc, Pinot Gris, Pinot Noir, Sémillon and Trebbiano are being produced. Though it currently represents a mere two per cent of British Columbia's area under vine, this region promises great potential. As winemaker Walter Gehringer of Gehringer Brothers Estate says: 'The risk of growing grapes in this northern environment are high, but the rewards are fruit flavours of an intensity not found in grapes of the southern regions.'

Although it is cool, wet and windy, another go-ahead region in Canada is its newest and second largest, Vancouver Island. While there is a small vineyard on Bowen Island, the majority of the wineries are based in the Cowichan Valley, though Venturi-Schulz is the only winery of note. You really have to think 'Germany' to capture the flavour of the styles of wine which are being made here and, as elsewhere, producers are keen to make wines which match Canada's reputation for fine food. And, only a short drive away, lies the mild and relatively damp Fraser Valley, with just six tiny farm wineries.

Unless I had seen the evidence for myself, I would have found it hard to believe that vines could be cultivated successfully in the cold, easterly, maritime province of Nova Scotia. However, grapes are grown in the Annapolis Valley where the Bay of Fundy creates a favourable mesoclimate. There are also a number of operations in Québec which do little more than bottle imported bulk wine, and the remainder are merely small cottage wineries.

Highlights of History

1860

The first vineyards are planted in the Okanagan Valley.

1866

Three Kentucky farmers plant eight hectares of Isabella vines and establish Canada's first commercial winery, Vin Villa, on Pelee Island in Lake Erie.

1890

There are now 41 commercial wineries in the country, of which 35 can be found in Ontario.

1913

The Horticultural Research Centre of Ontario launches its programme to develop hybrid grape varieties.

1916–27

Prohibition is in force in Canada. However, owing to some clever political wangling, wine is exempt from the anti-alcohol edict, a move designed to protect the livelihood of grape-growers.

1926

Hungarian winemaker Dr Eugene Rittich persuades Jesse Willard Hughes to plant grapes on his farm in the Okanagan Valley.

1927

The provincial liquor boards are set up, a system whereby the sale and distribution of all alcoholic drinks is controlled by the government.

1946

French chemist Adhemar de Chaunac imports several dozen French hybrid varieties from France along with 100 vinifera cuttings.

Post Second World War

More and more vineyards are established in response to a dramatic increase in demand for wine from the new wave of European immigrants.

1965

Château-Gai is the first winery to export to the UK. Two years later, the French government successfully sues the company over its use of the term 'Champagne'.

1972

The hybrid grape Seibel 9549 is renamed DeChaunac in honour and recognition of his pioneering work.

1975

Inniskillin gains a commercial licence, the first to be granted since 1929.

1977

Canadian wineries are authorized to open tasting rooms from which to sell their wines directly to the public for the first time. This year also sees the planting of the first vinifera vines in the Okanagan Valley on the Inkameep Indian reservation.

1978

Québec Province permits the sale of wine in grocery stores.

1988

The Vintners' Quality Alliance (VQA) is formed in Ontario and an appellation system is introduced. British Columbia follows in 1990.

Early 1990s

The government monopoly on the sale and distribution of alcoholic drinks is relaxed in Alberta, and some privately owned franchises are given permission to distribute wine. The liquor board continues to control prices, however.

The most encouraging sign for the future success of Ontario's wine industry lies in the very active programme of research into grape-growing.

one-third was produced from vinifera) comes from white varieties, which fare better in the average years in this cool climate region.

The majority of the vineyards are concentrated on the Niagara Peninsula (which is actually further south than Burgundy). Here, a temperate mesoclimate, nutrient-rich soils and good air circulation created between Lake Ontario and the protective Niagara Escarpment (a 30–50m/98–164ft-high ridge which runs through the Peninsula comprising a number of important geological 'benches' of different soils), allow the growth of vinifera vines.

The principal grape varieties, Baco Noir, Cabernet Franc, Cabernet Sauvignon, Chardonnay, Gamay, Gewürztraminer, Merlot, Pinot Blanc, Pinot Noir, Riesling and Vidal, are turned into cracking wines (given the right site) by producers such as Cave Spring, Château des Charmes, Henry of Pelham, Hernder, Hillebrand, Inniskillin, Marynissen (the first to plant Cabernet Sauvignon in Canada, in 1978), Pillitteri, Reif (where they are experimenting with Zinfandel), Strewn, Thirty Bench and Vineland.

The north side of Lake Erie (the shallowest and warmest of all the Great Lakes) is also a marvellous haven for grapes, which enjoy more hours of sunshine than anywhere else in Canada. Lake Erie's scenic Pelee Island, where the growing season can be 30 days longer than the mainland, is home to 200 hectares of vines, too.

Vintners' Quality Alliance (VQA)

If you want to be sure that you are buying the best that Canada can offer, then you need to look for bottles which carry the special VQA seal of quality. The VQA charter (introduced in Ontario in 1988, but also in force in British Columbia since 1990) not only sets the regulations, but also ensures that the wines live up to approved standards via a testing and grading panel. A distinction is made between two quality levels:

Provincial Designation – where the wines must be made from one or more *Vitis vinifera* or vinifera hybrid grapes (from an approved list) which are grown solely within the designated province. If the wine is labelled as a varietal, then it must contain at least 85 per cent of the variety named. All grape varieties must have reached a minimum level of ripeness at the time of picking.

Geographic Designation – a more stringent appellation based on Designated Viticultural Areas (DVAs) whereby a minimum of 85 per cent of the grapes must come from the viticultural area named on the label. Should a producer wish to designate a particular vineyard, then the site must be within a recognized viticultural area and 100 per cent of the grapes must come from that vineyard. Similarly, wines described as 'Estate Bottled' must be made entirely from the produce of vines owned or controlled by the winery in one of the designated viticultural areas. Only the classic European grape varieties can be used and, once again, a minimum of 85 per cent of the wine must be made from the variety/varieties named on the label. Minimum sugar levels have been set for vineyard designated and estate bottled wines, as well as dessert and Icewines.

Harvested grapes at Hillside Cellars, Okanagan Valley, British Columbia.

British Columbia

Developed in the 1970s, the British Columbian wine industry may be young and may be small, but it is tremendously dynamic nevertheless. Producers have even proved that it is possible to grow grapes successfully above the 50th parallel, way up at the northern end of the 130km (80m) long Okanagan Valley, where it would normally be considered too cold for quality grape production. While the winters are indeed bone-chillingly cold here, the deep, vineyard-warming Okanagan Lake, the summer heat and an abundance of intense sunshine make this feat achievable. Aromatic white varieties such as Ehrenfelser, Gewürztraminer, Pinot Gris and Riesling do particularly well, and some Chardonnay and Chenin Blanc is grown, too. Top wines, however, are created from Pinot Blanc and Pinot Noir, and Icewine is another local speciality, as one might expect.

South of the Okanagan Lake, things are quite different, though, to the extent that completely different wines are produced. To put this into some kind of perspective, you can easily sight scorpions and rattlesnakes amongst the Ponderosa pine and sagebrush. It is so sandy-soiled, so hot and so arid that 'the beach' is Canada's only true desert. Red varieties thrive here as a result, with Cabernet Sauvignon and Merlot showing the greatest flair, though the finicky Pinot Noir seems to grow well here, too (indeed, it appears to feel at home in all of British Columbia's wine regions).

The Okanagan Valley is by far the largest and most important winemaking area in British Columbia, containing roughly 96.5 per cent of the province's vineyards. Top producers include Blue Mountain (which makes excellent sparkling wines, Chardonnay and Pinot Noir), CedarCreek (with highly acclaimed Riesling Icewine), Gray Monk (particularly good for Rotberger rosé, and also an official sight station for the Lake Monster Ogopogo!), Hainle (the first winery to produce Icewine in the Okanagan Valley), Hawthorne (best known for Gewürztraminer), Inniskillin (in partnership with the Inkameep Indian Band), Quail's Gate (specializing in Chardonnay, Late Harvest Optima, Pinot Noir and Riesling Icewine) and Sumac Ridge (with noteworthy Chardonnay, Gewürztraminer and Pinot Blanc), though it could be argued that Mission Hill is a good cut above the others in terms of progression. This probably has much to do with the presence of John Simes, former winemaker at Montana Wines in New Zealand, who declares: 'We have a total dedication to elevating the quality of all wines we produce. We believe that wines of the Okanagan Valley can compete with the best the world has to offer.'

Principal Grape Varieties

While there remains some dependence on non-vinifera and hybrid grapes, this is fast-shrinking in the wake of the colossal success and better understanding of vinifera varieties.

Baco Noir (also known as Baco 1)

Some very tasty wines can be made from this 1894 cross between Folle Blanche and *Vitis Riparia*. The first flavour to assail the senses is one of very smokey wood (almost like a dying bonfire), but the wines are also awash with a highly attractive, warm, deep taste of dark fruits.

Cabernet Franc

The most widely planted red vinifera variety in Ontario and the province's third most important vinifera variety overall.

Cabernet Sauvignon

A red variety which needs a long growing season. But it also demands one which is warm, which may explain why plantings of Cabernet Sauvignon are so relatively rare.

Chardonnay

While this grape is incredibly adaptable, top growers around the world believe that it performs best in cool conditions, so it suits Canada's climate admirably – indeed, it is the most important vinifera variety in Ontario.

Maréchal Foch

A hardy, early-ripening French hybrid developed from a *Vitis Riparia-Vitis Rupestra* hybrid and the Goldriesling vinifera grape, this variety remains enormously popular in Canada, giving fruity, light-bodied wines made for easy drinking.

Merlot

A delicious mix of cherry and blackberry flavours mark the characteristics of this early-ripening grape in Canada. Often used in blends.

Pinot Noir

This variety flourishes (relatively speaking) in British Columbia, and is showing much promise for the future.

Riesling

In taste, Canadian Riesling falls anywhere between the perfumed, full-bodied style which is made in France's Alsace region and the delicate, peachy, floral flavours which are the hallmark of Riesling from the Mosel region in Germany. While the whole spectrum of styles is made, much depends on its provenance and its creator. Its most glorious incarnation, though, is the rich, sweet, orange blossom flavoured Icewine. Riesling is the second most important vinifera variety in Ontario.

Vidal Blanc (otherwise called Vidal 256)

A thick-skinned French hybrid, Vidal is well-adapted to withstand the extra months required on the vine before it can be picked to be turned into Icewine.

Grapes to Watch ... Chenin Blanc (especially Icewines), Ehrenfelser (a Riesling and Sylvaner cross), Gamay, Gewürztraminer, Pinot Blanc, Pinot Gris, Sauvignon Blanc, Viognier.

Mexico

There is a paradox to Mexico. The vine has been planted here for longer than any other country in continental America; yet, in other respects, it is by far the newest American country to join the modern-day wine age.

While French vine cuttings were introduced to Mexico towards the end of the 19th century, the ravages of civil war brought the fledgling wine industry to an abrupt halt. Thanks to an endemic lack of interest in wine-drinking amongst Mexican nationals, the industry never fully recovered, in spite of government efforts to revive it. Ironically, it was the imposition of high taxes on imported wines and spirits which proved to be the most effective measure of all – it attracted investment from overseas companies who constructed their own wineries in Mexico (albeit with the intention of making brandy rather than quality wine), a cunning way of sidestepping the new laws. This was only back in the 1960s, so Mexico truly is the new kid on the block.

Along with the money came the expertise, of course, and soon viticulturists and oenologists alike were predicting a very bright future for Mexico. Though half of the country lies south of the Tropic of Cancer, the terrain is mostly mountainous and the mile-high altitude of the central plateau helps to keep temperatures down. Also, while there are extremes of dryness in some areas and wetness in others, it was felt that these problems could be overcome.

The dream has not turned into reality, however. Mexico produced 1.13 million hectolitres of wine in 1996 (the latest statistics available), but this is half the amount that was made in 1994. And, while there are some 50,000 hectares of vines in production, less than half of their yield is turned into wine (the remainder is sold as table grapes, dried fruit or grapes for brandy production). Indeed, nearly 70 wineries have closed down in the face of the lack of demand for their wines since 1980 and, in turn, many of the grape-growers who supplied them have replaced their vineyards with more profitable cash crops.

All is not gloom, however. The biggest companies, Bodegas de Santo Tomás (in joint venture with Wente from California), Casa Madero, Casa Pedro Domecq, Chateau Camou, L.A. Cetto and Monte Xanic, are creating some exciting wines. L.A. Cetto, for example, has invested over US$25 million over the last six years and is now making some 90,000 hectolitres of wine of export quality each year (and these

Principal Grape Varieties

While a number of different grape varieties are grown (see below), and while one can say that the red varieties dominate thanks to the hot climate, there are no clear quality leaders apart from Cabernet Sauvignon (which is often blended with Merlot). Chardonnay, Nebbiolo, Petite Sirah, Sangiovese and Zinfandel can also make good wines in the hands of top producers.

Barbera, Bola Dulce, Cabernet Sauvignon, Cardinal, Carignan, Chenin Blanc, Colombard, Grenache, Malaga, Malbec, Merlot, Mission (aka Criolla), Muscat, Nebbiolo, Palomino, Perlette, Riesling, Rosa del Péru, Ruby Cabernet, Sauvignon Blanc, Trebbiano, Valdepeñas, Zinfandel.

It is difficult to predict the future prospects of Mexican wine. However, if demand surges, then there is still plenty of land to exploit.

wines are exported to 20 different countries). Casa Madero has also recently employed the services of a Flying Winemaker to create wines for a UK food and wine retailer. There is certainly a strong will amongst these top producers to make better wine and win orders both at home and abroad.

It is difficult to predict the future prospects of Mexican wine. If it catches on with wine drinkers around the world and demand surges, then there is still plenty of land to exploit. But Mexico has to compete with the rest of the New World, and while it can currently achieve this well enough on price, the industry lacks infrastructure and marketing clout by comparison with its more sophisticated rivals, so it may never progress further. More importantly, any wine-producing country needs the support of a strong domestic market if it is to move forward – and Mexico clearly lacks this.

Highlights of History

1521

The vine is planted, grown from seed imported by Cortés, and wine is soon produced, making Mexico the oldest wine-producing country in the whole of the American continent.

1593

Don Francisco de Urdiñola establishes Mexico's first commercial winery – Marqués de Aguayo – at Parras.

1825

The Mexican government takes control of all missionary properties – and, with them, their vineyards.

1888

Mexico's first truly commercial winery, Bodegas de Santo Tomás, is founded in Baja California.

1910

Many vineyards are destroyed during the ten years of civil war which commences in this year.

1926

L.A. Cetto is founded in Baja California, way ahead of the general revival in winemaking which did not really commence until the 1940s.

1946

Nazario Ortiz Garza, Mexico's single largest wine and brandy producer, becomes Secretary of Agriculture and he encourages the planting of more vineyards throughout the country.

Post Second World War

The government imposes stiff tariffs on all imported wines which is to stimulate the domestic wine industry even further. This action also encourages foreign wine companies to set up wineries in Mexico in order to circumvent the prohibitive taxes.

South America

South America produces wines to match its exotic cultures and volatile nature. It is a huge continent of vast untapped resources, with a wine industry in its infancy, just waiting to explode.

Latin Passions

South American wine – the legacy of the Conquistadors

There are lots of bright things emerging from the South American wine industry. Large tracts of unexploited land which do not require irrigation are being courted by foreign investment and the influence of the Flying Winemakers is making a huge impact across the continent.

The fourth-largest continent on earth, South America stretches 7,400km (4,600m) from north to south and spans a width of 5,150km (3,200m). It is home to the Andes, the longest mountain chain in the world, and the Amazon Basin is the world's largest area of tropical rain forest. Indeed, I remember being fascinated by the geography of South America as a young child (along with tales of flesh-eating piranhas that inhabit South American waters!) and can still picture the crude 'jungle' scenes which I painted in my primary school days.

What I certainly did not learn until much later, however, was the significance of South America in global wine terms. We may not have had the opportunity to drink its wines in our own homes until relatively recently, but since the Spanish (and, in parts, Portuguese) Conquests in the 16th century, there has always been a strong wine-drinking culture in South America, second only to Europe in historical interest.

At first, wine was supplied by Spain itself, but one only has to imagine the condition in which it arrived, after a long and hazardous journey, to appreciate why the Conquistadors soon demanded vine cuttings to make wines of their own. And, as South American countries gained their independence, it became absolutely imperative to produce wines domestically.

Early records indicate that Peru was the first South American country to establish viticulture on any systematic scale and it appears that it was influential in disseminating the vine to other parts of the continent. But it must be remembered that the modern-day interpretation of borders was irrelevant at that time. Where did the so-called frontiers between countries lie then, especially when most of the continent was being controlled by the Spaniards anyway? Today, one can safely say that Peru is lagging behind the times compared with Argentina (who produce volume), Chile (who produce quality) and even Brazil or Uruguay (where the vine arrived relatively late in the scheme of things).

COSTA RICA
PANAMA
TRINIDAD & TOBAGO
Caracas
VENEZUELA
Orinoco
Magdelena
Bogotá
GUYANA
SURINAM
FRENCH GUIANA
COLOMBIA
Orinoco
Branco
Caquetá
Negro
Quito
ECUADOR
Japurá
Amazon
Belém
NORTH ATLANTIC OCEAN
Tapajós
Tocantins
Fortaleza (Ceara)
Maranon
Japurá
Madeira
Paranaiba
Xingu
Ucagali
Araguaia
Purus
Recife (Pernambuco)
São Francisco
Aripuana
N
BRAZIL
Lima
PERU
Salvador
Mamoré
Brasília
La Paz
BOLIVIA
Belo Horizonte
PACIFIC OCEAN
Paraná
PARAGUAY
Rio de Janeiro
São Paulo
CHILE
Asunción
Salado
Pôrto Alegre
Córdoba
SOUTH ATLANTIC OCEAN
ARGENTINA
URUGUAY
Rosario
Mendoza
Montevideo
Buenos Aires
Santiago
Colorado
Negro
Main towns/cities
Land up to 200m/660ft
Land 200–1,000m/660–3,280ft
Land above 1,000m/3,280ft
Chubut
Principal rivers
Lakes
FALKLAND ISLANDS
0
500
1,000
1,500 Miles
0
500
1,000
1,500
2,000
2,500 Kilometres

Chile

We all know by now that a daily dose of red wine can protect against heart disease and cancer. But a recent report from the University of Glasgow has revealed that Chilean Cabernet Sauvignon does a much better job of it than, say, *French* Cabernet Sauvignon. Great news for the Chilean wine industry, but not so good for the French...!

The ironic thing about this discovery is that Chilean wine made from the classic French grape varieties probably tastes more authentically French than its modern French counterparts. The early settlers managed to bring healthy vinifera vines to Chile before the outbreak of the notorious twin scourges of phylloxera and oidium (powdery mildew) which decimated the vineyards in France and elsewhere. While the Europeans were forced to graft their vines onto resistant American rootstock (which inevitably altered the flavour of the wine), the Chileans managed to escape this fate. Even today, one of the country's chief viticultural advantages is phylloxera-free vines (and some of the prototypes are now more than a century old), which also rarely suffer from disease or invasion by other pests, keeping the need for costly spraying down to a minimum. One complaint from growers, however, is that they feel frustrated by the delays to progress brought about by strict quarantine laws.

Another immense viticultural asset is the naturally favourable climate, soil and geography and, quite rightly, everybody raves about how Chile is so ideally placed to make European-style wines. The seasons are well-defined: precipitation is limited mainly to Chile's winter months (May to September); there are generous levels of summer sunshine; and temperatures are moderated by prevailing onshore winds from the Pacific and a rush of cold air sinking down from the Andes at night. The grapes therefore mature at a slow, leisurely pace, giving the perfect equilibrium of sugars and acids.

Chile's slim, 4,200km (2,600m) length (though the wine-producing regions occupy only a fairly tight 1,400km/870m-long band in the middle of the country), provides a number of different soil types, but it is those which are poor in organic matter that fulfil the grape-growers dream. Furthermore, when they are also well-drained, the vines are forced to dig deep for water, which helps to keep vine vigour in check – in other words, the plant's energy is used to produce fruit, not leaves. Having said that, though some vineyards are 'dry farmed', much of the country relies on irrigation during the summer months and the meltwaters of the Andes usually provide a limitless supply. Interestingly, though, a two-year drought (which gave rise to a shortage of irrigation water) made some growers sit up and realize that their grapes ripened better from the stress caused by lack of water – quite simply, they had previously been over-irrigating their vineyards.

A viticultural paradise is all very well and good as long as you know how to make the most of it. Instrumental in Chile's rise to fame has been the assistance which has come from abroad (especially from California and France) and many Chilean wineries have formed partnerships with foreign producers who have provided modern technology, financial resources and oenological expertise. For example, California's Robert Mondavi Winery has joined forces with Viña Caliterra, and both view their alliance as 'an ideal opportunity to realize a global vision of winemaking centred on an exchange of cultures and winemaking philosophies'. As R. Michael Mondavi, President and Chief Executive Officer, explains: 'We saw the same potential in Chile that we saw in Napa Valley 30 years ago. But most importantly, with Caliterra we saw people who are dedicated to producing wines that belong in the company of the greatest wines in the world.'

This is a tall order by anybody's standards, yet the adoption of the very best practices in both vineyard and winery – such as concentrating efforts on finding the best clones for each variety, properly planning new vineyard sites, canopy management, harvesting the grapes at their peak of ripeness, using top winemaking techniques to capture true fruit character, and so on – is a strategy which is more than beginning to pay off. The signals of approval in terms of international consumer response have been phenomenal. In the UK alone, for instance, imports of Chilean wine rose by an astounding 13.6 per cent between 1997 and 1998, accounting for 17.4 per cent of total Chilean wine exports.

Total wine production in 1998 was 5.27 million hectolitres (of which 740,000 hectolitres was exported) and there are currently 52 wineries registered by the Chilean Wine Export Association, though Wines of Chile International 'are aware of at least another ten wineries'. As for the area under vine, there are roughly 63,500 hectares of vineyards, though this is expanding rapidly. As Sebastian Odeja at Viña San Pedro says: 'Chile is expanding its vineyards by some 20 per cent each year' – indeed, it is common for leading producers to plant an extra 1,000 hectares of vines annually.

Chile is still very much red wine territory, but more whites are coming on line each year. While Cabernet Sauvignon, Chardonnay, Merlot and Sauvignon Blanc dominate the production of 'quality' wines, it is good to see ambitious and innovative companies like Viña Canepa (the number one Chilean supplier to the thirsty UK market) experimenting with some of the less usual varieties such as Chenin Blanc, Cinsault, Gewürztraminer, Malbec, Pinot Noir and Zinfandel.

Overlooking the vineyards of Errázuriz-Panquehue in the Aconcagua Valley, Chile.

Highlights of History

1548

The first vines are introduced by Father Francisco de Carabantes, who brings them from Cuzco in Peru.

1551

Spanish Conquistador Don Francisco de Aguirre becomes the first recorded grape-grower. In letters to the King of Spain, Carlos V, Pedro de Valdivia (who took possession of Chile in the name of Spain) refers to the widespread consumption of wine in La Serena and Santiago.

1678

The governor recommends that the ban on new plantings of vineyards is lifted (Chile is still part of Spain at this time and the 'mother country' is desperate to protect its own wine export trade). However, the wine is nothing more than a boiled drink sweetened with concentrated grape juice at this time.

1830

The government agrees to set up Quinta Normal, an experimental botanical nursery, at the behest of Frenchman Claudio Gay. Cuttings of European pre-phylloxera vinifera are imported as part of the project, which prove to be a godsend for the future.

1831

There are now 19,664,901 vines planted in the country, distributed from Coquimbo to Concepcíon. The Atacama region, a great wine producer in the 17th and 18th centuries, has lost importance.

1851

Spaniard Don Silvestre Ochagavía Echazarreta invites French oenologists (who also bring French vine cuttings) to his estate in Talagante, in order to advise him on the best ways of improving his winemaking methods and promoting quality in his wines.

1889

A Chilean wine wins the Grand Prize at the Great Exhibition in Paris.

1970s

Chile experiences a steep fall in the domestic demand for wine (owing to political and economic instability) and roughly half of the vineyards are uprooted in response.

1974

Following his *coup d'état*, General Augusto Pinochet repeals the restrictions on grape-growing and new vineyard plantings, which had been enforced by the land-reforming socialist, President Salvador Allende. But the country's following semi-isolation from the rest of the world means that true vitivinicultural advancement is postponed until the early 1980s.

1976

Spaniard Miguel Torres establishes a winery and, in spite of the prevailing difficulties, introduces stainless steel and new oak barrels into his winery, producing one of the first wines which does justice to the natural quality of Chilean fruit.

1982

Viña Canepa builds the largest state-of-the-art winery in South America to date.

1987

More than 10,000 hectares of vines are replanted with premium varieties.

Principal Grape Varieties

Chile has its workhorse grapes (the red País and the white Moscatel) and these are widely planted for use in domestic wine brands and the national grape spirit, *písco*. However, thanks to its history, the internationally popular 'classic' varieties are also well-established, which is a major advantage when it comes to exports.

Harvesting Cabernet Sauvignon grapes in the Maipo Valley, Chile. Cabernet Sauvignon is Chile's most bountiful and popular red grape and some spectacularly successful wines are resulting from the huge investment in this variety.

Cabernet Sauvignon

Chile's most popular red variety (it has even managed to overtake the ubiquitous País) with a current total of 15,995 hectares under vine (though this figure is set to rise further – indeed, it is probably out of date already!), and showing a special affinity with the Maipo Valley. The wines are characterized by wonderfully vivid, blackcurranty fruit and supple, velvety tannins. There is certainly little need to soften it by blending in Merlot, for example, though some producers prefer to add extra dimensions of flavour by doing just that. The full potential of this grape is now beginning to be realized in Chile's new wave of super-premium, oak-aged wines ... wines with a bottomless depth of flavour, good structure and great longevity.

Carmenère (also known as Grand Vidure)

The wine from this grape is so similar in taste to the plummy style of Chilean Merlot that for many years it was being sold as Merlot. Should I really be saying 'passing it off as Merlot' here? Well, it is possible that unscrupulous producers might have been tempted to do so. After all, would you have bought a wine made from such an obscure, 'never heard of it before' grape variety at the very beginning of the Chilean wine boom? Probably not. But you would have undoubtedly felt quite confident about purchasing a Chilean Merlot. To be absolutely fair, many producers did not actually know that it was Carmenère which was planted in their vineyards and truly believed it to be Merlot. Keep an eye out for these wines. They are virtually unique to Chile (even though it remains a legally permitted variety in Bordeaux) and they sport lovely spice and smoke flavours – in addition to those Merlotesque plums, of course.

Chardonnay

Well, what a transformation. Back in 1985, Chile could only boast five hectares of Chardonnay; today some 5,563 hectares are planted. Much work has gone into canopy management in the vineyards, and experiments with barrel fermentation have paid off, most especially in the Casablanca Valley. If you are particularly keen on a precise style of Chardonnay, however, then you have to choose your wine with care, as there are distinct variations between each region and, moreover, between each winery (it is trial and error here, I'm afraid). I must admit to feeling slightly fed up with the frequency with which some UK supermarkets chop and change between the producers who supply wine for their own labels; the label itself stays much the same, of course, but the wine inside the bottle can taste incredibly different. There are no identikit Chardonnays in Chile!

Chile provides a perfect home to the fashionable Merlot and it is achieving excellent results everywhere.

Merlot

Chile provides a perfect home to the fashionable Merlot and it is achieving excellent results throughout all of the wine regions. With 5,411 hectares planted, it is the second most important 'quality' grape and the third most important grape overall. It is sometimes blended with Cabernet Sauvignon, but, quite frankly, this is a waste of a grape which can make delectable wines when left to its own devices.

Sauvignon Blanc

Covering 6,576 hectares of vineyards, this is now Chile's top 'quality' white grape variety, with the cooler Casablanca region setting the finest example in the country. However, Sauvignon Blanc suffered many false starts in its Chilean career. Given its head, this variety will grow like topsy and the vines will be teeming with grapes come harvest time. This merely enhances its typically herbaceous flavours while forcing a compromise on the desired aroma and acidity in the finished wine. Until producers learned to curb Sauvignon's naturally high yields, it was assumed that it was this factor which was causing the distinct lack of finesse and mutations of flavour. On closer examination, however, it was discovered that most of the so-called Sauvignon Blanc vines were not Sauvignon Blanc at all. Rather, they were the inferior Sauvignonasse (also called Sauvignon Vert). Chile has now planted new clones (of the real thing, this time around) and the modern-day wines are far more subtle.

Grapes to Watch ... Cabernet Franc, Chenin Blanc, Cinsault, Gewürztraminer, Malbec, Nebbiolo, Pinot Noir, Riesling, Sangiovese, Sémillon, Syrah, Viognier, Zinfandel.

Some producers are now also creating ultra-premium, Cabernet-based wines, aiming to carve out a niche in the top end of the market. 1998 saw the release of Seña (an Irene Paiva of Viña Caliterra/Ed Flaherty of Errázuriz/Tim Mondavi of Robert Mondavi production) and Montes Alpha M, and we will soon be tasting Domus from Ignacio Recabarren and Viña Tarapacá's Millennium.

As the industry matures, we can expect a further flurry of activity of this kind (though one hopes that it will not be at the expense of the value-for-money wines which Chile is so adroit at making). I am also confident that producers will continue to evolve wines which possess a greater definition of regional personality ... especially as they move their vineyards off the flat plains and onto hillside sites, and continue to explore hitherto undeveloped areas.

Atacama

I have not yet discovered the answer as to why this particular part of Chile has been awarded status as a wine-producing region, because most of the grapes grown here are destined for the table or are turned into *písco* (a grape spirit). The Atacama Desert is renowned for being one of the most arid places on earth (no rainfall has *ever* been recorded at Calama, for instance), so this comes as no surprise.

Coquimbo

The relentless heat of this parched region has precluded the production of quality wine ... so far. The Limarí Valley is beginning to attract some attention, though – the steep slopes of the mineral-rich, mountainous terrain lend themselves to viticulture, as long as irrigation water can be channelled into the vineyards and sites with more forgiving microclimates are identified. Viña Francisco de Aguirre remains the only registered vineyard in the region. They planted their vines in 1992 and are now crafting wines from Cabernet Franc, Cabernet Sauvignon, Chardonnay and Merlot.

The Aconcagua Region

Lying to the north of Santiago, this region encompasses two sub-regions: Aconcagua Valley and Casablanca Valley.

Aconcagua Valley

Chile's most northerly quality wine region is dominated by a single producer, Viña Errázuriz (based in the Panqueheu area), who makes one of Chile's most acclaimed and elegant of Cabernet-based wines, Don Maximiano Reserva Especial, thanks to careful vineyard husbandry and clever winemaking. This is named after the estate's founder, Maximiano Errázuriz Valdivieso who, with the assistance of technical experts from Bordeaux, planted the first noble varieties in the Aconcagua Valley. Cabernet Franc, Merlot, Nebbiolo, Sangiovese, Syrah and Zinfandel are now beginning to yield good results, clearly reinforcing the suitability of this region to red varieties.

However, vineyard sites have to be chosen with care if one is aiming at quality (indeed, most of the region is given over to the production of table grapes): some 1,500m (4,900ft) or so above sea level, the Valley is dry and hot (temperatures often climb to 30°C/86°F in the summer), so cooler hillsides are best.

Casablanca Valley

An average altitude of 500m (1,640ft) above sea level, relatively poor soils on smooth slopes, cooling afternoon breezes which blow through the coastal mountains, a 20°C (68°F) difference between day and night temperatures, and cloud cover which gives a long ripening period ... perfect conditions for the cultivation of white grapes. Add to nature's bounty the human touch – careful management of the vineyards, low yields, harvesting at the right moment, rigorous methods of vinification and the skilful use of new barriques – and all this contributes to Casablanca's deserved reputation as Chile's premier white wine region. 'This whole Valley has just exploded', says winemaker Gaetane Carron, and there has certainly been no shortage of interest from foreign investors who wish to stake a claim in this exciting region which now has plantings of 1,400 hectares of vines.

While the hallmark of all Casablanca wines is highly concentrated varietal characteristics, it is Chardonnay (occupying no less than 80 per cent of vineyards) which stands out as possessing the most clearly defined regional style and winemakers such as Ignacio Recabarren at Viña Casablanca and Thierry Villard at Villard Fines Wines make stunning versions which are brimming with intense tropical fruit aromas and powerful, well-balanced citrus and spice flavours which tend to be a streak crisper than their Central Valley rivals. Viña Casablanca's Santa Isabella Estate also creates one of Chile's finest and most distinctive Sauvignon Blancs (to a ripe gooseberry and asparagus style with a zip of lemony acidity) and a voluptuous Gewürztraminer.

The bodega which produces the well-known Caliterra wines, north of Santiago.

A peaceful scene in the Viña Franciscan de Aguirre vineyards in the Casablanca Valley. Californian Michael Mondavi (whose family company invested almost US$10 million in its partnership with Viña Caliterra in 1996) thinks Casablanca 'has the opportunity of producing Pinot Noirs and Merlots that will compete with some of the best in the world'.

Some promising (albeit small) amounts of very good Cabernet Sauvignon, Merlot and Pinot Noir are also being made, though some producers (Villard, for example) are forced to buy in grapes from the Maipo Valley to fulfil orders (indeed, it speaks volumes that Villard exports all of its production).

The Central Valley Region

Forming the very heart of the Chilean wine industry, this vast basin is traversed in an east to west direction by a number of smaller valleys which offer a variety of mesoclimates depending on the influence of the sea and the mountains. Each river lends its name to an appellation (Maipo Valley, Rapel Valley, Curicó Valley and Maule Valley) and each possesses its own unique set of viticultural characteristics.

Maipo Valley

The Maipo Valley is Chile's oldest wine region, with the greatest concentration of vineyards in the country and, as such, many of the industry's most prestigious players are centred here – Canepa, Concha y Toro, Viña Santa Carolina, Santa Inés Vineyard, Viña Santa Rita, Viña Tarapacá and Viña Undurraga in particular leap to mind as being among the most innovative. They certainly benefit from an ideal growing environment – sandy, alluvial soils enriched by calcium deposits from the Maipo river, warm, dry summers, rainless autumns, mild winters, frost-free springs and a sun that

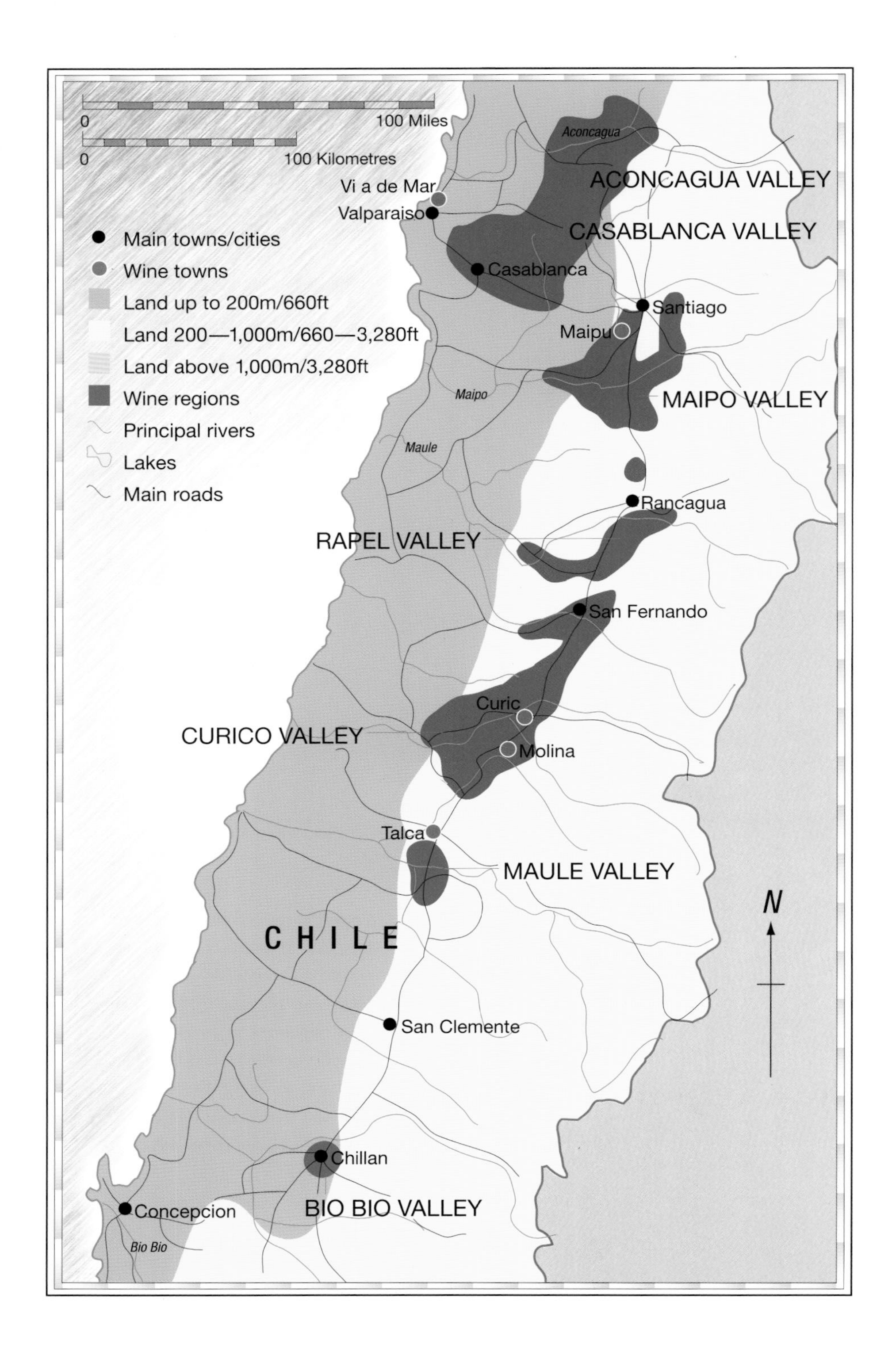

smiles on the Valley for most of the year, which encourages ripening.

While Cabernet Sauvignon is the principal variety grown, some very promising Chardonnay, Merlot, Pinot Noir, Sauvignon Blanc and Sémillon are emerging, too, including a Late Harvest Sémillon made under the Viña Carmen label.

The Maipo Valley is said to be one of the most exceptional grape-growing regions in the world and new developments are taking place all of the time. But there is a cloud on an otherwise sunny horizon: the insidious expansion of Santiago's suburbs. With it comes the human curse of urban smog which increases both temperature and precipitation.

Rapel Valley

Warm, sunny summers with cool, breezy nights, and winters with moderate rainfall. These climatic characteristics, along with the quality of the soils (rich loamy clay with patches of calcareous tuffeau in the south) and the purity of the irrigation water fed by the Los Cristales dam, combine to nurture one of the most exciting viticultural regions in the world. The region, which is divided into the Cachapoal and Colchagua Valleys, is now being flooded with boutique wineries making top-class wines and Viña Morandé has invested a colossal US$15 million in its Pelequen venture. All in all, this is quite a turnaround for an area which used to be a bulk supplier of grapes to other parts of the country.

Of the 8,000 hectares planted, some 5,000 are dedicated to red varieties (with Merlot showing the greatest promise) which seem to better match the terroir, though some Chardonnay and Sauvignon Blanc vines are cultivated, too.

This is still a relatively young area. Even as recently as 1991, Viña Bisquertt was still mostly making undistinguished table wines for local consumption (it is now building a reputation for fine Cabernet Sauvignon, Chardonnay and Merlot), and Viña Manent has only just installed stainless steel fermentation tanks to replace their very old and very large vats made of rauli wood (a native, evergreen beech that causes taint).

However, that worthwhile potential remains to be explored is exemplified by Viña Caliterra, who crushed their first vintage at their new state-of-the-art La Arboleda winery in 1998. They see red wines as the future of the Colchagua Valley and have planted 300 hectares of Merlot, Carmenère and Cabernet Sauvignon (plus experimental plots of Syrah, Malbec and Sangiovese) which they expect to harvest for the first time in the year 2000. The mighty Canepa has also bought 1,000 hectares of land here and intends to further the cause of Malbec. Other names to watch include Luís Felipé Edwards, MontGras, Sergio Taverso and Viña Manque. Cono Sur also makes a Burgundian-style Pinot Noir in the Chimbarongo area, even though it is a little hit-and-miss depending on the quality of the vintage.

A variety of factors combine to make Rapel Valley one of the most exciting viticultural regions in the world.

Curicó Valley

Many people firmly believe that the finest Chilean wines come from here, thanks to a magical combination of climate and soils. Well, my personal thoughts are that the whites from Casablanca are far superior; nevertheless, some extremely sound and interesting wines are indeed produced here.

The 15°C (60°F) variation between night and day temperatures suits white varieties well (especially in the foothills of the Coastal Mountain Range) and thus the region has developed a reputation for

The winery of Vina Aquitania in the Upper Maipo Valley. As Maipo is one of the warmest regions in the country, they are establishing vineyards further up the Andes' foothills where the nights are colder, which helps to improve grape acidity.

first-class and very modern Chardonnay, Gewürztraminer, Riesling and Sauvignon Blanc. But the warm climate and loamy clay soils make for good red wines, too. Excellent Cabernet Sauvignon, Malbec (especially from La Fortuna) and Pinot Noir is produced, and Merlot fairs particularly well – indeed, the Errázuriz El Descanso Estate has expanded its Merlot vineyards in the belief that they have found 'an exceptional match between grape variety, soil and climate'.

You can also find a drop or two of very classy champaña made by the traditional method from a blend of Chardonnay and Pinot Noir – Viña Valdivieso and Miguel Torres Estate make the most notable examples. With regard to the latter, it was Spaniard Miguel Torres who did much to revolutionize the Chilean wine industry. His success was due in part to the importance that he placed on tailoring wine styles to suit the international consumer, and many other producers have since followed his lead.

Maule Valley

Some pioneering work is afoot in this region, with Canepa (undoubtedly one of the most go-ahead wine estates in South America) at the helm. While white wine (made from Chardonnay, Sauvignon Blanc and Sémillon) predominates, its quality has been mutable and thus the Maule Valley is better known for the superiority of its red wines (most especially Merlot). While the summer daytime temperature can reach a toasting 32°C (88°F), it is moderated by cooling ocean breezes, funnelled up the Valley from the Pacific towards the Andes. More importantly, it drops by as much as 18°C (68°F) overnight. This gives model conditions for the production of superbly balanced fruit.

The Southern Region

Chile's southernmost wine outpost which, until recently, was overrun by the País grape owing to the relatively unfriendly climate. The Coastal Mountain Range offers no protection from the rain here and, consequently, it is very wet. Temperatures are much lower than those further north (indeed, there is a strong risk of frost) and the sun simply does not shine as much. While the region remains relatively unexploited as far as the classic grapes are concerned, some producers have taken great strides to produce a handful of quality wines.

Statistics Versus Change

It must be stated that all statistics quoted in this chapter have to be treated with a certain degree of caution. Chile is the only South American country to have established a generic promotional body in the UK (which is something that Argentina needs to tackle if it is to progress, I feel), but even their figures are dependent on information supplied by the Chilean Wine Export Association (to which not all wineries belong). Anyway, the sheer rate of development implies that the statistics are out of date almost as quickly as one can write them down!

Similarly, official classification systems which would equate to the French *Appellation Contrôlée* rules which govern hierarchical designations and minimum viticultural and vinification standards, for example, are rudimentary in South America. Efforts have been made in Chile, but everything changes as new areas are opened up (although I am not suggesting that this is a bad thing).

Chilean Appellations

A set of regional appellations has been put in place, and with it, a label integrity scheme. Owing to the speedy rate of development in Chile, however, this is likely to be updated in future years, but it currently covers five regions (north to south):

Atacama

Copiapó Valley
Huaso Valley

Coquimbo

Elqui Valley Region – Vicuña, Paiguano
Limarí Valley Region – Ovalle, Monte Patria, Punitaqui, Río Hurtado

Choapa Region – Salamanca, Illapel

Aconcagua

Aconcagua Valley Region – Panquehue
Casablanca Valley

Central Valley

Maipo Valley Region – Santiago, Pirque, Puento Alto. Buin, Isla de Maipo, Talagante, Melipilla
Rapel Valley Region – Cachapoal Valley
Sub-region – Rancagua, Requínoa, Rengo, Peumo
Colchagua Valley Region – San Fernando, Chimbarongo, Nancagua, Santa Cruz, Palmila, Peralillo
Curicó Valley Region – Teno Valley Sub-region – Rauco, Romeral (Teno)
Lontué Sub-region – Molina, Sagrada Familia
Maule Valley Region – Del Claro Valley Sub-region – Talca, Pencahue, San Clemente
Loncomilla Valley Sub-region – San Javier, Villa Alegre, Parral, Linares
Tutuvén Valley Sub-region – Cauquenes

Southern

Itata Valley Region – Chillán, Quillón, Portezuelo, Coelemu
Bío Bío Valley Region – Yumbel, Mulchén

Argentina

Corned beef, the Falklands War, *Evita*, polo ... these are the things which probably spring first to most people's minds on thinking of Argentina and wine is most likely way down the list. Yet Argentina is the fifth largest wine producer in the world, with over 2,000 wineries vinifying a mammoth 12,681 million hectolitres of wine from 210,639 hectares of vineyards – just one producer alone makes more wine than the whole of New Zealand!

Now before you jump to the conclusion that I am being a little slack in attention to detail here, the figures above relate to the 1996 vintage only (the latest statistics available, as I write). Interestingly, wine production has actually fallen by a remarkable 47 per cent over the last 20 years, so it would be foolish to suggest that any one vintage is representative of the whole anymore. This reduction, incidentally, is the result of a switch in allegiance from wine to beer in the domestic market. Argentinian wine consumption peaked at a mind-boggling 91.8 litres (20.2 gallons) per capita in 1970 (by comparison, the British were drinking a mere 2.89 litres/0.6 gallons a head), but this had decreased to 41.5/9.1 gallons litres per capita by 1998.

Under normal circumstances, one would assume that a drop in quantity would give rise to better quality, but this was not generally true of Argentinian wines until the mid-1990s. While many vineyards were grubbed up in the wake of shrinking domestic sales, high yields (anything up to 400 hectolitres per hectare against the 50 hectolitres per hectare figure generally accepted as the maximum limit for premium wine production) remained the order of the day in those which survived. These were very easy to achieve, with the help of naturally prolific grapes like Criolla Chica, Criolla Grande, Cereza, Cereza Grande, Pedro Giménez and Moscatel Rosada. The wines were pretty horrible, but poor quality never seemed to bother the Argentinians themselves, and they were the ones drinking the vast majority of them, after all. Even as recently as 1998, only five per cent or so of Argentinian wine was destined for export and four-fifths of that was grape concentrate or very ordinary bulk wine, though the balance is slowly shifting.

The gradual but radical decline in domestic wine sales, coupled with a burgeoning interest in Argentina from speculative world wine markets seeking out the next 'great unexploited unknown', is now driving producers towards developing a stronger export market, and they have simultaneously realized that they must improve their standards if they are to meet the demands of very choosy international buyers. There has subsequently been a rush to embrace new technology in the wineries, to put an end to over-irrigation, to introduce better rootstocks, clones and canopy

Ploughing by mule to maintain irrigation channels is still a commonplace sight in Argentina, especially where there is no room for machinery.

management techniques, and to cultivate more of the classic 'international' grapes which make the wine that people want to drink. There is a certain irony here, however: there is no doubt that some of the best Argentinian 'new wave' wines are coming from Malbec and Torrontés, grapes which are considered as Argentine specialities – and long may they stay planted; growers worldwide are often too quick to rip out their really interesting (often indigenous) vines, only to replace them with yet more rows of Chardonnay and Cabernet Sauvignon.

The true key to progress (and to secure a long-term future for the industry) has been the foreign investment which is streaming into the country. For example, on-site crushing facilities are being built in an effort to improve the quality of the must. As Carlos Tizio Mayer at Bodegas Norton says: 'You have to be careful with your fruit between harvesting and crushing' – Argentina's summer heat is so powerful that the grapes can easily be oxidized during what can be a long road journey from vineyard to winery. As for the wineries themselves, they now gleam with stainless steel and their cellars are packed with new oak barrels (neither of which comes cheap) thanks to financial input by corporations such as Allied Domecq, IDV, Kendall-Jackson, Moët & Chandon, Pernod-Ricard, Seagram and Sogrape – and, even Chilean wine companies (such as Concha y Toro and Santa Carolina) are backing Argentina! (But does this mean that they have nothing to fear? A challenging thought...!)

It takes more than money to make good wine, of course, and to this end, outside expertise has been sought from experts such as consultant oenologist Michel Rolland and his viticultural

counterpart, Richard Smart. And when highly respected winemakers such as Tobias Ansted, Peter Bright, Ed Flaherty, Paul Hobbs, Jacques and François Lurton, David Morrison, Hugh Ryman, Hubert Weber and John Worontschak move in to make wine, then you know that things are on the up and up.

Argentina is still in its infancy as far as international recognition is concerned, but I am convinced that this country will go from strength to strength as it continues to realize the potential of its natural advantages (virtually phylloxera-free vines, healthy growing conditions, a long ripening season and great soils), learns how to identify and make the most of vineyard sites which are better-suited to quality winemaking, and gains a closer understanding of international markets. Furthermore, Argentina has one great asset which other New World countries can only envy: a seemingly bottomless well of red wine (of which there is a global shortage).

Once the world catches on to this, and as wine quality rises, prices are bound to rocket, but in the meanwhile, Argentina offers fantastic value for money. With the exception of Dr Nicolás Catena's inspirational Malbec and Chardonnay from Bodegas Esmerelda, you will not find premium quality (yet), but there are plenty of very reliable and immensely drinkable wines to be had.

Catamarca, Jujuy and Salta

Of Argentina's most northerly wine provinces, it is Salta which is the most significant (and most specifically its sub-region of Cafayate in the Calchaqui Valley). Producing roughly two per cent of the country's wine, it boasts the world's highest vineyards, up to 2,000m (6,500ft) above sea level. It is cooler up here (with a 22°C/70°F summer daytime mean which plummets to a refreshing nightly 12°C/54°F), though the sun shines 350 days a year. Add a moderate annual rainfall of 200mm (8in)

Highlights of History

1550

One view purports that the vine found its way into Argentina from Peru in this year. However, other sources think that the Spanish had already introduced vines back in 1541.

1556

An historical source claims that this is the year in which the vine is imported to Argentina for the first time ... from Chile! And yet more theories suggest that it came in from Bolivia, Mexico or even Siberia!

1557

Whatever the actual source of the vine, records show that a vineyard is established at Santiago del Estero by Jesuit missionaries, who turn their grapes into sacramental wine.

1591

The La Rioja region is planted with vines, but only towards the middle of the 20th century do the wines begin to make themselves known on the domestic market.

1810

Argentina becomes the first of South America's colonies to gain independence and European immigrants (mainly Italian and Spanish) flood to the country in its wake.

1885

This year sees the completion of the railway between Buenos Aires and Mendoza, thanks to the efforts of Don Tiburcio Benegas. Previously, horse-drawn carts were used to transport wine from the vineyards to the capital and they were often attacked by native Indians. The greatest significance, however, is the speedier and more efficient access to Argentina's ports, which thus allows the possibility of the shipment of wines overseas for the first time.

1895

Edmund James Palmer Norton, a railway engineer, falls in love with the beautiful countryside of northwestern Argentina and settles in Luján de Cuyo, Mendoza. He imports vines from France and builds a winery.

1913

Humberto Canale grows the first grapes in the Alta Valle of the Río Negro in remote Patagonia, an area which has essentially been made over to fruit production up until now.

1920s

Argentina has become the eighth richest nation in the world, though future economic depression will lead to a slump in foreign investments and a steep decline in the demand (and prices) for its exports.

1943

General Juan Domingo Perón comes to power and his ideals bring some respite to the depressed economy. This state of affairs is relatively brief, however, as the country's fortunes plunge once again in the wake of his ousting in 1955.

1960s

Bodegas Chandon is established in Agrelo. The location is chosen by Monsieur Renaud Poirier (Chef de Cave of France's Maison Moët & Chandon) for its optimum vineyard conditions. In the meanwhile, Nicolás Catena revolutionizes the wine industry by introducing the first 100 per cent varietal wine (Saint Felicien Cabernet Sauvignon).

Early 1980s

Inflation is running at nearly 1,000 per cent a year in Argentina (which has now dropped to 15th place in the league of developed nations).

1996

The wine business is thriving again and exports to the UK increase fivefold.

Principal Grape Varieties

The high yielding but poor quality Criolla Grande is the most widely planted grape in Argentina and the domestic market still laps up the wine it produces. It is not one which would suit 'western' palates, however, and, thankfully, Argentina is turning its attention to the international varieties of which we are all so fond.

Cabernet Sauvignon

This is the second most important variety after Malbec and I reckon that more and more of it will be planted as Argentina gets to grips with Cabernet's natural vigour and better learns how to use oak to complement the grape's natural concentration of tannins and fruit compounds. Cabernet Sauvignon has the propensity to be instantly recognizable wherever it is planted in the world. In Argentina, however, its flavour leans towards blackberries rather than blackcurrants, and it tends to have a very dense and savoury character. Of course, this may simply be a function of old-fashioned winemaking techniques and, as wineries continue to be modernized and upgraded, we may yet see different tastes coming through. Only time will tell if Argentinian Cabernet truly possesses a distinctly individual and national style.

Argentina is best known for its red wines, although whites are coming increasingly to the fore now that winemakers such as John Worontschak are involved in the industry.

Chardonnay

Only the foothills of the Tupungato have proved to be a truly consistent source of good Chardonnay so far – this is not to say that good Chardonnay is not made elsewhere, however. It has to be grown in sites which offer a natural brake to Chardonnay's willingness to turn grape acids into grape sugars as it races towards maturity – in other words, a cooler site will give a longer ripening season which, in turn, offers growers a better chance of picking the grapes at precisely the optimum time.

Malbec

The most widely planted and the most important 'quality' grape – indeed, I would go as far as saying that this is Argentina's finest grape of all. While the wine varies from the 'everyday' to the 'pretty special', it nevertheless gives a much richer and more seductive style than its French compeers. Malbec performs particularly well in Mendoza, where it has the potential to make wines which age well. Definitely a grape to follow.

Sauvignon Blanc

Argentina can support the cultivation of this grape as long as it is planted up in the hills – it appreciates cooler mesoclimates and microclimates (like Chardonnay, this has everything to do with grape acid retention).

To this end, the majority of the plantings are in Salta and Río Negro. Personally, I find that the wines lack the high acid crunch which I enjoy so much in some other countries' versions.

Torrontés

This is quite the most fascinating and eclectic of white grape varieties which Argentina offers and, furthermore, there are precious few places in the rest of the world where you will find it. Its signature is a delightful and astonishing aroma, and a naturally high acidity – provided it is handled properly in both vineyard and winery, that is. There are a number of sub-varieties: Torrontés Riojano is (not surprisingly) common to the La Rioja region, and the bigger-berried Torrontés Sanjuanino is planted mostly in San Juan; the rarer Torrontés Mendocino, however, is more likely to be found in Río Negro than Mendocino. The 'aromatic' varietals in general seem to be the least popular in terms of sales worldwide, so I hope sincerely that Argentina will not be tempted to give up on Torrontés in favour of something more fashionable but potentially less interesting.

Grapes to Watch ... Barbera, Cabernet Franc, Chenin Blanc, Merlot, Pinot Noir, Riesling, Sangiovese, Sémillon, Syrah, Tempranillo (often described as Tempranilla).

Malbec is Argentina's most important 'quality' grape – indeed, its finest grape of all, the wines giving a much richer and more seductive style than those of its French compeers.

(supplemented by controlled irrigation), and permeable, very sandy soils, and you have the recipe for virtually ideal growing conditions. The slow ripening cycle allows the development of concentrated varietal character in grapes such as Cabernet Sauvignon, Chardonnay, Chenin Blanc and Malbec, which have all been planted here with success. But it is the gorgeously aromatic Torrontés which has risen as the shining star. Look no further than Bodegas Etchart for the most lustrous example.

La Rioja

The first vines were planted in 1591, but it took until the 1950s before anyone took any notice of the wines. Today, the most significant wineries include Bodega La Rioja (who make a curious Torrontés-Barbera blend) and the Cooperativa La Riojana (responsible for half of the province's production, from Barbera, Cabernet Sauvignon, Malbec, Merlot and Torrontés).

San Juan

If you were transported here from the *USS Enterprise*, you would be forgiven for thinking that you had landed on the moon, such is the surreal nature of the landscape. You would come back to earth with a bump very soon, however, when the baking heat hit you (summer temperatures can climb to 42°C/108°F). In spite of this, San Juan is Argentina's second largest grape-growing area, with more than 46,000 hectares of vines, though quality is low and much of the crop is turned into concentrated must, sherry or brandy. Chardonnay, Syrah and Viognier are showing promise in the cooler Ullun, Zonda and Tulum Valleys and some better wines are emerging from producers such as Peñaflor and Santiago Graffigna.

Mendoza

Hugging the eastern foothills of the Andes, Mendoza is by far the largest and most important wine region of Argentina. It produces 75 per cent of the nation's wines, a colossal 95 per cent of the country's exports and is home to no less than 1,000 registered wineries and 30,000 separate growers.

As ever, the best fruit comes from the cooler, higher slopes, most especially those of the

The huge Peñaflor winery, said to be the world's third largest, at Maipú in Mendoza.

Tupungato volcano (the second highest mountain in the Americas), though winter frost and early summer hail can be a problem here. The 15°C (60°F) diurnal range offers grapes the chance to ripen for longer, thus increasing the concentration of aroma, flavour and acidity (much undervalued in Argentina) in the finished wine. Chardonnay, Merlot and Pinot Noir do especially well, alongside Cabernet Sauvignon, Chenin Blanc, Sauvignon Blanc, Syrah and Torrontés. Most notable, however, is Malbec (especially when the wine is barrel-aged) and Tempranillo (La Agrícola and Tittarelli make Argentina's finest wines from this grape). Planting continues apace in this area and the result of better rootstocks and clonal selection is showing through in the improved quality of the wines.

But the Italian grapes also thrive in Mendoza, which is not surprising considering the country's history. Many of the original immigrants hailed from Piemonte, bringing with them Barbera and Sangiovese *et al* in an attempt to keep their culture alive. Paradoxically, some of the 'Italian' bodegas are now beginning to establish a reputation for their 'non-Italian' varietals. Simonassi Lyon and Pascual Toso, for example, make robust, pepper and leather-styled Cabernet Sauvignon and perfumed Riesling (and the former also produces an outstandingly peachy Chenin Blanc and a good Malbec), and, under the Luigi Bosca label, Leoncio Arizu makes delicious, citrussy Chardonnay and superb Syrah, having pioneered clonal and canopy experiments over the past 20 years.

Others, such as Valentín Bianchi, are creating unusual blends from French and Italian grapes – their so-called Elsa's Vineyard Mendoza Malbec actually contains 15 per cent of Barbera. Talking of which, the very modern Bodegas Norton (the first wine estate to be located south of the Mendoza river, in 1895) arguably makes the best Barbera wine in the Americas (alongside a very prestigious, long-lived Malbec).

No matter where you are in the world, improvement in quality demands vast injections of capital, of course. Even as far back as 1973, it took the giant Peñaflor company (one of the world's largest winery groups) ten million dollars to upgrade the Trapiche estate when they acquired it. Trapiche now makes excellent examples of Argentinian Cabernet Sauvignon (firm, fruity and meaty with the structure to age well) and Chardonnay (fermented and matured in oak barriques to give a rich and complex wine with considerable body).

In the hunt to identify the best terroirs for each grape variety, Mendoza has also established itself as the forerunner in the development of specific sub-regions, such as Lavalle, Luján de Cuyo, Junin, Maipú, Rivadavia, San Carlos, San Martín, San Rafael, Santa Rosa and Tupungato – indeed, official bodies have been set up to regulate production and they are now controlled denominations of origin (Luján de Cuyo became the first in 1993, led by the highly quality-conscious José Luis Goyenechea). What appears to be transpiring is that areas of high altitude (Tupungato, for instance) are best for white grapes, while the reds prosper in the relatively lower Luján de Cuyo and Maipú. The biggest drawback to development is proving to be the shortage of water for irrigation.

Río Negro and Neuquén

It is often said that where the apple will ripen, the vine will happily follow – and this region provides a prime example. Located towards the south of the country in Patagonia, the climate is cool and dry (with a favourably long growing season) and the soils are chalky, conditions which have encouraged the cultivation of Cabernet Sauvignon, Chardonnay, Merlot, Pedro Giménez (sic), Petit Verdot, Sauvignon Blanc, Sémillon, Torrontés and even some Pinot Noir. Owing to its size, Humberto Canale is considered the most important winery here. A third of their wines is exported, so they are doing a good job on the whole, though my money would be spent on the modern, clean, fresh and fruity whites (and, in particular, their Sauvignon Blanc) rather than the slightly tough and tart reds. This is a region to keep an eye on – it offers enormous potential given more exposure to investment.

The house of Bodegas Navarro Correas at Maipú, Mendoza, Argentina.

Other Countries

Chile and Argentina are responsible for the vast majority of South American wine output – and certainly lead the international export tables by miles – but many of the other countries in South America have produced wine for centuries, albeit principally for domestic consumption. Growth is slower, but it is coming....

Bolivia

A decade ago, writers were not kind about the standards of Bolivian wine. One can understand why. The climate is decidedly tropical, problems with rot and phylloxera are endemic, and the soils are too fertile for the production of quality wine – indeed, most of the 20,000 hectolitres of wine made each year are turned into *písco* brandy. However, the UK is now importing small amounts of wines made from Cabernet Sauvignon, Merlot and Syrah at the Vinos y Viñedos La Concepción Estate and they have a certain curiosity value if nothing else (provided you are prepared to spend a minimum of £5.99/$9.99!).

A 200-year-old vine at Valle de la Concepción, Bolivia. Vines might have been grown for a long time in this mid-South American country, but sadly the winemaking industry remains primitive.

Brazil

It is amazing what money can do. Brazil's winemaking history featured nothing but a litany of failure until the 1970s, when companies such as Martini & Rossi and Moët & Chandon stepped in. They planted new vineyards with classic grape varieties (Cabernet Franc, Cabernet Sauvignon, Chardonnay, Gewürztraminer, Merlot, Sémillon *et al*) and opened up new wineries stuffed with state-of-the-art winemaking equipment. More recently, Flying Winemaker John Worontschak has made wine for an important UK supermarket at the mega-sized Vinicola Aurora co-operative whose 1,000 members are responsible for a third of total vineyard plantings and a mighty 95 per cent of all Brazilian wine exports (of which most goes to the USA). Today, Brazil is the third most important South American wine producer.

Producers have had their work cut out, however. Brazil's very wet, hot, sub-tropical climate (which can easily support five crops within a two year period) is anathema to *Vitis Vinifera*, and the more tolerant American

Many South American vintners still traverse their vineyards on horseback – the traditional method of getting around in this part of the winemaking world.

hybrids and *Vitis Labrusca* still eclipse vinifera by eight to one. The high humidity causes no end of trouble with fungal diseases. The clouds have a nasty habit of emptying their load during the harvest, so farmers tend to pick earlier than they should in order to avoid diluted crops ... but this practice gives grapes which are too acidic, a factor that is further exacerbated by the presence of leafroll virus in the vineyards which reduces grape sugar content.

One can only assume that the large multinationals know what they are doing. While everyone wants to be the person to 'discover' the next New World wine country, no-one is going to pump lots of money into an area unless the potential is really worth exploiting (the many devices which can be deployed in the vineyard and in the winery to outwit nature's shortcomings are costly).

Over half of Brazil's 60,000 hectares of vineyards are found at the southern tip of the country in the Rio Grande do Sul province, but, as ever, precise vineyard location is crucial. To this end, the better wines come from vines grown 700m (2,300ft) up in the hilly Serra Gaucha region, and from the communes of Santana do Livramento and Pinheiro Machado in the smaller Frontera region bordering Uruguay and Argentina.

The prevailing conditions are challenging enough, but Brazil is now facing a bureaucratic marketing obstacle. A new piece of European Union legislation came into force in September 1998 which stipulates that geographical origin must be stated on the labels of quality wines. Countries which have not designated and/or registered their wine regions can only sell their wines as table wines ... Brazil has not yet done this.

Colombia

The wine industry here was established in the 1920s and the number of major wineries now stands at 15, using grapes from 1,500 hectares of vines which are cultivated mainly in the Cauce Valley. To be honest, the statistics about Colombian livestock are more impressive – the country has almost as many cows as people ... 26 million! By tradition, the Colombians have a taste for sweet fortified wines (indeed, the first so-called wines were made from a blend of bananas, pineapple juice and dried grapes!). Some Chardonnay and Cabernet Sauvignon is grown, but the quality is dubious – hardly surprising in a difficult climate which requires hand-defoliation of vines in order to mimic some kind of dormancy (essential to quality).

The quintessentially South American entrance to the Tacama Winery in the Ica Valley of Peru. Topographical conditions and vine disease cause problems, but the Peruvian industry is making progress.

Ecuador

To say that the amount of land under vine is tiny is no exaggeration. Just 50 hectares of the native Nacional Negra and Moscatel Morado varieties are planted along parts of the breeze-cooled coastal areas, while a further 200 hectares can be found in the even chillier, mountainous Imbabura, Pinchincha, Cotopaxi, Tungurahua, Canar Azuay and Loja provinces. However, 'breeze-cooled' and 'chillier' must be put into context – the tropical climate permits three crops each year.

Peru

As far back as the 1960s, Professors Peynaud, Riberau-Gayon and Rives came to the conclusion that as long as vines were planted at high altitudes (which host a dry climate with warm days and cool nights), then Peru was 'well suited to wine

Highlights of History

1532

The Portuguese introduce the vine to Brazil and, two years later, the Spanish take vine cuttings to Ecuador.

1537

Vineyards are established in Paraguay, but the wine industry never takes off.

1547

Peru becomes the very first South American country to establish any kind of methodological viticultural *modus operandi* and, by the 1560s, an estimated 40,000 hectares of vines have been planted.

1626

Viticulture is introduced to the province of Rio Grande do Sul in Brazil by the Jesuits, but the vineyards are destroyed when the monasteries are dissolved.

1822

Brazil gains its independence, which gives a further boost to domestic wine production.

1840

The hybrid Isabella grape is planted with much success in Brazil's Rio Grande do Sul region.

1870

Italian immigrants bring Italian vine cuttings (such as Barbera, Bonarda, Moscato and Trebbiano) to Brazil, planting them in the Serra Gaucha region. In Uruguay, Pascual Harriagues, Luis de la Torres and Francisco Vidiella pioneer the planting of the Tannat grape. By now, commercial wine production is in full swing.

1885

Some 50,000 vines are planted at Establecimiento Juanicó in Uruguay.

1888

Phylloxera is discovered in Peruvian vineyards.

1913

Uruguay's Irurtia winery produces its first wine.

1920s

The commercial wine industry is founded in Colombia.

1944

Santa Rosa Estate produces Uruguay's first Cabernet Sauvignon.

1960s

Peru seeks advice from French viticulturists Professors Peynaud, Riberau-Gayon and Rives.

1969

Cabernet Sauvignon is grown in Brazil for the first time.

1970s

Multinational corporations begin to invest in the vineyards and wineries of Brazil, bringing about vast improvements, and Peru also sees progress in the identification of suitable planting material.

1984

Non-South American wine exports are prohibited in Colombia, which forces a renewed interest in domestic wine production.

1988

The Instituto Nacional de Vitivinicultura (INAVI) is created in Brazil to improve wine quality.

1996

Establecimiento Juanicó makes Uruguay's first botrytized wine, which is released in 1998.

Uruguay recognizes that it is too small to be able to match the likes of Chile or Argentina and thus aims to establish quality at a relatively higher level.

growing in conditions which are exceptional in the world'. Nevertheless, problems with phylloxera and high rates of oxidation meant that most of the production (an annual 18,000 hectolitres from 14,000 hectares of vines) was distilled into *písco* brandy. Today, the Chinca, Moquegua and Ica regions are beginning to make headway with Cabernet Sauvignon, Chenin Blanc, Colombard, Malbec and Sauvignon Blanc, thanks to good clones and an intriguing irrigation system which is fed via sets of large, deep pools developed over 500 years ago. Viña Tacama is the top exporter and Flying Winemaker John Worontschak has also worked his magic in the country.

Uruguay

Uruguay produces an annual 90 million litres (20 million gallons) of wine (albeit that only a tiny proportion of this can be considered as quality wine) and there is a very buoyant export market. The UK takes 45.8 per cent of all exports owing to the long history of trade links between Britain and Uruguay.

The leading producers (Castel Pujol, Castillo Viejo, Irurtia, Juanicó and Stagnari) make some very acceptable wines from numerous different varieties of grape, but the most widely planted in Uruguay's 22,000 hectares of vineyards is the thick-skinned, juicy Tannat, which gives lovely wine well worth tasting (especially now that better, virus-free clones are in place). This variety was imported at the beginning of the century by the Catalans, and it has adapted well to the humid climate.

The Uruguayans have confirmed that successful wine can be made as long as the vines are planted in suitable locations (the rolling hills in the temperate region of Canelones near Montevideo in the south is favourite), irrigation is prohibited, the vines are trained properly (as a result of careful research, over 50 per cent of growers now use the Lire system), yields are limited and modern vinification techniques using decent equipment are applied.

Venezuela

There are probably more anacondas and alligators here than vines – just 450 hectares are planted, producing some rather tasty table grapes, but that is about it. Having said that, since 1985 Bodegas Pomar has made a Bordeaux-style Sémillon and Sauvignon Blanc wine, and another Cabernet Sauvignon-Syrah-Tempranillo blend. I cannot vouch for its quality, but what I do find fascinating is the way in which the labels give the year *and the month* in which the grapes were harvested – this is because they have two harvests a year.

South Africa

South African wines have never been as exciting as they are today. Not only are they of superb quality, but we now have the widest choice of wines available in the Cape's 333-year-old winemaking history.

Southern Comfort

An eclectic range of warm reds and cool whites

South Africa is currently the sixth largest wine producer in the world. Following the lifting of sanctions, export volumes have increased a breathtaking fifteen-fold and Cape wines are now imported by no less than 50 countries.

As Her Majesty the Queen was moved to say in 1995 during her first official visit to South Africa under Nelson Mandela's presidency: 'I have come back to see for myself what is nothing short of a miracle.' Without wishing to comment on South African politics, it is safe to say that the new regime has also brought about something of a minor miracle to the country's wine industry. Since the end of sanctions, export volumes have increased fifteen-fold and Cape wines are now imported by no less than 50 countries (the UK is the most important market). South Africa is currently the sixth largest wine producer in the world (representing 3.4 per cent of global volume) with 260 cellars annually making some five million hectolitres of quality wine of all styles from 110,000 hectares of vines.

These statistics are all the more impressive for having been achieved by a country with no tangible wine-drinking culture of its own. But how has the industry coped with such a precipitous rise in demand, especially when it was effectively isolated from the rest of the wine world during the years of sanctions? And does quality necessarily parallel quantity? Some would say that South Africa has tried to run before it has learned to walk, but the facts speak for themselves.

Looking at supply and demand, the consumer trend is emphatically towards red wine and yet 88 per cent of South African vineyards are planted with white varieties (it is easy to forget that these were – and still are – the backbone of Cape brandy and fortified wine production). Furthermore, the world wants premium varietals such as Chardonnay and Cabernet Sauvignon, yet these represent only 17 per cent of total vineyard area (by comparison, this figure is 80 per cent in Australia).

If this is not problematical enough, the industry has had to cope with shortfalls in harvests, severe viral infection in the vineyards (leafroll, corky bark and fanleaf) and a legacy of extremely poor clones, the outcome of strict government

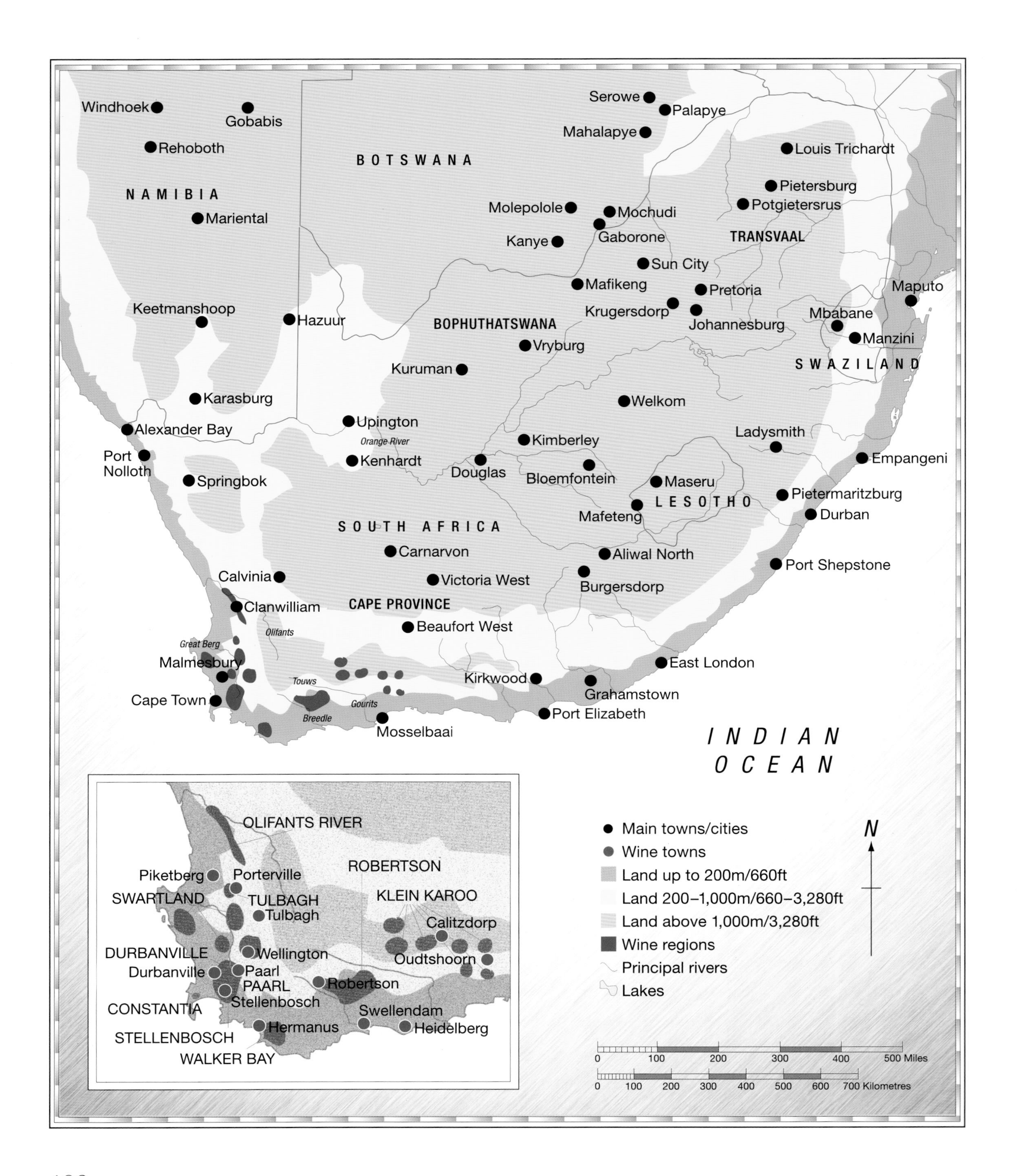

Windhoek
Gobabis
Rehoboth
NAMIBIA
Mariental
BOTSWANA
Serowe
Palapye
Mahalapye
Louis Trichardt
Pietersburg
Potgietersrus
Molepolole
Mochudi
Kanye
Gaborone
TRANSVAAL
Sun City
Mafikeng
Pretoria
Krugersdorp
Johannesburg
Maputo
Mbabane
Manzini
SWAZILAND
Keetmanshoop
Hazuur
BOPHUTHATSWANA
Vryburg
Kuruman
Karasburg
Welkom
Alexander Bay
Upington
Orange River
Kimberley
Ladysmith
Port Nolloth
Kenhardt
Douglas
Bloemfontein
Empangeni
Springbok
Maseru
LESOTHO
Pietermaritzburg
Mafeteng
Durban
SOUTH AFRICA
Carnarvon
Aliwal North
Port Shepstone
Calvinia
Victoria West
Burgersdorp
Clanwilliam
CAPE PROVINCE
Beaufort West
Great Berg
Olifants
Malmesbury
East London
Kirkwood
Grahamstown
Cape Town
Touws
Gourits
Breedle
Port Elizabeth
Mosselbaai
INDIAN OCEAN
OLIFANTS RIVER
Piketberg
Porterville
ROBERTSON
SWARTLAND
TULBAGH
Tulbagh
KLEIN KAROO
Calitzdorp
DURBANVILLE
Wellington
Oudtshoorn
Durbanville
Paarl
PAARL
Robertson
CONSTANTIA
Stellenbosch
Swellendam
Hermanus
Heidelberg
STELLENBOSCH
WALKER BAY
Main towns/cities
Wine towns
Land up to 200m/660ft
Land 200–1,000m/660–3,280ft
Land above 1,000m/3,280ft
Wine regions
Principal rivers
Lakes
N
0 100 200 300 400 500 Miles
0 100 200 300 400 500 600 700 Kilometres

restrictions on the import of rootstock material. Since the relaxation of these controls, the demand for healthy rootstock of new clones has led to immense shortages, a factor which has perhaps impeded development by far more than any other.

On a more positive front, growers are taking advantage of the opportunity to replant vineyards in locations which better suit the noble grapes – and simultaneously grabbing the chance to re-trellis vines, recondition the soil and so on. While the Cape is blessed with an almost ideal growing environment overall, with almost optimum weather conditions, there is still enough variation in soil and climate to make this exercise more than worthwhile and we are now beginning to drink the rewards.

The Neethlingshof Estate at Stellenbosch in Cape Province produces several good red and white wines from its extensive vineyards.

New Agricultural Products Marketing Act (1997)

The South African wine industry is beginning to make the adjustment to new free market rules. The withdrawal of subsidies will be difficult to come to terms with, but it is envisaged that the ensuing competitive edge will lead to industry improvements overall.

Ironically, however, a protectionist 25 per cent tariff has been imposed on all wine imports (which also penalizes domestic producers who blend bulk imports with domestic varieties), thus neutralizing some of the country's free market aspirations.

All this comes at a time when there is a shortage in domestic wine supplies – particularly for reds – owing to harvest shortfalls, a growth in exports and (not insignificantly) the emergence of a new middle class across the country which now likes to drink wine with dinner.

The South African wine industry will be facing the new millennium with the task of increasing production levels to meet the demands of a growing domestic market while continuing to pursue the trends of the international marketplace, particularly as it foresees a slowing down in demand from Europe and therefore needs to concentrate its market development efforts in the United States, Africa and Asia.

These forward-thinking initiatives are being reinforced by the founding of agencies like the Wine Industry Network for Expertise and Technology (WINETECH), and many of the winemaking areas have set up their own local associations to exchange ideas on best viticultural and oenological practice in addition to attempting to identify the best sub-regions or sites for the various grape varieties. Improvement in quality is also being brought about as a result of foreign investment and through the conversion of co-operatives (which account for 85 per cent of production) to companies, whereby the growers have a personal stake in the end product.

Progress in the vineyards, and within the infrastructure of the industry itself, is extremely encouraging. But South Africa has to firmly grasp the marketing nettle, too. If demand is so hard to fulfil, then why stretch oneself thin by supplying 50 different countries? Has the investment in wine tourism been money wisest spent? Did South Africa lose a marketing trick by switching to Bordeaux-style blends from the more traditional Cabernet Sauvignon-Shiraz blend (albeit less fashionable)? More importantly, however, is the question of selling prices: South Africa must turn its attention away from the bottom end of the market. I can do no better than to quote the very forthright South African winemaker Jabulani Ntshangase: 'We can sell on export all the good wine we can make. We just need more of the good stuff and no more of the cheap junk.' I could not agree more.

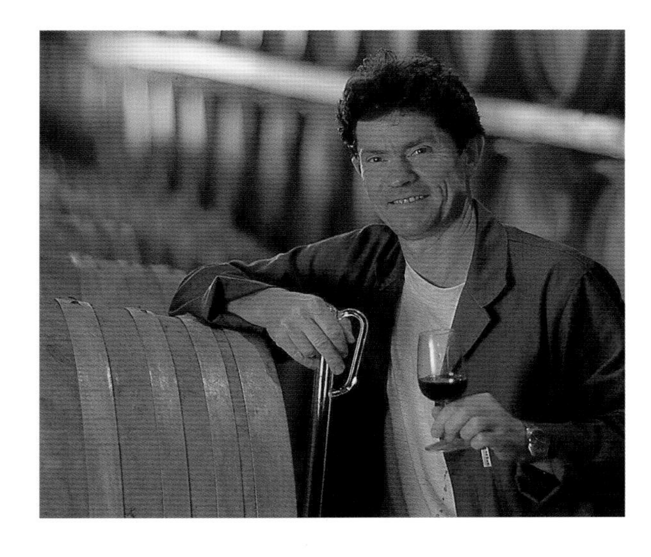

Gyles Webb, head winemaker at Thelema Mountain vineyards.

Principal Grape Varieties

Cabernet Sauvignon

This grape has become increasingly popular and, with plantings doubling between 1984 and 1994, Cabernet Sauvignon now covers some five per cent of South Africa's vineyards. Given the right clone and site, it delivers wines with minty, herby flavours backed up by plenty of cassis fruit, though they invariably need some time in the barrel, and the very best also demand long haul bottle ageing to reach their peak. The tough, 'green', tarry, old clone examples should disappear soon – important with a grape that is so sensitive to international consumer judgment. Cabernet also performs well when blended with Cabernet Franc and Merlot (or, indeed, with Shiraz).

Cape Riesling

This is what South Africans call Crouchen Blanc and it should not be confused with the superior Rhine Riesling. Nevertheless, it is much liked in South Africa (nearly four per cent of the vineyards are planted with it compared with just 0.9 per cent of Rhine Riesling) and, when made by quality-conscious producers, can offer dry, fruity, grassy, steely-backboned wines that sometimes develop attractive honey flavours with age.

Chardonnay

The last ten years or so have seen an explosion in the number of new plantings of Chardonnay. Growers have been quick to capitalize on the consumer popularity of this easy-to-grow variety and it now represents four per cent of the total vineyard area. This grape lends itself to barrel-fermentation and ageing which give greater depths of flavour. But results have been mixed: avoid any Chardonnay that tastes particularly oaky, as this usually indicates that oak has been used to disguise the thin flavours of a poorly-made wine. As Jan Momberg of the Middelvlei Estate in Stellenbosch observes: 'Oak should be likened to background music. If you want to hear it you can, but it should not intrude.'

Above: Punching down the grape skins on open tanks of Pinotage at the Kanonkop Estate, Stellenbosch. This helps to extract more flavour.

Left: Both red and white Hanepoot are used to make South Africa's sweet dessert wines. Nearly six per cent of the nation's vineyards are planted with the variety.

The high natural acidity of Chenin Blanc means that it can be grown almost anywhere in the country, producing an incredible variety of different wines.

Chenin Blanc (also known as 'Steen')

Chenin Blanc is the most widely planted 'workhorse' grape variety in South Africa, occupying 28.5 per cent of total vineyard area. Its high natural acidity means that it can be grown almost anywhere in the country (even in the hotter districts) and its versatility produces a number of styles ranging from dry to sweet, from still to sparkling, and it is even used to make white port and brandy. However, the results can all be a little staid unless the wines are either made from grapes picked from old, low-yielding bush vines or they are given special treatment in the winery. For example, extended lees contact (a process which allows the wine to rest on its post-fermentation sediment for longer than normal) and judicious use of oak, can add extra flavour and personality.

Cinsaut (formerly 'Hermitage')

Until the mid-1960s, Cinsaut used to be South Africa's most planted grape and it has only recently been overtaken by Cabernet Sauvignon as the country's most planted red variety (plantings are now down to 4.4 per cent of total vineyard area). 'Light and easy-drinking' best sums up the kind of wine it produces – in other words, it is not very exciting when bottled as a single variety, so it tends to be used in blends to speed up maturation.

Colombard (usually written as Colombar)

South Africa's second most important grape in terms of vineyard plantings, making up 10.5 per cent of the total. Like Chenin Blanc, it has a naturally high acid content, so is perfect for warm areas like the Breede River Valley, though it is susceptible to rot and oidium (powdery mildew). The wines are usually very fresh and bright with mouth-tingling astringency, and some versions boast enticing tropical fruit aromas and flavours.

Merlot

Introduced to South Africa in 1981, Stellenbosch and Paarl in particular are now growing even more of this early-ripening variety, although it still only occupies a lowly 1.8 per cent of total plantings. It can show finesse when bottled as a single variety, especially if it is allowed some new oak ageing. However, it has not abandoned its important role in the medley of grapes used to make Bordeaux-style blends, where it pads out the austerity of Cabernet Sauvignon.

Muscat of Alexandria (also known as Hanepoot)

Both red and white Hanepoot are commonly used to make South Africa's sweet dessert wines and nearly six per cent of the nation's vineyards are planted with the variety. This contrasts with the 0.7 per cent plantings of the finer Muscat de Frontignan (also described as Muscadel).

Pinotage

At one time, growers could not rip out their Pinotage vines fast enough; they saw no future for a variety which was condemned by a party of visiting British Masters of Wine in 1977 as giving coarse wine 'with a flavour of rusty nails'. Today, this cross between the noble but fussy Pinot Noir and the hardier, higher-cropping Cinsaut is now being replanted with fashionable gusto – though it still represents only 2.7 per cent of the vineyard area. More often than not, it used to be turned into fresh, fruity, juicy wines made expressly for early drinking. This style is still being made, but providing the grapes are picked at optimum ripeness, that fermentation is carried out rapidly and at a high temperature (28°C/83°F), and that the new wine sees a little oak, producers are now making Pinotage which has the potential to mature into complex and very exciting wines.

Sauvignon Blanc is on the up again once more in South Africa. Other grapes to watch include Bukettraube, Cabernet Franc, Gewürztraminer, Malbec, Pinot Noir, Viognier and Zinfandel.

Rhine Riesling (also called 'Weisser Riesling')

This grape has adapted well to South Africa's climate and soils and its wines are definitely a cut above those made from Cape Riesling. Styles vary from bone dry (which can be good) to honey sweet (invariably excellent and often possessing great longevity).

Sauvignon Blanc (occasionally labelled Blanc Fumé when oaked)

Following a dip in popularity, this variety is on the up and up again (currently accounting for 4.5 per cent of Cape vineyards) and is improving in quality with each vintage. While it gives all the dry, aromatic, grassy characteristics one would expect, South African Sauvignon leans towards a ripe, pungent and peppery style.

Grapes to watch ... Bukettraube, Cabernet Franc, Gewürztraminer, Malbec, Pinot Noir, Ruby Cabernet, Sémillon, Shiraz, Viognier, Zinfandel.

Autumnal vineyards and the manor house of South Africa's oldest winemaking estate, Groot Constantia, Cape Province.

Constantia

Known locally as the 'Cradle of the Cape Winelands', the historic Constantia district is not only home to South Africa's oldest wine estate (Groot Constantia), but also offers some of the country's most dynamic and consistent wines.

Grape-growing conditions are ideal, thanks to the cooling maritime effects of onshore breezes from False Bay and the Atlantic, and the afternoon shadows cast by the mountains. Both help to slow down the grape ripening process, giving wines of greater concentration and finesse. There is also plenty of winter rain (in excess of 1,000mm/33in per annum), so irrigation is not a word to have entered the wine vocabulary around here. The chief disadvantage is the richness of the soils, which tends to encourage vigorous growth; pruning and crop thinning are therefore essential to quality.

On the whole, the white wines of Constantia are the safest consumer bet, in my view. Sauvignon Blanc, in particular, performs extremely well here, especially when made by thoughtful producers such as Steenberg Vineyards, and Chardonnay has also been universally successful with local growers. Reds have not yet been perfected, however, though Klein Constantia Estate makes a decent

Highlights of History

1652

Dutchman Jan van Riebeeck arrives at the Cape of Good Hope in 1652 and establishes the first European settlement at Table Bay (now Cape Town) as a victualling station for the Dutch East India Company (an extremely useful stopover point for the Company's merchant fleet during the long passage of the 'Spice Route' from Holland to the East). He recognizes the area's potential for grape-growing and imports a shipment of vine cuttings in 1655.

1659

'Today, praise be to God, wine was pressed for the first time from Cape grapes.' These words from the diary of van Riebeeck, who has made the wine himself. This inspires the Free Burghers (those liberated from Company service) to plant vineyards inland, though success is limited owing to viticultural ignorance.

1679

Wine-loving Simon van der Stel is appointed Commander of the Settlement and establishes the town of Stellenbosch and the Groot Constantia farm (which he turns into a model wine estate with a reputation for fine wines which continues to this day).

1680–1690

French Huguenots fleeing religious persecution arrive in the Cape (settling in Stellenbosch, Paarl and the Franschhoek Valley) bringing with them first-hand knowledge of viticulture and vinification.

1761

Sweet red and white Constantia wines begin to be exported, gaining popularity amongst the European aristocracy (the only people who could afford to pay the exorbitant prices).

1806

Following the Battle of Blaauwberg, the British claim their second (more permanent) occupation of the Cape and a new market for Cape wines is opened up, with modest exports beginning more or less immediately.

Fine wines have been produced in the Cape since Simon van der Stel established the world-famous winemaking town of Stellenbosch in the late 17th century.

1825

Prohibitive tariffs on French wines in Britain brings about increased imports of Cape wines (reaching a staggering 45,000 hectolitres by 1859) and the colony's wine industry prospers. This happy state of affairs lasts until the Palmerston government reduces taxes on French wine imports in 1861 and, by 1865, Cape wine imports have been reduced to just 4,200 hectolitres.

1885

The vine disease phylloxera appears in the Cape, soon ravaging the vineyards.

1906

The first South African co-operatives are founded in an attempt to salvage the ailing wine industry via collective bargaining and marketing, and a pooling of technical knowledge and resources.

1910

The Act of Union is declared and the Boer Republics (Orange Free State and Transvaal) and the British colonies (Cape Province and Natal) are incorporated into a new country, the Union of South Africa.

1918

In response to a growing problem of overproduction, the Ko-operatieve Wijnbouwers Vereniging van Zuid-Afrika Beperkt (KWV) – the Co-operative Winegrowers' Association – is formed.

1925

South African viticulturist Professor Abraham Izak Perold crosses Pinot Noir and Cinsaut to create a new grape, Pinotage, which remains South Africa's only indigenous cultivar. However, the first Pinotage wine does not appear in bottle until 1961.

1948

The National Party comes to power and the apartheid policy is brought into force throughout South Africa.

1950s–1960s

The 'Natural Wine Revolution', an unprecedented enthusiasm for semi-sweet table wines, causes a slump in production of the fortified wines which have dominated the market up until now. Indeed, the Stellenbosch Farmers' Winery brand 'Lieberstein' becomes the world's largest-selling bottled wine – sales grow from nearly 30,000 litres (6,600 gallons) in 1959 to 31 million litres (6.8 million gallons) by 1964. In its wake, Chenin Blanc takes over from Sémillon as the most widely planted grape (the latter made up some 90 per cent of all plantings in the late 1920s and early 1930s). High demand also brings about important and long-lasting changes in the South African wine industry: the introduction of cold fermentation, the installation of stainless steel fermentation and storage vessels, and high-speed bottling lines.

1970

A survey reveals severe viral infection in a shocking 99 per cent of the country's vineyards.

1973

The Wine of Origin legislation is implemented countrywide.

1984

KWV sets up facilities to develop certified clonal material.

1986

The Vine Improvement Board is founded. This institution not only recommends the correct clone for each grape variety, but also propagates new, virus-free rootstock and 'cleans up' diseased rootstock via a process known as thermotherapy (heat treatment).

1990

President F.W. de Klerk announces the release of Nelson Mandela.

1994

South Africa holds its first full-race elections on 27 April.

1995

Wine estates are permitted to buy in grapes from elsewhere, though they have to be vinified separately and any claim to origin monitored carefully.

Shiraz and, along with Buitenverwachting (which rather evocatively translates as 'beyond expectation'), it can also turn out hearty Cabernet Sauvignon.

Much depends, of course, on the precise choice of vineyard location. Most of the vineyards cling to the sides of the 600m (1,950ft) high Constantiaberg which provides a great number of diverse slope angles and microclimates. There is certainly much opportunity to pair each grape variety to its optimum terroir, and I am positive that we will see far more premium red wines from Constantia in the future – after all, the technology is already in place in the wineries; they just need slightly better grapes.

An interesting twist to modern-day viticulture is the fierce determination of Martin Moore of the Groot Constantia Trust (established in 1993) to re-create the red dessert Muscat wine which made the estate so famous all those years ago. I have yet to taste the results, but I am sure they will be as fascinating as Klein Constantia Estate's similarly motivated white Muscat rendition, Vin de Constance.

Stellenbosch

The fertile soils of the broad Eerste River Valley and a favourable Mediterranean climate convinced Governor Simon van der Stel that this district offered the ideal growing environment for vines, way back in 1679. Today, Stellenbosch remains at the heart of the Cape wine industry, boasting the greatest (and ever growing) concentration of wineries in any one South African winemaking area – currently some 84 in total – and many of the country's classiest wines.

Many South African whites boast enticing tropical fruit aromas and flavours.

The question which naturally arises, of course, is: 'What makes Stellenbosch so special?' This almost defies answer because the district cannot easily be summed up in any one defining statement. Vineyards can be found just about everywhere, from the valley floors to the high reaches of the rugged mountain slopes, planted on 50 different soil types (ranging from loam to granite), in as many disparate mesoclimates. Indeed, one can only talk about climate in the broadest of terms here: the summer heat (around 20°C (68°F) average) is tempered by sea breezes, and rain (which falls mostly in winter) affects mountain vineyard sites more than others (to the extent that irrigation is vital in some parts). There is no doubt, however, that van der Stel's original assessment was very sound – vines of all predispositions prosper here, though it can be said that some grapes fare better than others and that the very best wines hail from vines planted in the mountain foothills.

Logic also dictates that Stellenbosch cannot claim any single wine style as its own – and this is

The barrel maturation cellar at the Stellenzicht Estate in Stellenbosch. The winery is one of the most modern in South Africa.

truly the case. While Stellenbosch has been revered traditionally for the high quality of its red wines, the tide is now turning for the whites, too, and some stunning wine is being made. Chardonnay and Sauvignon Blanc from producers such as Eikendal Vineyards, Jordan Vineyards, Morgenhof, Mulderbosch Vineyards, Neil Ellis Wines, Saxenberg, Thelema Mountain Vineyards and Vergelegen stand out particularly. Among the reds, Cabernet Sauvignon, Merlot, Pinotage, Shiraz and Bordeaux-style blends have all proved their worth (and the list of excellent producers is very long). However, Stellenbosch's reputation rests on its superb Zinfandel (Blaauwklippen is the Cape's top producer) and Pinot Noir (L'Avenir and Kanonkop Estates arguably create South Africa's benchmark examples).

As for the future, we can expect further development of the Helderberg/Somerset West area of the district, which is beginning to acquire a kind of sub-regional status for its wines.

L'Avenir Estate, in the lee of the Simonsberg Mountains, Stellenbosch. One of South Africa's most prestigious Pinot Noirs is crafted here.

Durbanville

This is one of the coolest vine-growing areas in South Africa, benefiting from the chilly air which blows in off Table Bay (just 15km/9m away), which not only moderates the summer heat, but also keeps the vineyards dry (thus minimizing the risk of fungal disease).

One might automatically jump to the conclusion that a dry vineyard equals thirsty vines, but this is not the case here. While rainfall averages only 500mm (16in) each year, early morning dew moistens the soils. And the soils themselves – predominantly granite-based – are deep and well-drained, although they nevertheless retain water well and the need for irrigation is therefore precluded.

Almost all of the vineyards are planted on the slopes of the Tygerberg Hills and growers are keen to match each grape variety to its prime location. As a result, Durbanville has long been renowned for the high quality of its premium red wines, though the whites (most especially the very complex and fruity Sauvignon Blanc from Nitida Vineyards) are also beginning to grab interest.

If all of this sounds far too perfect, then, yes, there is a downside ... Cape Town's suburban sprawl. Durbanville's vineyards are under threat of being engulfed by the concrete jungle. Perhaps we should rush out and buy these wines whilst we still can?

Paarl

For sheer diversity of wine styles, Paarl simply cannot be beaten. The spectrum ranges from crisp, delicate whites right through to rich, weighty, fortified wines, and there are luscious dessert wines, brilliant bubblies and plenty of good reds along the way. Paarl currently supports 20 per cent of South Africa's entire plantings and, all in all, some 22 different grape varieties are cultivated – and there are probably even more tucked away out of the limelight.

Paarl is one of South Africa's leading wine districts and home to one of the most famous wineries in the world: KWV.

You do not have to be a wine expert to appreciate that it requires an extraordinary set of soils and mesoclimates (not to mention microclimates) to achieve this, given the fussiness of most varieties as to where they are grown – and Paarl provides this.

The mix of soils (mainly decomposed granite with areas of clay-based, sandy loam, outcrops of Table Mountain sandstone near the river, and weathered Glenrosa shales to the northeast) have encouraged growers to plant vines just about everywhere: vineyards sprawl across the wide, flat bed of the Berg River Valley and climb up into the gentle foothills and steeper slopes of the craggy Paarlberg, Simonsberg and Klein Drakensteinberg mountains which fringe it.

There is also a good spread of mesoclimates. While the summers are generally long, hot and sticky, the mountain sites are cooler as a rule and, though there is plenty of rain overall (often reaching 650mm/25in a year), most of it falls in the southeast corner of the district, so irrigation is frequently required elsewhere.

There is no doubt that Paarl is one of South Africa's leading wine districts and it is also home to some of the country's most prestigious and innovative producers. KWV and the Nederberg (of Nederberg Auction fame) dominate by virtue of their size and reputation, but it is the smaller estates which form the backbone of the Paarl wine industry. They make good wines from almost every variety, using fruit from their own vineyards and rarely buying in grapes.

Chardonnay is very much the mainstay here and top of the range examples have emerged from Backsberg Estate, Fairview Estate and Glen Carlou amongst others. Other white varieties to show particular promise are Sauvignon Blanc (especially from Villiera Estate), Riesling (a good off dry wine is made by De Leuwen Jagt), and Nederberg has proved that a Noble Late Harvest style is possible from a blend of Chenin Blanc and Muscat de Frontignan.

By tradition, Paarl has always been considered as the headquarters of South African white wine, but Charles Back of Fairview takes a different view: 'I think Paarl is basically a red wine area. I see Shiraz, not Cabernet Sauvignon, as the future of Fairview.' He is not alone in this view in that Landskroon Estate and Simonsvlei do great things with this grape, too. But this is not to dismiss Cabernet Sauvignon – all three

The cellars of the internationally renowned KWV company at Paarl, Cape Province.

A view over the Dieu Donné ('God Given') vineyard to the historical Franschhoek Valley beyond.

produce excellent wines from this variety, along with Backsberg, Boland Vineyards International and Sonop Winery. Other star red wines are being turned out from Merlot (especially from Backsberg, Bodega, Fairview, Veenwouden and Villiera) and Pinotage (Backsberg, Diamant, Fairview and Sonop), while Glen Carlou makes one of South Africa's best Pinot Noirs.

Paarl means 'pearl' in Afrikaans owing to the way in which the Paarlberg seems to glisten after rainfall; many of its wines have an elegance and sophistication to match its name.

Franschhoek

Wine has been made in the 'French Corner' ever since the Franschhoek Valley was settled by the Huguenots in 1688 and, even today, its French heritage remains very strong (in spite of the recent invasion of English-speaking growers!).

Technically, Franschhoek is a ward within the Paarl appellation, but it possesses its own very distinct character. For a start, it is substantially wetter and cooler than the rest of Paarl, thanks to the influence of the lofty Wemmershoek, Groot Drakenstein and Simonsberg mountains, which virtually encircle the valley, and the cooling winds which sweep down the valley during the summer. The lower temperature is very welcome because it restricts vegetative growth and allows the grapes to ripen more slowly (extracting more aroma and flavour in response).

Some vines are still planted on the poorer, sandy alluvial valley floor, but the best vineyards are found on the valley slopes where the weather is even cooler and the soils (clay and sand on the lower slopes, turning into rocky sandstone and granite as the land rises) make the vines work harder and naturally restricts yields – indeed, as Achim von Arnim at Cabrière Estate proclaims: 'Marginal soils give discreet, elegant wines.'

By tradition, Franschhoek is white wine country (with a long history of growing Sémillon, in particular), but, over the last few years, there has been much progress with red varieties. Cabernet Sauvignon, Merlot, Pinot Noir and Shiraz have all produced exceptional results, and L'Ormarins Estate's Bordeaux-style blend is now one of the very best in South Africa (which just goes to prove that careful matching of variety to mesoclimate and soil does yield better wines). Until recently, wine production was dominated by Boschendal Estate, but there are now 26 separate wineries in operation – it is becoming a very fashionable area and land prices are rising accordingly. I believe that there is much potential

Wine of Origin Legislation

The South African Wine of Origin legislation operates in a similar way to the French *Appellation Contrôlée* system: it guarantees the origin, grape variety and vintage of the wine in the bottle (which must be 85 per cent of the stated origin/variety/vintage). However, unlike France, there are no controls governing yields, methods of pruning, and so on.

There are roughly 50 official appellations which range from large regions to tiny wards – but it is complicated, to say the least. In essence, regions are divided into districts which are further sub-divided into wards (generally in decreasing order of size). However, some regions have wards but no districts, and some wards are self-contained, forming neither part of a district nor region ... and so on. Furthermore, there is a new 'Cape' appellation which covers the whole of the Cape province.

Another crucial area of wine legislation concerns the use of the term 'Estate' (the smallest appellation, if you like). Estates have to be registered (voluntarily) and they can only use grapes grown on that estate; that is, they cannot buy in grapes and use them to make 'Estate' wine. In fact, most producers are forced to buy in grapes from dedicated grape growers in order to supplement their own production (and there are even 'virtual' wineries which have no land of their own), which can be an advantage if you have some kind of deficiency of terroir.

The most important point to bear in mind regarding both sets of legislation is that neither guarantees quality. It is the reputation of the producer which is critical.

still to be tapped in Franschhoek provided the right clones are planted in the right site ... and so long as farmers can afford to pay for 'the right site'.

Wellington

Strictly speaking, Wellington is merely a ward encompassed within the Paarl district, but it does deserve a few words of its own. Not only is it South Africa's nursery – almost all new vines now being planted across the country have been nurtured here – but it is also home to a number of important co-operatives.

Cape Wine Cellars springs to mind immediately. Founded by Wamakersvallei Winery, Wellington Wynkelder, Bovlei Winery and Boland Vineyards International, in association with the South African Dried Fruit Co-operative, it supplies own label wines (often vinified by Flying Winemakers) to the important British supermarket trade, made from grapes supplied by 305 farmers.

Some producers are also beginning to market wines of intrinsically finer quality – Pinotage from Wellington Wynkelder and Wamakersvlei, and Bovlei's Cabernet Sauvignon, are pointers to a very auspicious future.

Worcester

A decade ago, Worcester was declared South Africa's Champion Wine District ... but I, for one, am not sure why! While a few delicate and fruity wines were (and continue to be) made here from Chenin Blanc, Colombar and Hanepoot, most of the grape production has traditionally been turned into sweet fortified wines and brandy – indeed, the area is home to the KWV Brandy Cellar, the largest of its kind in the world. The accolade was more likely merited by Worcester's extensive viticultural size (forming approximately 19

Perfect Growing Conditions

Most of South Africa's vineyards are based within a 160km (100m) reach of Cape Town. The climate here is excellent: the growing season is eight months long, with sun-drenched summers cooled by sea breezes; most of the rain falls in winter (between May and August); frost and hail are rare; and the nights are cool, which promotes the storage of sugar in the grapes.

The northern and eastern regions are much drier – indeed, the few degrees of latitude which bring these areas closer to the equator make a substantial difference between day and night, and summer and winter, temperatures.

Vineyards stretch across the wide, flat bed of the Berg River Valley in Paarl, climbing up into the gentle foothills and steeper slopes of the jagged Paarlberg, Simonsberg and Klein Drakensteinberg mountains which flank it.

Predators like the African lynx and cheetahs stalk their prey in the gently undulating contours of the Langeberg, Drakensberg and Sonderendberg mountains.

per cent of South Africa's total vineyard area) and its contribution to the national grape crop (around 25 per cent).

Strangely enough, its size is probably the key to its future. Because Worcester covers such a large proportion of the scenic Breede River Valley and its tributaries, there is no such thing as a regional climate or soil pattern. Quite the opposite, in fact – there are marked variations throughout the district. For example, the amount of rain which falls on a vineyard (anything from 200–800mm/8–32in per annum) depends entirely on its proximity to the mountain ranges which border the district on three sides (albeit that some vineyards have to be heavily irrigated because they hardly receive any rain at all). And, while summer temperatures average out at around 24°C (75°F), the exact site temperature will have everything to do with how it is affected by the cool, late-afternoon, southeasterly winds which are funnelled up the valley.

Providing the co-operatives (which dominate the district) are willing to make their best efforts in the winery and the grape-growers are sensible about site selection, there is every reason to plant a wider selection of noble varieties. The promising results which have emerged so far from Pinotage, Merlot and Cabernet Sauvignon vindicate this point of view.

Robertson

On visiting Robertson, one cannot help but think about the trailblazing explorers of South Africa and what they discovered in this picturesque district of the Breede River Valley. So much of it is unspoiled ... antelope, steenbok, pheasants and guinea fowl roam at wild in the scrub, and there are even predators like the African lynx and cheetahs stalking their prey in the gently undulating contours of the Langeberg, Drakensberg and Sonderendberg mountains. I doubt that much has changed since the pioneering years.

What would not have been found in this district at that time, however, was the vine. Here, viticulture is very much a 'man-made', 20th-century innovation and only became feasible with the construction of the Brandvlei Dam. A means of irrigation is essential when summer temperatures can reach a sweltering 40°C (105°F) and the average rainfall is a lowly 250mm (10in), because the mountains shield the valley from precipitation.

Nature does lend a helping hand in other respects, however: the calcareous soils of the district are packed full of lime which promotes healthy vines with sound root structure; the nights witness a dramatic drop in temperature, which intensifies grape acids; and the strong, afternoon southeasterlies protect the grapes from the ubiquitous problem of sunburn.

At first, the vineyards were planted on the flat Breede River valley floor, owing to the prohibitive cost of pumping water up to the cooler, higher, rockier slopes where vine quality would be better. In the early development of this district, however, this did not matter – the majority of the wines were simply turned into

Hand-harvesting Chardonnay grapes for sparkling wine in Robertson.

brandy or fortified wines anyway, so it was an advantage to grow the vines in the hotter spots where yields would be high. Chenin Blanc and Colombar were the most popular varieties for this job.

The picture is quite different today, though. While some producers (such as Van Zylshof Estate) are now creating better wines from Chenin Blanc and Muscat (in all of its forms), many of the old vines are being ripped out and replaced with more sophisticated varieties (including reds); the vineyards are moving up into the hills; growers are breaking away from the co-operatives and setting up on their own (not that I am suggesting that there is anything wrong with the co-operatives); the grapes are often harvested at night when temperatures are low (cooler juice makes better wine); and more wineries are carrying out their own bottling which is always an improvement.

Perhaps the best summing-up of this exciting district is provided by Kobus van der Merwe, cellarmaster at Clairvaux Wines: 'We aim to produce the "big six" cultivars, namely Sauvignon Blanc, Chardonnay, Merlot, Cabernet Sauvignon and Shiraz.' This is by no means a maverick objective and we can already reap the rewards of drinking world-class Chardonnay from the likes of De Wetshof Estate (perhaps the best Chardonnay producer in South Africa), Graham Beck Winery, Rietvallei Estate, Van Loveren, Weltevrede Estate (which translates rather wonderfully as 'well satisfied') and Zandvliet Estate. Among the reds, Zandvliet produces one of the Cape's best Shiraz wines, and Springfield Estate is showing that

Mechanical harvesting of Cabernet Sauvignon grapes on Madeba Farm at the Graham Beck Winery, Robertson. Studies have proved that the machine can be better than man when it comes to harvesting grapes.

'Grandpa's Vineyard'

'Grandpa's Vineyard', a 70-year-old block of red Muscadel vines on the Weltevrede Estate, has been declared a National Monument, the first vineyard to be awarded this special status. In 1926, Klaas Jonker, founder of Weltevrede, planted 16,000 red Muscadel vines. As demand for sweet wines fell, however, most of them were uprooted in 1986. A mere 780 vines were retained in commemoration of Grandpa Klaas, and their grapes still contribute to the Estate's 'Oupa se Wyn' ('Grandpa's wine').

The extensive vineyards of the De Wetshof Estate at Robertson, Cape Province. Chardonnay is quite the best grape grown here and is turned into striking wine, arguably the best of its kind from South Africa.

Cabernet Sauvignon is promising when planted in the right location. Graham Beck is also creating some delicious sparkling wines.

Klein Karoo

The kind of climate which features relentlessly hot summers with precious little annual rainfall (under 200mm/8in) would normally rule out viticulture. But a wine culture was established here during the 18th century when growers realized that the stark ridges and peaks of the Swartberg Mountains to the north and the Langeberg and Outeniqua ranges in the south offered a degree of protection from the sun. And, as long as they planted the vines in the deep, red, alluvial soils on the river banks, the aridity problem could be overcome via irrigation.

In those days, of course, just managing to cultivate any vines at all was an achievement in itself. The quality of the grapes, however, was quite a different matter, which is why Klein Karoo became primarily a producer of brandy and (still very good) fortified wines.

More recently, noble grape varieties (Chardonnay, Riesling and Sauvignon Blanc) and new production techniques have been introduced in the cooler, damper, eastern end of the region near Mossel Bay by Boplaas, Die Krans and Ruiterbosch Mountain

Vineyards. The results so far are encouraging and we are likely to hear more from this area in the future.

Overberg (formerly Caledon)

This is South Africa's 'coolest climate' territory – at least as far as viticulture is concerned. The average daily temperature during the ripening period is a modest 20°C (68°F) at most, and there is no doubt that the vines do not see as much sunshine as other areas thanks to the shade of the mountains (which means that the grapes ripen late in the season). Furthermore, the vineyards closest to the sea are chilled even more by stiff winds.

What this adds up to is an ideal maritime mesoclimate for grape varieties which positively relish cooler conditions, and the district is therefore the source of some of South Africa's flagship Chardonnay, Pinot Noir and Sauvignon Blanc.

Soils vary from sandstone to weathered shales, watered by anything from 500–750mm (20–30in) of rain each year, and it is the level of natural watering that determines the exact siting of each variety. Of equal importance, however, is the move by pioneering producers like Hamilton Russell Vineyards and Bouchard-Finlayson Wines to plant their vineyards with new, improved clones (most especially Pinot Noir).

South Africa's most southerly vineyard district, which encompasses the wards of upland Elgin and coastal Walker Bay, is certainly the 'New World' of South Africa: in spite of the fact that it covers a large area, there are currently only ten producers

KWV

The Ko-operatieve Wijnbouwers Vereniging van Zuid-Afrika Beperkt (KWV) – the Co-operative Winegrowers' Association – was set up originally to overcome the challenging problem of over-production which was rife at the beginning of the century.

At one point, this dynamic enterprise represented no less than 4,919 growers and there is no doubt that it brought about invaluable reforms. However, KWV was soon acting as administrator, watchdog and policeman of the Cape wine industry as a whole, and while it was banned from competing as a producer on the domestic market, it became by far the largest exporter of South African wines, a stranglehold position which some argued created a conflict of interest.

Another criticism levelled at KWV concerned the minimum price mechanism (launched in 1940). Growers were paid a minimum price for 'good' grapes and were also guaranteed payment for any surplus grapes which were then turned into brandy or grape concentrate. This was an excellent arrangement for the grower, but one which encouraged high yields of grapes of generally indifferent quality.

Restrictions on the development of quality were encouraged by the introduction of the quota system, whereby KWV dictated who could plant grapes and where. Consistency of production was sought above all else when permission was granted to open up new vineyards; the exploitation of marginal areas offering potential quality but no other guarantees was therefore proscribed.

The quota system was abolished in 1993, the demise of the fixed minimum price policy followed in 1995 and, in the wake of the New Agricultural Products Marketing Act in 1997, and an amendment to the Wine and Spirits Act, KWV was finally converted into a company, handing over its administrative responsibilities to a new, non-profit-making Wine Industry Trust. However, by virtue of its size and its new freedom to compete internally, KWV remains a powerful force within South Africa, especially now that the quality of its wines has improved significantly.

operating here and, apart from Hamilton Russell (which was established in the 1970s, apparently illegally under the old KWV regime), they have all been founded in the 1990s.

Watch this district for the opening up of even more vineyards ... and its promising start at making very attractive Pinotage.

Tulbagh

It is amazing how wine quality can be elevated by just a simple modification to viticultural practice. In the bad old days, the sheer heat of the Tulbagh Valley during the picking season caused a rapid deterioration in the condition of the grapes between the vineyard and the vat – in consequence, the resulting wines were flabby and lacking in flavour. But the introduction of night harvesting changed all that. The temperature is 10°C (50°F) lower and the much fresher grapes can retain more of their natural fruit and aroma. The cooler Winterhoek Mountains, which surround the valley on three sides, can also be used to advantage, of course. On the whole, Tulbagh is known for its white wines, though a number of interesting reds are now coming on stream. Drostdy Winery, for example, is making good Merlot, and both Kloofzicht and Lemberg Estates have produced tasty Pinotage. Even more exciting is Krone Borealis, a Pinot Noir-Chardonnay based Cap Classique method fizz, from the pioneering Twee Jonge Gezellen Estate.

The cool mesoclimate and terrain of the Winterhoek Mountains are best suited to the premium varieties.

Swartland (formerly Malmesbury)

This district is best known for its top-notch fortified wines and robust, full-bodied and deeply coloured reds, the direct result of its mesoclimate: hot and dry. Plant some of the same grape varieties on

The Blue Crane of Breede River Valley

There is a lovely story behind the symbol featured on Goedverwacht Estate's wine labels, which depicts the blue crane (South Africa's national bird). It is officially listed as an endangered species, but it used to be a common sight in the Breede River Valley. The tale goes that Estate workers once found a baby blue crane wedged under a bridge next to one of their vineyards. Having rescued it, they nursed the bird back to health and then returned it to the wild. Now, 'at the end of the day, when the sun sets the valley alight with colour, you can spot the cranes coming over. Then, it is as if one of them hangs back a bit, calling a little louder to ensure that everything is fine at Goedverwacht'.

the granitic mountain slopes, however, and the beneficial influence of the cooling west coast sea breezes is felt – the wines positively bound forward in quality.

In fact, the degree of difference in temperature is quite startling. While temperatures can hit a blistering 40°C (105°F) at the peak of summer in the lowlands, the wind-chill factor cuts this figure in half in the Kasteelberg and Perdeberg mountains. This has encouraged a vast expansion in vineyard plantings over the past decade and a half, in a district traditionally dominated by wheat and sheep. Watch out in future, too, for increased cultivation in the coastal area around Darling, which is showing signs of potential.

So, which grapes are currently doing best? Chenin Blanc, Colombar and Sauvignon Blanc lead the way as far as the white varieties are concerned, while Pinotage is prominent amongst the reds (especially from the Swartland Wine Cellar). It is also important to remember that many South African producers do not necessarily abandon their old favourites when they start to embrace the new-wave styles. While exports of table wine from this district are steadily increasing, the traditional fortified wines are still hugely important. This is exemplified by Allesverloren Estate who, in addition to making succulent Cabernet Sauvignon and Shiraz, also continue to create a late bottled vintage 'port' which is widely regarded as South Africa's finest.

Olifants River

Growers in this blisteringly hot and dry region have proved just what can be achieved with careful canopy management (by using the vine's leaves to shade its grapes from the scorching heat of the sun), astute control of flood irrigation and modern winemaking techniques. From a position of churning out solid but generally uninspiring bulk wines, Olifantsrivier is now beginning to realize its potential for better quality.

Vredendal Winery, South Africa's largest and most progressive co-operative, is a good case in point. While it handles a whopping 60,000 tons of fruit each year (to put this into perspective, this is more than New Zealand's total annual crop!), it has now turned its attention to separately vinifying wines from individual vineyard plots where the character of the terroir is allowed to be expressed.

The Sparkling Wine Industry

'Méthode Cap Classique' is South Africa's answer to Champagne – the bubbles are created via a secondary fermentation in the bottle. Any potential argument between France and South Africa over the use of the term 'Champagne' was settled relatively early on (in the late 1960s) and involved crayfish, of all things! France agreed to buy South African crayfish in return for South Africa's pledge to boycott all use of French wine terms on their wine labels.

Sparkling wine (Méthode Cap Classique or otherwise) is not new to South Africa, but its first dedicated sparkling wine house, Bergkelder's House of J.C. le Roux, opened in the Devon Valley in Stellenbosch as recently as 1998. Approximately 64 hectares of vineyards have been planted with Pinot Noir and Chardonnay (the classic grapes for quality fizz) and it is envisaged that something in the region of five to six million bottles of sparkling wine will be produced annually.

J.C. le Roux was also the first South African vintner to create sparkling wines from Sauvignon Blanc and the first to make a red sparkling wine.

Vineyards in the scorching Olifants River valley, with the Gifberg Mountain in the background.

The Bergkelder

A number of leading Cape wine estates have an unusual partnership agreement with the Bergkelder. The winemakers produce wines to their own personal style from grapes grown on their own estates, thus ensuring that the distinctive character and individuality of each wine is maintained. The best of these wines is then aged and marketed by the Bergkelder, along with its own Alto, Fleur du Cap, Grünberger, Here XVII, Kupferberger, Le Bonheur, Pongrácz, Stellenryck and Uitkyk labels.

The Bergkelder (so named because its cellars are tunnelled into the side of the Papegaaiberg Mountain) has an incredible reputation: not only was it the first to introduce the practice of maturing wines in small, new, French oak barrels (in 1715), but it is also one of the most technologically advanced wineries in the southern hemisphere, with sophisticated oenological laboratories and extensive rootstock nurseries.

Bergkelder Partners:

Allesverloren
Jacobsdal
La Motte
Meerendal
Middelvlei
L'Ormarins
Rietvallei
Theuniskraal

They have also introduced a revolutionary 'total quality' programme which impacts on the whole winemaking process, including a requirement that farmers must properly house their workers before the co-operative will even consider paying top prices for their grapes. Motivation of this kind is certainly driving quality upwards and clearly demonstrates how it is possible to coax good wines from a region not blessed with the best of natural grape-growing conditions.

Orange River

South Africa's most northerly and very isolated wine-producing area presents a sun-scorched and extremely arid landscape. But it is one where lush, green vineyards flourish on highly fertile soils, thanks to much irrigation from the Orange River. Yields are extremely high (350 hectolitres per hectare versus the national average of 77) and all wines are made in bulk by local co-operatives, contributing some 12 per cent of the nation's crop.

A few good wines are made in Andalusia and Douglas (near Kimberley), but these are negligible.

Wine Buyer's Guide

A personal selection of some of the top-performing New World producers, though any shortlist such as this is difficult to compile because the overall standard is generally so high. The greater the number of stars (one to five), the better the wine; the 'v' suffix denotes those producers who offer particularly good value for money.

Argentina

Etchart ***(v)

Mendoza and Salta Owned by Pernod-Ricard, who have made considerable investment in this two-winery operation. International winemakers advise on style and production methods.
BEST WINES: *Cafayate Cabernet Sauvignon, Cafayate Barrel-Fermented Chardonnay, Cafayate Torrontés (one of Argentina's best), Rio de Plata Malbec*

Finca Flichman **

Mendoza Originally established in 1873, but refounded at the turn of the century by Don Sami Flichman. Heavy investment in two wineries has brought about huge improvements to wines which are highly fruit-driven.
BEST WINES: *Cabernet Sauvignon, Malbec, Syrah*

Nicolás Catena ***(v)

Mendoza Dr Nicolás Catena has arguably been the most influential man in steering the Argentinian wine industry into modernity. There is no doubt that his group produces consistent wines of world class quality. Labels: Alamos Ridge, Alta Catena, Bodegas Esmerelda, La Rural, Libertad, Rutini and Trumpeter.
BEST WINES: *Alta Catena (super-premium, highly concentrated, fruit-driven Cabernet Sauvignon, Chardonnay and Malbec made only in the best years), Bodegas Esmerelda (Cabernet Sauvignon, Chardonnay, Malbec), Alamos Ridge (good value Cabernet Sauvignon, Chardonnay, Malbec), La Rural (Malbec, Merlot)*

Norton **

Mendoza Originally founded by an English railway engineer back in 1895, this state-of-the-art enterprise is now owned by Austrian businessman Gernot Langes-Swarvski. One of the few bodegas not to employ a consultant winemaker, and they also have Carlos Tizio Mayer, one of Argentina's best viticulturists, tending their vineyards. Great value, highly fruity wines, red and white, oaked and unoaked, are made from a wide range of grapes.
BEST WINES: *Barbera, Malbec Reserva, Merlot, Norton Privada (top of the range blend of Merlot, Cabernet Sauvignon and Malbec), Sangiovese, Sémillon-Chenin Blanc, Torrontés*

Peñaflor **(v)

Various locations Argentina's largest producer making a very wide range of wines – from bulk wines for the domestic market, to premium quality under the Trapiche label (see separate entry). Flying Winemakers Peter Bright and John Worontschak have brought about huge improvements in quality.
BEST WINES: *Oak Cask Malbec, Tempranillo*

Trapiche **(v)

Mendoza Angel Mendoza and international wine consultant Michel Rolland, harnessed the very best quality from estate-grown grapes from vineyards in the Maipú and Tupungato Valleys. Trapiche is the premium label of Peñaflor.
BEST WINES: *Iscay (Malbec-Merlot, 50 per cent each), Medalla Cabernet Sauvignon-Malbec, Medalla Chardonnay, Oak Cask Malbec*

Weinert ***

Mendoza Very traditional winery, now partially owned by Dr Nicolás Catena, making wines of terrific quality, most particularly the reds. Owing to long periods of barrel ageing before release, these are not at all 'international' in style – their flavours are very dense, powerful and oaky, maybe over so for some. Weinert was the first Argentine producer to reduce yields in order to improve wine quality.
BEST WINES: *Carrascal (blend of Cabernet Sauvignon, Malbec and Merlot), Weinert Cabernet Sauvignon, Weinert Malbec*

Australia

All Saints ***

Rutherglen, Victoria See Brown Brothers.

Bailey's ***

Milawa, Victoria See Mildara Blass.

Bannockburn ***(v)

Geelong, Victoria One of Geelong's top wineries, best known for two Burgundian-style classics – gamey Pinot Noir and Meursault-like Chardonnay – from top winemaker Gary Farr. He brings an elegance and complexity to his wines as a result of invaluable annual experience at Domaine Dujac in Burgundy.
BEST WINES: *Cabernet Sauvignon-Merlot, Chardonnay, Pinot Noir, Shiraz (made to a Rhône style)*

Barossa Valley Estates **

Adelaide Plains, South Australia See BRL Hardy.

Best's ***(v)

Grampians, Victoria Viv Thomson crafts well-balanced wines from ancient vineyards. The whites are fairly tropical in style; the reds tend to be quite dense, especially Shiraz, made from old vines.
BEST WINES: *Cabernet Sauvignon, Chardonnay, Thomson Reserve Shiraz*

BRL Hardy ***

South Australia Australia's second largest wine producer, with seven wineries throughout South Australia, based at the historic Chateau Reynella where Thomas Hardy himself began his career as a nineteenth-century cellar hand. They show particular strength in blending grapes and/or wines from several areas giving results of consistently fine quality across a spectrum of price points. An ever-expanding group which is always looking for ways to improve standards. Brands: Barossa Valley Estates, Berri Estates, Chateau Reynella, Hardys, Leasingham, Renmano and Yarra Burn.
BEST WINES: *Bankside Grenache, Bankside Shiraz, Chateau Reynella Basket-Pressed Shiraz, E&E Black Pepper Shiraz, Eileen Hardy Chardonnay, Leasingham range (Clare Valley), Nottage Hill Chardonnay, Nottage Hill Shiraz, Siegersdorf Riesling, Thomas Hardy Cabernet Sauvignon, Tintara Grenache, Tintara Shiraz*

Brokenwood ***

Lower Hunter Valley, New South Wales Fast-growing, ultra-premium producer making voluptuous reds and delicious whites. Only the low yielding Graveyard Vineyard wines are 100 per cent Hunter Valley; the others are rather eclectic blends of Hunter Valley and other regions' grapes. Also owns Seville Estate in the Yarra Valley.
BEST WINES: *Cricket Pitch Cabernet Sauvignon-Merlot, Cricket Pitch Sauvignon Blanc-Semillon, Graveyard Hunter Valley Shiraz, Rayner Vineyard McLaren Vale Shiraz, Seville Estate Yarra Valley Cabernet Sauvignon*

Brown Brothers ***(v)

Milawa, Victoria Old family business producing a vast range of outstanding single varietal wines across a number of different styles – their Riesling, for example, is available in both bone dry or sweet, botrytized versions. Highly innovative, they are also developing a successful line of Italian varietals. Grapes for their premium wines are sourced from their King Valley and Whitland vineyards. Brown Brothers also own All Saints winery in Rutherglen.
BEST WINES: *All Saints Muscat, All Saints Tokay, Barbera, Chardonnay, Dry Muscat, Koombahla Cabernet Sauvignon, Noble Riesling, Semillon, Tokay, Whitland Gewürztraminer, Whitland Riesling*

Cape Mentelle ****(v)

Margaret River, Western Australia The innovative, California-trained David Hohnen is the Australian who founded New Zealand's famous Cloudy Bay winery. At Cape Mentelle, he creates wonderful Cabernet Sauvignon, though the Chardonnay can be even better. All of his wines possess elegance and finesse, although the fruit is allowed to shine through. Veuve Clicquot is now the major shareholder. Second label: Trinders Vineyard.
BEST WINES: *Cabernet Sauvignon, Chardonnay, Semillon-Sauvignon Blanc, Shiraz, Trinders Vineyard Cabernet Sauvignon, Zinfandel*

Chapel Hill ****

McLaren Vale, South Australia Boutique winery known for really big, chunky wines. The celebrated Pam Dunsford is the winemaker.
BEST WINES: *Coonawarra Cabernet Sauvignon, Eden Valley Chardonnay, Eden Valley Riesling, McLaren Vale Shiraz, McLaren Vale Verdelho, The Vicar (blend of Coonawarra Cabernet Sauvignon and McLaren Vale Shiraz)*

Chateau Reynella ****

McLaren Vale, South Australia See BRL Hardy.

Chateau Tahbilk ***

Goulburn Valley, Victoria Victoria's oldest winery and vineyard, established in 1860. Also owns the oldest producing Shiraz vines in the world and has one of the largest single holdings of old Marsanne vines in the world.
BEST WINES: *1860 Vines Shiraz, Chimera (joint venture with James Halliday), Four Sisters (joint venture with Trevor Mast), Longleat (partner brand with Mark Schulz), Marsanne, Riesling*

Coldstream Hills ***

Yarra Valley, Victoria See Southcorp.

Cullen ****

Margaret River, Western Australia Mother and daughter team making super-intense wines of great finesse. One of the original Margaret River wineries going from strength to strength.
BEST WINES: *Cabernet Sauvignon-Merlot, Chardonnay, Pinot Noir, Sauvignon Blanc, Semillon Reserve*

D'Arenberg ***

McLaren Vale, South Australia A producer whose acclaim grows with each successive vintage. Chester D'Arenberg Osborn combines traditional and modern methods to sculpt wines of great finesse and expression from very low yielding, geriatric Grenache and Shiraz vines.
BEST WINES: *Custodian Grenache, Dead Arm Shiraz (named after the Dead-Arm vine disease; growers cut the vine off, leaving a stump, but Osborn continues to use his gnarled, stumpy vines which yield some of his best fruit each year), Ironstone Pressings (Grenache-Shiraz blend), The High Trellis Cabernet Sauvignon, The Other Side Chardonnay, Twenty Eight Road Mourvèdre*

De Bortoli ***(v)

Yarra Valley, Victoria/Riverina, New South Wales De Bortoli bought the former Chateau Yarrinya winery to become the Yarra Valley's largest producer. The regular range is divided into De Bortoli, Gulf Station and Windy Peak. Large amounts of everyday quaffing wine are made at their Riverina winery.
BEST WINES: *Black Noble, Noble One Botrytis Semillon (Australia's best Sauternes-style dessert wine), Yarra Valley Chardonnay*

Delatite ****(v)

Grampians, Victoria Cool, isolated mountain vineyards give very fine, delicate, beautiful wines. Winemaker is Rosalind Ritchie.
BEST WINES: *Cabernet Sauvignon, Devil's River (Bordeaux-style blend), Gewürztraminer, Pinot Noir, Riesling (dry and sweet), Shiraz*

Domaine Chandon **(v)

Yarra Valley, Victoria Moët & Chandon foresaw the possibility of making premium, traditional method sparkling wine in Australia back in 1985 when they approached consultant Dr Tony Jordan for help (he has since moved on). Chardonnay and Pinot Noir are sourced from cool areas across South Australia, and turned into complex wines which are given long yeast ageing.
BEST WINES: *Domaine Chandon (Aussie label), Green Point (export label)*

Evans & Tate ***

Margaret River, Western Australia Well-made, high quality, fruit-driven wines from exciting winemaker Brian Fletcher. Grapes come from the Margaret River region itself plus Swan District.
BEST WINES: *Cabernet Sauvignon, Chardonnay, Merlot, Riesling, Sauvignon Blanc-Semillon, Semillon, Shiraz*

Evans Family **

Hunter Valley, New South Wales One to watch. Until recently, production from Len Evans' own, very tiny vineyard was negligible and was virtually all sold at the vineyard gate. Since selling Rothbury, however, the Evans Family brand is being expanded big time, using bought-in grapes.
BEST WINES: *Chardonnay, Gamay, Pinot Noir, sparkling (made at Petaluma)*

Grosset ****

Clare Valley, South Australia Tiny amounts of superb, hand-made wines capable of long ageing are made by perfectionist Jeffrey Grosset.
BEST WINES: *Gaia Cabernet Sauvignon-Merlot, Piccadilly Chardonnay, Piccadilly Pinot Noir, Polish Hill Riesling, Watervale Riesling*

Hardys **(v)

See BRL Hardy.

Henschke *****

Eden Valley, South Australia Fifth generation family business founded by Silesian immigrant Johann Christian Henschke in 1862. One of Australia's finest producers, renowned for the legendary, single vineyard Shiraz 'Hill of Grace', which regrettably sells out within minutes of release. Husband and wife team Stephen and Prue Henschke form a dynamic partnership: she is the viticulturist, he the winemaker.
BEST WINES: *Cabernet Sauvignon, Chardonnay, Eden Valley Riesling, Eden Valley Semillon, Hill of Grace Shiraz, Johann's Garden Bush Vine Grenache-Mourvèdre-Shiraz, Mount Edelstone Shiraz*

Houghton **(v)

Swan District, Western Australia Two labels, Houghton and Moondah Brook, from this big operator, WA's largest. Houghton Supreme (called Houghton White Burgundy at home) is one of Australia's best-selling white wines. Their Moondah Brook vineyards in the northerly Gingin area (cooled by a famous sea breeze known as the 'Fremantle Doctor') is of special note for its good value single varietal Verdelho. Budget brand: Wildflower Ridge.
BEST WINES: *Jack Mann Commemorative Cabernet Sauvignon, Moondah Brook Verdelho, Supreme (Chenin Blanc-Chardonnay-Verdelho)*

Howard Park **

Mount Barker, Western Australia Wines to lay down – they are all incredibly dense and well-textured. Second label: Madfish Bay.
BEST WINES: *Cabernet Sauvignon-Merlot, Chardonnay, Madfish Bay Shiraz, Riesling*

Lake's Folly ****

Lower Hunter Valley, New South Wales In the 1960s, pioneering Sydney surgeon, Dr Max Lake, led the Hunter Valley into a new era. His winery was bang up to date, he introduced

new oak and created wines which reflected the true expression of the region by planting Cabernet Sauvignon and Chardonnay in traditional Shiraz territory. Today, under son Stephen's direction, it continues to produce complex, long-lived wines of great sophistication.
BEST WINES: *Cabernet Sauvignon, Chardonnay*

Leasingham **(v)
Clare Valley, South Australia See BRL Hardy.

Leeuwin Estate ****
Margaret River, Western Australia State-of-the-art winery with prices to match. Worth it though, as these are truly classy wines indeed. The whites are better than the reds where quality can be a little patchy owing to vintage variation.
BEST WINES: *Chardonnay (flagship wine), Pinot Noir, Prelude Cabernet Sauvignon, Riesling*

Lindemans ***(v) See Southcorp.

McWilliam's **(v)
Upper Hunter Valley and Riverina The premium wines of this family firm hail from Mount Pleasant, but they also master quaffing wines of high standard in Riverina. Also own Brand Laira label.
BEST WINES: *Brand Laira Cabernet Sauvignon, Brand Laira Chardonnay, Brand Laira Shiraz, Elizabeth Hunter Valley Semillon (bargain)*

Mildara Blass
Various locations Owned by the giant Fosters brewing group since 1996, this is one of the top five industry players embracing Andrew Garrett, Bailey's (Milawa – best known for weighty dessert wines), Balgownie, Ingoldby, Krondorf, Maglieri, Rothbury Estate, Saltram, St Hubert's, Tisdall, Wolf Blass, Yarra Ridge and Yellowglen (for sparklers). Len Evans founded the Rothbury Estate in 1968 with the aim to make one red wine (Syrah) and one white (Semillon). Evans left when Mildara Blass bought him out in 1996.
BEST WINES: *Bailey's Shiraz, Bailey's Winemaker's Selection Muscat, Bailey's Winemaker's Selection Tokay, Balgownie (sparkling), Hunter Valley Reserve Shiraz (Rothbury label), Jamieson's Run range, Mamre Brook Cabernet Sauvignon, Mamre Brook Chardonnay, Mamre Brook Shiraz, Mount Ida Reserve Shiraz (Tisdall), Rothbury Brokenback Chardonnay, Rothbury Brokenback Semillon, Rothbury Brokenback Shiraz, Saltram No 1 Shiraz (Barossa), Wolf Blass Black Label (top of range Cabernet blend), Wolf Blass Gold Label (off dry Riesling), Wolf Blass President's Selection, Wolf Blass Show Reserve Coonawarra Cabernet Sauvignon, Wolf Blass Yellow Label (cheap and cheerful Cabernet blend), Yarra Ridge range, Yellowglen Cuvée Victoria, Yellowglen Vintage Brut, Yellowglen 'Y'*

Mitchelton ***(v)
Goulburn Valley, Victoria See Petaluma.

Montrose **
See Orlando Wyndham.

Moss Wood ****
Margaret River, Western Australia Produces some of Australia's finest, richest and most polished wines.
BEST WINES: *Cabernet Sauvignon, Chardonnay, Pinot Noir, Semillon (oaked and unoaked)*

Mountadam ***
Eden Valley, South Australia The pioneering David and Adam Wynn make fabulous, complex wines from grapes grown high up on the steeper slopes of the valley. Other labels: David Wynn and Eden Ridge.
BEST WINES: *Chardonnay (Burgundian style), David Wynn Patriarch Shiraz*

Mount Hurtle **(v)
McLaren Vale, South Australia This is where energetic, high profile Flying Winemaker Geoff Merrill comes home to roost. He does not rest for long though – he is equally well known for premium wines under his own name, and everyday drinking wines under the Mount Hurtle label.
BEST WINES: *Geoff Merrill Cabernet Sauvignon, Geoff Merrill Semillon-Chardonnay, Mount Hurtle Grenache Rosé*

Mount Langi Ghiran ***(v)
Grampians, Victoria Trevor Mast is winemaker and part owner and in 1997 was made Winemaker of the Year by Robert Parker. The estate is farmed organically and biodynamic trials are taking place in conjunction with the Department of Agriculture with varying degrees of success.
BEST WINES: *Cabernet Sauvignon, Chardonnay, Pinot Grigio, Riesling (Mast trained at the Geisenheim Institute in Germany, so no surprise that this is one of Australia's best), Shiraz (the star)*

Mount Mary ****
Yarra Valley, Victoria Impeccable winemaking from Dr John Middleton. His very fine quality wines are much sought after – shame that only tiny amounts are made.
BEST WINES: *'Cabernets' (Cabernet Sauvignon-Cabernet Franc-Merlot blend), Chardonnay, Pinot Noir, Triolet (Sauvignon Blanc-Semillon-Muscadelle)*

Orlando Wyndham ***(v)
Various locations Australia's third largest wine group, owned by Pernod-Ricard. Jacob's Creek is its most successful and famous incarnation, but other labels to look for are Craigmoor, Gramps, Hunter Estate, Montrose, Morris, Richmond Grove, Saxonvale, Wickham Hill and Wyndham Estate.
BEST WINES: *Jacaranda Ridge Coonawarra Cabernet*

Sauvignon, Jacob's Creek range, Mick Morris Liqueur Muscat, Montrose Cabernet Sauvignon, Montrose Poet's Corner, Montrose Shiraz, St Helga Eden Valley Riesling, St Hugo Coonawarra Cabernet Sauvignon, Steingarten Eden Valley Riesling, Wyndham 555 Shiraz

Passing Clouds *(v)

Bendigo, Victoria Passing Clouds has been one of Victoria's stars for many years. Top winemaker Graeme Leith has opinions as interesting as his wines.
BEST WINES: *Cabernet Sauvignon-Shiraz, sparkling wines*

Penfolds *****(v)

See Southcorp.

Penley ***

Coonawarra, South Australia Concentrated stunners from this hi-tech winery.
BEST WINES: *Hyland Chardonnay, Phoenix Cabernet Sauvignon, Riesling, Shiraz-Cabernet Sauvignon*

Petaluma ****(v)

Adelaide Hills, South Australia Brian Croser, one of Australia's most influential winemakers, pioneered the cool and humid Piccadilly Valley adjacent to Adelaide. Apart from making outstanding still wines under the Petaluma and Bridgewater Mill labels, he teamed up with Bollinger to create 'Croser', a top quality, traditional method sparkling wine from Chardonnay and Pinot Noir. All Petaluma-branded wines can be cellared for at least five years. Bridgewater Mill wines are ready earlier. Petaluma also owns Mitchelton (Goulburn Valley) and Knappstein (Clare Valley).
BEST WINES: *Croser, Mitchelton Blackwood Park Riesling, Mitchelton Oaked Marsanne, Mitchelton Preece Cabernet Sauvignon, Mitchelton Preece Chardonnay, Mitchelton Print Label Shiraz, Mitchelton III (Rhône-style blends, red and white), Petaluma Chardonnay, Petaluma Clare Valley Riesling, Petaluma Coonawarra Cabernet Sauvignon-Merlot, Petaluma Merlot (arguably Australia's best)*

Peter Lehmann ***(v)

Barossa Valley, South Australia A four-strong team of winemakers produces good wines of excellent value under the Peter Lehmann label, though the best fruit is reserved for the pinnacle of the range, the Cellar Collection. These wines, released in small quantities only, are well known for their staying power. Owns only one vineyard – Stonewell – so the vast bulk of the grapes are bought-in.
BEST WINES: *Cellar Collection Stonewell Shiraz (old vines), Clancy's Gold Preference (Shiraz-Cabernet Sauvignon-Merlot), Peter Lehmann Eden Valley Riesling, Peter Lehmann Vine Vale Grenache*

Pierro **

Margaret River, Western Australia
Rapidly rising, exciting star making top-notch (expensive!) Chardonnay – easily one of Australia's best – alongside fine Sauvignon Blanc, Semillon and Pinot Noir. Second label (from bought-in grapes): Fire Gully.
BEST WINES: *Chardonnay, Sauvignon Blanc-Semillon*

Pipers Brook ****

Tasmania First division winery under the helm of the pioneering Dr Andrew Pirie, who takes full advantage of the cool climate to produce an exciting range of stunning, stylish wines under Pipers Brook and Ninth Island labels.
BEST WINES: *Cabernet Sauvignon (Tamar Valley), Chardonnay, Gewürztraminer, Opimian (Bordeaux-style red), Pinot Gris, Pinot Noir, Pirie (sparkling), Riesling, Sauvignon Blanc*

Plantagenet ***

Mount Barker, Western Australia Regional specialists whose best grapes go into their benchmark Mount Barker wines. Sparkling wine is also made. Gavin Berry is winemaker.
BEST WINES: *Cabernet Sauvignon (recently voted one of Australia's top 20 Cabernets), Chardonnay, Pemberton Pinot Noir, Riesling, Shiraz*

Reynolds ***

Hunter Valley, New South Wales New – and very promising – winery creating richly-textured wines from Orange vineyard grapes.
BEST WINES: *Cabernet Sauvignon, Semillon, Shiraz*

Richard Hamilton **(v)

McLaren Vale, South Australia Dr Richard Hamilton was one of the original McLaren Vale winemaking pioneers back in 1837. His great-grandson, Burton Hamilton, added to the vineyards in 1947, planting Grenache and Shiraz vines. Today, the family's properties (including Leconfield in Coonawarra) provide for their entire production. Winemaking is overseen by Ralph Fowler.
BEST WINES: *Burton's Vineyard Grenache-Shiraz, Leconfield Cabernet Sauvignon, Richard Hamilton Reserve Merlot*

Rockford ****

Barossa Valley, South Australia Hugely deep and powerful red wines made from Robert 'Rocky' O'Callaghan's very old, low yielding vines. One white and a delicious red fizz complete this cult range.
BEST WINES: *Basket Press Shiraz, Dry Country Grenache, Sparkling Black Shiraz, 1886 Vine Vale Riesling*

Rosemount ***(v)

Hunter Valley, New South Wales Highly successful, large-scale winery of international fame. Established in 1969 by Robert Oatley and family in the Upper Hunter Valley, Rosemount has grown to include vineyards in the Adelaide Hills,

Coonawarra, Langhorne Creek, McLaren Vale, Mudgee and Orange regions. They are now developing an exciting range of single vineyard wines (Rose label). Winemaker is the celebrated Philip Shaw.
BEST WINES: *Coonawarra Cabernet Sauvignon, Balmoral Shiraz, Mountain Blue Shiraz-Cabernet Sauvignon, Rose Label McLaren Vale Shiraz, Rose Label Orange Chardonnay, Rose Label Yarrawa Sauvignon Blanc, Roxburgh Show Reserve Chardonnay*

Rothbury ****(v)

Hunter Valley, New South Wales See Mildara Blass.

Scotchman's Hill **(v)

Geelong, Victoria A relative newcomer, this is one of Geelong's most important wineries, making Burgundian-style, value for money Chardonnay and Pinot Noir from locally-sourced grapes. Keep both for up to five years – if you want; they taste good young, too.
BEST WINES: *Chardonnay, Pinot Noir*

Seaview **(v)

McLaren Vale, South Australia See Southcorp.

Seppelt ***

See Southcorp.

Shaw & Smith ****(v)

Adelaide Hills, South Australia Shaw & Smith began over lunch in 1989 when cousins Martin Shaw (former Flying Winemaker) and Michael Hill Smith (Australia's first Master of Wine) decided to realize a long-held dream to make wine together. Unlike many Australian winemakers who produce a wide range of wine styles, Shaw & Smith specialize in two grape varieties only: Chardonnay and Sauvignon Blanc.
BEST WINES: *Reserve Chardonnay, Sauvignon Blanc, Unoaked Chardonnay*

Southcorp

Australia's biggest wine company, created in 1994, with a ubiquitous presence owning many of the country's top brands including Devil's Lair, Great Western, Hungerford Hill, Lindemans, Penfolds, Seaview, Seppelt, Tollana, Tulloch and Wynns. Coldstream Hills is a member of the stable, but James Halliday still rides this particular horse.

Penfolds is one of the best and most consistent companies around, enjoying a reputation for super-premium, eclectic red wines. Penfolds enjoys particular fame for its mastery of the Shiraz grape in the form of Grange. Long before anyone even dreamed of modern, gutsy, fruit-driven reds from Australia, a quirk of fate set Max Schubert off on his quest to make a great red wine following a visit to Bordeaux. Schubert's legendary first vintage of Grange Hermitage in 1951 was made from Shiraz and was called 'Hermitage' after the Rhône's finest Syrah wine. Grange became, and is still, one of the world's greats.

Bin 65 Chardonnay is the most popular brand of the Lindemans portfolio. Hunter Valley wines were their original speciality, but they are now making excellent wines from Padthaway and Coonawarra grapes. Leo Buring and Rouge Homme are Lindemans-owned wineries, both making terrific wines of excellent value.

Originally based in the McLaren Vale, the Seaview winery was called 'Hope Farm' by its first owner George Pitches Manning. After changing ownership several times, Hope Farm was renamed 'Seaview' during the 1950s by the California-born W. B. Chaffey and winemaking pioneer F. H. Edwards. Their winery was one of the first to release a varietal-labelled table wine, Seaview Cabernet Sauvignon. Today, Seaview is best known for great value sparkling wines made from McLaren Vale Chardonnay and Pinot Noir, though still wines – Chardonnay and Shiraz-Cabernet Sauvignon – are made, too. Sister company Seppelt is also famous for sparkling wines (matured in historic underground cellars), but winemaker Ian MacKenzie turns his hand to creating good still wines, too.
BEST WINES: *Adam Wynn Samuels Bay Malbec, Briarston Cabernet Sauvignon-Merlot, Coldstream Hills Chardonnay Reserve, Coldstream Hills Pinot Noir Reserve, Devil's Lair Chardonnay, Edwards & Chaffey fizz, John Riddoch Cabernet Sauvignon (Wynns), Lindemans Bin 65 Chardonnay, Lindemans Bin 70 (Semillon-Verdelho-Sauvignon Blanc-Chardonnay), Lindemans Cawarra Unoaked Chardonnay, Lindemans Limestone Ridge Shiraz-Cabernet Sauvignon, Lindemans Padthaway Chardonnay, Lindemans Pyrus, Michael Shiraz (Wynns), Penfolds Bin 128 Coonawarra Shiraz, Penfolds Bin 389 Cabernet Sauvignon-Shiraz, Penfolds Bin 407 Cabernet Sauvignon, Penfolds Bin 707 Cabernet Sauvignon, Penfolds Grange, Penfolds Kalimna Bin 28 Shiraz, Penfolds Yattarna Chardonnay (the 'White Grange'), Richardson's Red Block (Cabernet blend from Rouge Homme), Rouge Homme Chardonnay, Rouge Homme Shiraz-Cabernet Sauvignon, Seaview (sparkling), Seppelt Great Western Brut (sparkling), Seppelt Rutherglen Show Muscat, Seppelt Salinger (sparkling), Seppelt Sparkling Shiraz*

St Hallett ****

Barossa Valley, South Australia Grows half of its needs and purchases the balance from Barossa vineyards. The collectors' wine is Old Block Shiraz, so named because it is made from 70- to 100-year-old vines, yielding tiny, concentrated juice.
BEST WINES: *Barossa Grenache, Blackwell Shiraz, Eden Valley Riesling, Faith Shiraz, Gamekeeper's Reserve (Shiraz-Grenache-Mourvèdre-Touriga Nacional), Old Block Shiraz, Poacher's Blend (blend of Semillon, Chardonnay, Riesling and several others), Semillon Select*

Tim Adams ****(v)

South Australia No vineyards, but grape selection vigorous. Brilliant wines as a result.

BEST WINES: *Aberfeldy Shiraz, Botrytis Riesling, Clare Valley Semillon, Riesling, The Fergus*

Torbreck *****

Barossa Valley Dave Powell has spent the last five years rejuvenating some ancient, abandoned vineyards and here are the results – absolutely gorgeous.
BEST WINES: *Run Rig Shiraz-Viognier, The Steading*

Tyrell ***(v)

Hunter Valley, New South Wales Vat 47 was Australia's first commercial Chardonnay. A very traditional winery with superb Lower Hunter Valley vineyards.
BEST WINES: *Vat 1 Semillon, Vat 9 Shiraz, Vat 47 Chardonnay*

Vasse Felix ***

Margaret River, Western Australia One of the original Margaret River trailblazers. Noted for powerful, long-lived Cabernet Sauvignon which are nevertheless approachable young. Second label: Forest Hills (Mount Barker grapes).
BEST WINES: *Classic Dry White (Chardonnay-Semillon-Sauvignon Blanc), Forest Hills Chardonnay, Forest Hills Riesling, Vasse Felix Barrel-Fermented Semillon, Vasse Felix Cabernet Sauvignon, Vasse Felix Noble Rot Riesling, Vasse Felix Shiraz*

Wendouree ****

Clare Valley, South Australia You need patience with these wines because they age for ever in top years. Based on Cabernet Sauvignon, Malbec, Mourvèdre and Shiraz, only tiny amounts are produced from antique vines.
BEST WINES: *Muscat (sweet)*

Wirra Wirra ****

McLaren Vale, South Australia The idiosyncratic Greg Trott creates fantastic, ageworthy reds which could almost pass as European except the fruit is riper. Whites and sparklers are good, too.
BEST WINES: *Original Blend (Grenache-Shiraz), RSW Shiraz, The Angelus (Cabernet Sauvignon)*

Wolf Blass ***

Barossa Valley, South Australia See Mildara Blass.

Wynns ****

Coonawarra, South Australia See Southcorp.

Yalumba ****

Barossa Valley, South Australia Alias S. Smith & Sons or 'All the land around' in Aborigine. Best known for crowd pleasing sparkling Angas Brut and wonderful Oxford Landing range, but this big firm, owned by the Hill Smith family, also produces premium wines under the Heggies Vineyard, Hill Smith Estate, Pewsey Vale and Yalumba labels, and a super premium Yalumba Viognier from Eden Valley and Barossa vineyards is due to be released in 1999. Also owns Nautilus in New Zealand. Director of winemaking is Brian Walsh.
BEST WINES: *Angas Brut, Heggies Vineyard Botrytis Riesling, Heggies Vineyard Riesling, Hill Smith Estate Botrytis Semillon, Oxford Landing Black Grenache, Oxford Landing Cabernet Sauvignon-Shiraz, Pewsey Vale Riesling, The Antipodean (Sauvignon Blanc-Semillon-Viognier), The Menzies (Coonawarra Cabernet Sauvignon), The Octavius (Shiraz), The Signature (Cabernet Sauvignon-Shiraz), Victoria Museum Release Muscat, Yalumba Bush Vine Grenache, Yalumba Cuvée One Pinot Noir-Chardonnay (sparkling), Yalumba 'D' (sparkling), Yalumba Museum Show Reserve Liqueur Muscat*

Yarra Yerring *****

Yarra Valley, Victoria Boutique winery run by the eccentric, legendary Bailey Carrodus who since 1969 has been making quite extraordinary, memorable, individualistic wines, among the most concentrated and profound in Australia. Definitely wines to lay down.
BEST WINES: *Chardonnay, Dry Red No 1 (Cabernet-based), Dry Red No 2 (Shiraz-based), Dry White No 1 (Semillon-Sauvignon Blanc), Pinot Noir, The Underhill Shiraz*

California

Arrowood ****(v)

Sonoma Valley Cabernet Sauvignon to lay down and big, oaky, supple Chardonnays for drinking young. Keep an eye on their Malbec, Merlot, Pinot Blanc and Viognier, too. Dick Arrowood has done well since he set up this winery in 1988. Second label is Domaine de Grand Archer (!).
BEST WINES: *Cuvée Michel Berthoud Reserve Cabernet Sauvignon, Cuvée Michel Berthoud Reserve Chardonnay, Domaine de Grand Archer Chardonnay (good value)*

Au Bon Climat ****

Santa Maria Valley Larger than life winemaker Jim Clendenen makes larger than life wines. He is passionate and outspoken, but his wines carry the weight of his conviction. He makes Pinot Noir as if he taught the Burgundians everything they know, making several powerful Pinot Noirs each vintage. Also creates interesting wines from Bordeaux varieties (Vita Nova label) and Italian varieties (Podere dell' Olivos label).
BEST WINES: *Pinot Noir, Parabla (Nebbiolo with four years in barrel), Reserve Chardonnay*

Beaulieu ***(v)

Rutherford The old timers of Napa, Beaulieu Vineyard (BV) make benchmark Cabernet Sauvignon. The most famous and ageworthy wine is Georges de Latour Private Reserve Cabernet Sauvignon, named after the man who founded the winery in 1900. BV have expanded their range to include less expensive wines from Napa, Carneros, Central Coast and North Coast. The

late and great André Tchelistcheff was winemaker/consultant here for decades. Now owned by Guinness/Grand Met.
BEST WINES: *Georges de Latour Private Reserve Cabernet Sauvignon, Rutherford-Napa Clone 6 Cabernet Sauvignon, Tapestry (Bordeaux-style red)*

Beringer ****

Napa Valley Big company owning Chateau Souverain (Sonoma), Chateau St Jean (Sonoma), Meridian (San Luis Obispo), Napa Ridge (Sonoma) and Stags' Leap Winery (Napa), producing the whole gamut of California styles. The wines are consistently good, from inexpensive White Zinfandel to top drawer Cabernet Sauvignon. A current California fashion is to build cool cellars by digging deep into the hillsides, but the Beringer brothers had the same idea back in 1876 – their hand-built winery is still used today for storing and ageing the wines. Beringer-branded Chardonnays tend to be fat and heavily oaked, but the massively fruity Cabernets are of premium quality. Second label: Hudson Estates.
BEST WINES: *Bancroft Vineyard Howell Mountain Merlot, Beringer Alluvium (Bordeaux-style red), Beringer Appellation Collection Cabernet Sauvignon, Beringer Howell Mountain Bancroft Ranch Merlot, Beringer Private Reserve Cabernet Sauvignon (Knights Valley), Beringer Sbragia Chardonnay, Chabot Cabernet Sauvignon, Chateau St Jean Belle Terre Single Vineyard Chardonnay, Chateau St Jean Botrytized Riesling, Chateau St Jean Robert Young Single Vineyard Chardonnay, Lemmon Ranch Cabernet Sauvignon, Meridian Edna Valley Chardonnay, Meridian Paso Robles Syrah, Stags' Leap Winery Petite Syrah*

Bonny Doon *****(v)

Santa Cruz Mountains The original Rhône Ranger, Randall Grahm pioneered stunning Rhône-style wines in California and has since turned his hand to Italian grapes, too. Definitely one of America's most iconoclastic, innovative and exciting winemakers. Currently, the winemaking facility is in downtown Santa Cruz with a vineyard in Soledad (Monterey County). The lion's share (80 per cent) of grapes are bought-in from vineyards located throughout the state and from Washington state, as well. Unfortunately, the Santa Cruz Mountains vineyard succumbed to Pierce's Disease.
BEST WINES: *Bloody Good Red, Ca' del Solo, Cardinal Zin, Le Cigare Volant (Grenache-Syrah), Le Sophiste (white blend of Rhône grapes), Old Telegram (100 per cent Mourvèdre)*

Cain Cellars ****

St Helena One of the new elite. Manager/winemaker Chris Howell blends the five classic Bordeaux varieties into a traditional structure more akin to the Classed Growths of Bordeaux than the big-fruit Californians. High altitude, classic varieties and a commitment to real quality are proving a winning formula.
BEST WINES: *Cain Five*

Calera ****

Mount Harlan Josh Jensen is creating classic single vineyard Pinot Noirs, arguably California's finest. But they are not elegant Burgundian styles; they are rich, heavyweight, blockbusting wines which demand cellaring for a number of years.
BEST WINES: *Jensen Single Vineyard Pinot Noir, Mills Estate Pinot Noir, Mount Harlan Chardonnay, Reed Single Vineyard Pinot Noir, Selleck Single Vineyard Pinot Noir, Viognier*

Caymus ****

Rutherford Charlie and Lorna Wagner acquired the land for their Napa Valley vineyard in 1941. Shortly thereafter, they began to sell their grapes to local wineries. In 1972, Charlie, Lorna and son, Chuck, started to make their own Cabernet Sauvignon, noted for its benchmark rich, ripe, ageworthy personality. Second label: Liberty School.
BEST WINES: *Mer & Soleil Monterey Chardonnay, Special Selection Cabernet Sauvignon, Zinfandel*

Chalone Vineyard ***

Chalone The oldest vineyard in Monterey County with some plantings of Chardonnay and Chenin Blanc dating back to 1922. Back in the 1960s, the late Dick Graff made his wines in a chicken shed high above the Salinas valley; today, Chalone owns Acacia, Carmenet, Edna Valley Vineyard, Gavilan and Canoe Ridge (Washington State). Chalone Chardonnay and Pinot Noir is crafted in an exquisite Burgundian style – Graff was one of the first to import Burgundy barrels. The Pinot Noir is slow-evolving and needs cellaring for up to 15 years to reap its true rewards.
BEST WINES: *Acacia St Clair Vineyard Pinot Noir, Chalone Vineyard Chenin Blanc, Chalone Vineyard Pinot Blanc, Chalone Vineyard Reserve Chardonnay, Chalone Vineyard Reserve Pinot Noir*

Chateau Montelena ****

Napa Valley Winemaker Michael Grgich brought this prestigious winery back to life in the 1970s – it had been abandoned for many decades. His luxurious wines are long-lived and utterly delicious.
BEST WINES: *Calistoga Estate Cabernet Sauvignon, Chardonnay*

Clos du Val ***

Stags Leap While the Carneros Chardonnay is very good, the reds are better, particularly top-notch Stags Leap Cabernet with its impressive longevity, though Merlot, Pinot Noir and Zinfandel are also tasty.
BEST WINES: *Cabernet Sauvignon, Chardonnay, Merlot, Pinot Noir, Zinfandel*

Dehlinger ****

Russian River Valley Pinot Noir is the speciality here – and very good it is, too, in a rich, fruity style. One of the very best.

Repays keeping for anything up to ten years.
BEST WINES: *Chardonnay, Pinot Noir, Syrah, Young Vine Cabernet Sauvignon*

De Loach ***

Russian River Valley Former fireman Cecil de Loach had not intended to make wine. Seeking a place to retire in 1970, he bought 10 hectares of vineyard land simply because it was the cheapest country property that you could buy. Today, his 20 wine, 80,000 case range sells out persistently. Winemaker is Dan Cedarquist.
BEST WINES: *OFS (Our Finest Selection) Chardonnay, OFS Pinot Noir, Papera Single Vineyard Zinfandel, Pelletti Single Vineyard Zinfandel*

Diamond Creek ****

Napa Valley California's first Cabernet-only estate vineyard, established 1968. Comprises three adjoining sites: Volcanic Hill, Red Rock Terrace and Gravelly Meadow. Since each site differs in exposure and soil composition, the wines are bottled under the three different vineyard names. Snapped up quickly, owing to their outstanding and highly consistent quality. Needs five years cellaring, and will happily last a further ten.
BEST WINES: *Gravelly Meadow Cabernet Sauvignon, Red Rock Terrace Cabernet Sauvignon, Volcanic Hill Cabernet Sauvignon*

Domaine Chandon ***

Napa Valley Moët & Chandon's California fizz factory. Second label: Shadow Creek.
BEST WINES: *Carneros Blanc de Blancs, Etoile Rosé, NV Reserve*

Domaine Mumm ***

Napa Valley Things could have turned out differently for this joint Mumm-Seagram venture if Greg Fowler, now Senior Winemaker, had not decided to study oenology at Davis University – the course suited his busy football training schedule!
BEST WINES: *Blanc de Blancs, Blanc de Noirs, Cuvée Napa Brut Prestige, DVX (luxury label), Winery Lake (single vineyard)*

Dominus Estate ****

Napa Valley Big Bordeaux influence in the Cabernet-dominant wines now that Christian Moueix (director of Bordeaux's Château Pétrus) owns the historic Napanook vineyard and winery. Winemaker is David Ramey who crafts wines which are more Pomerol than Napa – divine, indeed. Drink between five and 15 years.
BEST WINES: *Dominus*

Duckhorn ***

St Helena While this winery's reputation has been built on black cherry-styled Merlot (two or three are made every year), Dan Duckhorn is also creating wines from Cabernet Sauvignon and Sauvignon Blanc from Yountsville, Howell Mountain and St Helena fruit (amongst the most sought after in California). Second label: Decoy (!)
BEST WINES: *Howell Mountain Merlot, Migration (Bordeaux-style red), Napa Valley Cabernet Sauvignon, Paraduxx (Zinfandel-Cabernet Sauvignon), Three Palms Vineyard Merlot, Vine Hill Vineyard Merlot*

Fetzer **(v)

Redwood Valley Whilst the huge Fetzer empire produces good wines at all price levels, it is the Bonterra range which shines. These have been made from organic grapes since 1988 and the wines taste better for it. Owned by distilling giant Brown-Forman.
BEST WINES: *Bonterra range, Dry Gewürztraminer, Sundial Chardonnay, Valley Oaks Cabernet Sauvignon*

Franciscan ***(v)

Oakville Cabernet Franc, Cabernet Sauvignon and Merlot are the classic grapes which form the prime focus here, though Chardonnay and Zinfandel are tasty, too. A new parcel of hillside land, the Lewis Ranch (also in Napa), has just been bought – it has never been planted with vines before. Other labels: Estancia (using fruit from Monterey and the Alexander Valley), Mount Veeder and Quintessa.
BEST WINES: *Cabernet Sauvignon, Cuvée Sauvage Chardonnay, Quintessa (Bordeaux-style red), Rutherford Meritage (Bordeaux-style red), Zinfandel*

Frog's Leap ***

St Helena Organic, small scale producer making wines with lovely punchy fruit. Whites should be drunk within two to three years, reds up to six or seven. Wonderful motto: 'Time's fun when you're having flies!'
BEST WINES: *Cabernet Sauvignon, Merlot, Sauvignon Blanc, Zinfandel*

Gallo ***(v)

There are two sides to this leviathan (the largest wine company in the world selling 40 million cases annually): the mainly bulk wine operation based in the San Joaquin Valley, and the fine wine facility in Sonoma which is doing great things with its very classy, ageworthy, single vineyard wines. Apart from the E&J Gallo and Sonoma ranges, there are also the Anapamu, Gossamer Bay, Marcellina and Zabaco labels. A new range of varietals made in Italy is due to be launched under the Ecco Domani label.
BEST WINES: *Gallo Sonoma Cabernet Sauvignon, Gallo Sonoma Chardonnay, Garnet Point range, Frei Ranch Zinfandel, Turning Leaf range*

Grgich Hills ****

Rutherford Founded in 1977 by winemaker Miljenko Grgich (the same one who made the Bordeaux-beating Ch Montelena

during the famous Paris blind tasting) and vineyard owner Austin Hills of the Hills Brothers coffee family. The range is eclectic and the wines beautifully put together. The Cabernet can be aged for 20 years, the Chardonnay for five.
BEST WINES: *Cabernet Sauvignon, Chardonnay, Riesling (sweet), Sauvignon Blanc, Zinfandel (Sonoma grapes)*

Heitz ****

Oakville Long-established, premier league winery, best known for its fabled Martha's Vineyard and Bella Oaks Cabernet Sauvignons. Phylloxera delivered a crippling blow in the early 1990s, but the team is very much focused once again on producing some of California's finest wines.
BEST WINES: *Bella Oaks Cabernet Sauvignon, Martha's Vineyard Cabernet Sauvignon, Trailside Vineyard Cabernet Sauvignon*

Iron Horse ****(v)

Russian River Valley Four stars for top flight, long-lived sparkling wines made from Chardonnay and Pinot Noir. Three stars for the still wines. Second label: Tin Pony (!).
BEST WINES: *Blanc de Blancs (sparkling), Brut (sparkling), Cabernet Sauvignon (Alexander Valley grapes), Chardonnay, Pinot Noir, Sauvignon Blanc (Alexander Valley grapes), Viognier*

Jordan ****

Alexander Valley Fantastic, opulent, biscuity fizz (made by Tom Jordan and daughter Judy) plus a Cabernet Sauvignon bearing the marvellous ripe fruit characteristics of California and the cigar box, cedar notes of Bordeaux. One to age for ten years or so. Chardonnay is promising.
BEST WINES: *Cabernet Sauvignon, J (sparkling)*

Kendall-Jackson ***

Lake County The K-J portfolio is an empire which is expanding at a faster rate than even Gallo or Robert Mondavi. With projects in Argentina, Chile and Tuscany, Jess Jackson has no plans to slow down, even though he is now 67. Currently developing Pinot Noir at three of his wineries. Most wines are blends from a number of regions. Also in charge of Artisans & Estates – labels include Cambria, Camelot, Cardinale, Edmeades, Hartford Court, La Crema, Robert Pepi and Stonestreet.
BEST WINES: *Cambria Chardonnay, Cambria Pinot Noir, Edmeades Zinfandel, Hartford Court Zinfandel, La Crema Chardonnay, La Crema Pinot Noir, Vintners Reserve Chardonnay (which sold over 1.6 million cases in 1998)*

Kenwood ***

Sonoma Valley Terrific producer whose reputation has been built on deeply concentrated, deliciously gutsy reds which are enjoyable on release, but well worth cellaring. Their Sauvignon Blancs are now amongst California's best, too.
BEST WINES: *Jack London series (single vineyard wines named after the author Jack London whose ranch is now a national park in Sonoma Valley), Mazzoni Single Vineyard Zinfandel, Nuns Canyon Single Vineyard Zinfandel, Sonoma County Chardonnay, Sonoma County Sauvignon Blanc (superb), Sonoma Valley Artist Series Cabernet Sauvignon (a collectors' item since its first vintage in 1975), Sonoma Valley Cabernet Sauvignon*

Niebaum-Coppola ***

Rutherford Not everything can be improved by throwing money at it, but Francis Ford Coppola has injected lots of the stuff to turn this hobby into a major – and very successful – concern.
BEST WINES: *Rubicon (Cabernet Sauvignon-based trailblazer)*

Ravenswood ***

Sonoma Valley Joel Peterson is celebrated for Zinfandel – it has massive personality, hence the winery slogan 'No Wimpy Wines'! Can be kept for 15 years. Other wines include Cabernet Sauvignon, Chardonnay and Merlot, but leave these alone.
BEST WINES: *Dickerson Vineyard Zinfandel, Old Hill Ranch Single Vineyard Zinfandel (Sonoma Valley), Old Vines Zinfandel, Wood Road Belloni Single Vineyard Zinfandel (Russian River Valley)*

Ridge *****

Santa Cruz Mountains Who would imagine that a winery owned by a Japanese pharmaceutical company could produce the ultimate of top class estate wines? But winemaker Paul Draper crafts powerful, utterly heavenly, unbeatable old vine Zinfandel and benchmark Cabernet. Both need time in bottle – anything from seven to 17 years.
BEST WINES: *Bridgehead Mataro, Dusi Zinfandel (San Luis Obispo), Geyserville Zinfandel, Lytton Springs Zinfandel (Sonoma), Monte Bello Cabernet Sauvignon (Santa Cruz Mountains), Mourvèdre, Pagani Ranch Zinfandel, Paso Robles Zinfandel, Santa Cruz Mountains Merlot, York Creek Petite Sirah, York Creek Zinfandel (Napa)*

Robert Mondavi *****

Napa Valley Robert Mondavi, zealous pioneer of varietal labelling, cold fermentation and oak ageing, founded his Oakville winery in 1966 and has been empire-building ever since. Today's portfolio encompasses Byron Vineyards in Santa Maria (acquired 1990), La Famiglia di Robert Mondavi (Italian varietals), Mondavi Coastal Series, Mondavi Woodbridge, the standard Robert Mondavi varietals and, of course, the extraordinary, world classic Opus One, born of a joint venture between Mondavi and Baron Philippe de Rothschild in 1979. There are also projects in Chile (with Caliterra), France ('Vichon Mediterranean' label in Languedoc) and Italy (working with Frescobaldi to produce super-Tuscan 'Luce'). All in all, Mondavi offers a spectrum of wines to suit every palate and purse.
BEST WINES: *Byron Pinot Noir, Opus One, Robert Mondavi Cabernet Sauvignon Reserve Unfiltered, Robert Mondavi*

Chardonnay Reserve, Robert Mondavi Pinot Noir Reserve

Saintsbury ****

Carneros Textbook Chardonnay and Pinot Noir since the early 1980s, made by David Graves and Richard Ward using Carneros fruit only.
BEST WINES: *Chardonnay Reserve, Garnet Pinot Noir (lighter style for early drinking), Pinot Noir Reserve (will improve for five years plus)*

Schramsberg *****

Napa Valley The best traditional method sparkling wine in California. They do nothing else and have honed their craft to an outstanding level of excellence as a result. The winery was established in 1862 by German émigré Jacob Schram. Vineyards replaced scrub oak on the high slopes of the Napa Valley, and a network of underground cellars was tunnelled into the hillside. The estate became a California historical landmark in 1957.
BEST WINES: *Blanc de Blancs, Blanc de Noirs (ageworthy), J. Schram (luxury cuvée), Schramsberg Reserve Brut*

Simi ***

Alexander Valley Zelma Long breathed a new lease of life into this old winery when she took the helm as winemaker in 1979. Vastly underrated winery now owned by Moët & Chandon.
BEST WINES: *Cabernet Sauvignon, Chardonnay Reserve, Sendal Sauvignon Blanc-Sémillon*

Spottswoode ****

St Helena Small, family-owned, organically-farmed estate dating back to the 1800s. All attention is focused on producing extremely limited quantities of two wines: Cabernet Sauvignon and Sauvignon Blanc. Both are dreamy.
BEST WINES: *Cabernet Sauvignon, Sauvignon Blanc*

Stag's Leap Wine Cellars ****

Stags Leap Producer of one of California's exceptionally seductive, cassis-flavoured, ageworthy Cabernets, this winery leapt to fame in 1976 when Stag's Leap Wine Cellars Cabernet Sauvignon 1973 beat top Classed Growth Claret in the historic blind tasting in Paris. SLV and Fay are the most famous vineyard sites. Made only in exceptional vintages, Cask 23 is the flagship wine which incorporates the best reserve wines of both SLV and Fay Vineyards. Chardonnay, Merlot , Riesling and Sauvignon Blanc are also made well. Second label: Hawk Crest.
BEST WINES: *Cask 23 Cabernet Sauvignon, Chardonnay, Fay Vineyard Cabernet Sauvignon, SLV Reserve Cabernet Sauvignon*

Williams Selyem ****

Russian River Valley Until 1990, Pinot Noir was the only wine made by Burt Williams and Ed Selyem, and much sought after it is, too. Excellently made to a traditional style, it boasts oodles of smoky fruit. They are now making very promising Chardonnay and Zinfandel and, as with Pinot, the fruit is bought-in. All wines age well (five years plus). Now owned by John Dyson of New York's Millbrook Vineyards and Winery.
BEST WINES: *Allen Single Vineyard Pinot Noir, Rochiolo Single Vineyard Pinot Noir*

Canada

Château des Charmes ***

Niagara Peninsula One of Canada's most progressive producers, founded in 1978 by Frenchman Paul-Michel Bosc, it was the first in Canada to plant a vinifera-exclusive vineyard, the first in Canada to pioneer the use of French oak barrels for ageing and the first in the world to plant transgenic vines. Premium wines hail from the St David's Bench and a wide number of varieties are grown.
BEST WINES: *St David's Bench Cabernet Sauvignon-Merlot, St David's Bench Chardonnay, Riesling Icewine*

Henry of Pelham ***

Niagara Peninsula Low yields from the Speck family's vineyards, planted to make the most of the unique mesoclimate of the Niagara Bench.
BEST WINES: *Baco Noir, Proprietor's Reserve Riesling, Reserve Chardonnay, Riesling Icewine*

Inniskillin ****

Niagara Peninsula Between them, agronomist Donald Ziraldo and oenologist Karl Kaiser have put Canada on the global wine map. While the winery was founded in 1975, it took until 1989, when Inniskillin won the Grand Prix d'Honneur at Vinexpo for its Icewine, for the world to sit up and notice Ontario wines. Owned by Vincor International, Canada's biggest winery. Also have vineyards and a winery in the Okanagan Valley.
BEST WINES: *Alliance Chardonnay, Alliance Pinot Noir, Inkameep Vineyard range (Okanagan), Inniskillin Chardonnay, Inniskillin Pinot Gris, Inniskillin Pinot Noir, Klose Vineyard Chardonnay, Vidal Icewine*

Marynissen ***

Niagara Peninsula John Marynissen had been growing grapes for 40 years before he opened his winery in 1990, giving him some of the oldest vines in the region – indeed, he was the first in Canada to plant Cabernet Sauvignon (in 1978). Lovely wines from a lovely man.
BEST WINES: *Cabernet Sauvignon, Chardonnay, Vidal Icewine*

Mission Hill ***

Okanagan Valley Dating back to 1981, Anthony von Mandl established the first family-owned, commercial winery in the Okanagan Valley. New Zealander John Simes – formerly chief winemaker for Montana – became winemaker in 1992 who gives his Antipodean stamp to the wines.

BEST WINES: *Grand Reserve Chardonnay, Grand Reserve Pinot Blanc*

Pelee Island Winery ***

Pelee Island Pelee Island on Lake Erie has the longest growing season in Canada and German-trained winemaker, Walter Schmoranz, makes the most of it. Exciting wines.
BEST WINES: *Chardonnay, Gamay-Zweigelt, Gewürztraminer, Pinot Gris, Pinot Noir, Riesling*

Quail's Gate **

Okanagan Valley Ben Stewart, third generation of Okanagan fruit farmers, opened a winery in the 1980s and since 1994 Aussie winemaker Jeff Martin has been on board to create exceptional wines.
BEST WINES: *Chenin Blanc, Family Reserve range, Late Harvest Riesling, Limited Release Chardonnay, Limited Release Pinot Noir, Riesling Icewine*

Reif Estate ****

Niagara Peninsula If it had not been for the fact that I was staying in a guest house next door to this estate and therefore happened to meet Klaus Reif by chance, I would have missed a treat. A Geisenheim graduate and 13th generation winemaker from Neustadt, his uncle, Ewald Reif, who purchased this property in 1977, asked Klaus to join him a decade later. The Reif style is highly technical, but is nevertheless fruit-driven to a fantastic result. 100 per cent estate wines.
BEST WINES: *Cabernet Sauvignon, Chardonnay, Gewürztraminer, Icewine, Merlot, Riesling*

Southbrook Farms ***

Niagara Peninsula Bill Riedelmeier's long-standing fruit and vegetable farm became home to a thriving winery in 1991 under the direction of Brian Croser (of Petaluma in Australia) and Klaus Reif. While he makes delicious wines from grapes, his fruit liqueurs cannot be beaten.
BEST WINES: *Cassis, Framboise*

Sumac Ridge ***

Okanagan Valley British Columbia's first estate winery, founded in 1980 by Harry McWatters and Bob Wareham, who have done much to bring the province's wines to the attention of international markets. Until recently, production was centred on white wines, but the acquisition of 47 hectares of vineyards in Oliver in the southern 'beach' area now allows for the making of red wines.
BEST WINES: *Gewürztraminer Reserve, Merlot, Pinot Blanc, Steller's Jay Cuvée Brut (bottle fermented fizz)*

Chile

Caliterra ***

Curicó See Errázuriz.

Canepa ***

Maipo Founded by Don José Canepa in 1930. Early access to modern technology over the years has enabled Canepa to maintain its position as one of the leaders of the modern Chilean wine industry – indeed, they constructed South America's largest state-of-the-art winery in 1982. BRL Hardy has recently teamed up with them to launch the mid-priced Mapocho range. Also own Vinicola Mondragón (Montenuevo, Peteroa and Rowan Brook brands).
BEST WINES: *Casablanca Sauvignon Blanc, Magnificum (Cabernet Sauvignon), Rancagua Private Reserve Cabernet Sauvignon, Rancagua Private Reserve Chardonnay, Rancagua Private Reserve Malbec, Rancagua Private Reserve Merlot*

Casa Lapostolle ***

Rapel French investment by the Marnier-Lapostolle family of Grand-Marnier fame who have invested more in this Rabat family-owned winery in three years than most wineries invest in a lifetime. This includes financing the winemaking input of globe-trotting French consultant Michel Rolland. Casa Lapostolle's first vintage was in 1994. Stellar winemaking.
BEST WINES: *Cabernet Sauvignon Rosé, Chardonnay, Cuvée Alexandre Merlot*

Concha y Toro ***(v)

Maipo Large, hugely reliable spectrum of wines spanning different qualities and price levels from Chile's largest winery. Top of the range is the relatively new, gracefully-styled super-premium release called Almaviva, the result of a joint venture between Concha y Toro and Baron Philippe de Rothschild. Also owns the dynamic Cono Sur company which makes good value wines with strong personalities. Recent innovations include hiring Adolfo Hurtado as chief winemaker. This plus heavy investment in the vineyard form part of the quest towards modernization. Second labels (Concha y Toro): Casillero del Diablo, Santa Emiliana and budget brands Andes Peak and Walnut Crest. Second labels (Cono Sur): Isla Negra and Tocornal.
BEST WINES: *Casillero del Diablo Merlot, Concha y Toro Almaviva Cabernet Sauvignon, Concha y Toro Amelia Chardonnay (Casablanca), Concha y Toro Don Melchor Private Reserve Cabernet Sauvignon (Rapel), Concha y Toro Sauvignon Blanc (Casablanca), Cono Sur Isla Negra range (also uses fruit from Argentina), Cono Sur Pinot Noir (Chimbarongo), Cono Sur Pinot Noir (Rapel), Cono Sur Viognier, Marqués de Casa Concha Merlot (Rapel), Trio range (crafted by Ignacio Recabarren).*

Cono Sur ***

Chimbarongo See Concha y Toro.

Errázuriz ****(v)

Aconcagua Errázuriz was founded in 1870 when Don Maximiano Errázuriz planted his first vineyard in the Aconcagua Valley. Still family-owned, it is run by Eduardo Chadwick, a direct descendent of Don Maximiano. The whole ethos is focused on the production of world class quality wines, sourced from their own vineyard estates. The concept of terroir is central to the Errázuriz philosophy, whereby each of their four estates grows only those varieties which can excel in the particular soil and microclimates. These are managed by Pedro Izquierdo who works hand in hand with winemaker Ed Flaherty in a joint quest to produce Chile's finest wines.

Errázuriz also owns Caliterra, one of the leading Chilean brands in both the UK and US, which is getting better with each vintage (especially as they now use a higher percentage of Casablanca Valley grapes in the whites). In fact, this 1996 alliance between Errázuriz and Robert Mondavi was launched originally to sell budget-priced wines worldwide, but they have moved up a notch or ten since: Seña, the product of a single estate (the Don Maximiano vineyard in the Aconcagua Valley), is an ultra-premium wine which tastes like a high profile Napa Cabernet Sauvignon. Made from a blend of Cabernet Sauvignon, Merlot and Carmenère, though the proportion of each changes with each vintage.

BEST WINES: *Caliterra Chardonnay Reserva, Caliterra Merlot, Caliterra Sauvignon Blanc Reserva, Caliterra Tribute Chardonnay (Casablanca), Errázuriz Chardonnay (Casablanca), Founder's Reserve Don Maximiano Cabernet Sauvignon, Seña*

Luís Felipé Edwards ****(v)

Colchagua These wines sing out with fruit, yet they are incredibly well-balanced. Totally underestimated.

BEST WINES: *Chardonnay, Reserve Cabernet Sauvignon*

Montes ***

Curicó Premier producer Aurelio Montes seems to have the knack of infusing his wines with freshness and flavour, well removed from the old rustic style of traditional Chilean wines. Established in 1988 by four partners with years of experience in winemaking, their philosophy was to produce the best wines in the country, a goal which has defined Montes since its inception. Its high standards have set the pace for Chile in the international market. They own four estates – three in Curicó and one in Colchagua.

BEST WINES: *Late Harvest Gewürztraminer-Riesling, Montes Alpha range, Montes Fumé Blanc, Montes Malbec, Montes Sauvignon Blanc*

Valdevieso ***(v)

Curicó Huge investment from the Mitjan group at both its Lontué winery and Curicó vineyards. Californian Paul Hobbs is the major consultant, with Raphael Brisbois advising on the production of Chardonnay- and Pinot Noir-based bottle fermented sparkling wines. Wines are sold in the US under the Stonelake label.

BEST WINES: *Caballo Loco (multi-varietal blend), Cabernet Franc, Malbec, Reserve Chardonnay, Reserve Merlot, Reserve Pinot Noir*

Viña Carmen ***

Maipo See Viña Santa Rita.

Viña Casablanca ****(v)

Casablanca Top producer, courtesy of famous winemaker Ignacio Recabarren. Famed for its white wines from the Casablanca Valley, but reds from Cabernet Sauvignon and Merlot fruit sourced in Lontué, Maipo, Rapel and San Fernando are very promising. Sister winery to Viña Santa Carolina.

BEST WINES: *Santa Isabel Estate Chardonnay, Santa Isabel Estate Gewürztraminer, Santa Isabel Estate Sauvignon Blanc*

Viña La Rosa ***

Rapel Cabernet Sauvignon, Chardonnay, Merlot and Sauvignon Blanc are planted on this Peumo Valley estate (founded by Don Gregorio Ossa in 1824) alongside oranges, peaches and avocados. All wines are estate grown and bottled. The new showpiece winery is one of the most modern in Chile and Ignacio Recabarren consults. Labels: Casa Leona and La Palma.

BEST WINES: *La Palma range*

Viña Santa Carolina ***

Maipo Long established sister company to Viña Casablanca with a fine range of wines, Santa Carolina was founded in 1875 by Louis Pereria with vineyards located in the Casablanca, Lontué, Maipo and San Fernando Valleys. Winemaker María del Pilar Gonzalez produces fresh, fruity white wines, as well as rich and elegant reds, currently being exported to more than 40 countries worldwide, making Santa Carolina one of the leading export wineries.

BEST WINES: *Late Harvest Sémillon-Sauvignon Blanc, Reserve Sauvignon Blanc*

Viña Santa Rita ***

Maipo One of Chile's top seven exporters, thanks to heavy investment by wealthy industrialist Ricard Claro over the last few years. Santa Rita's Maipo and Rapel wineries are now amongst the most technologically advanced in Chile. Developments in canopy management allow Santa Rita's winemakers Andres Ilabaca and Cecilia Torres to create wines with a new concentration of fruit and varietal character. Ownership of extensive plantations in all of Chile's main grape-growing areas enables Santa Rita to offer stable pricing. Also owns Viña Carmen (Chile's oldest brand) whose wines define the Chilean character, thanks to the talents of one of Chile's great winemaking stars, Alvaro Espiñoza, and the recently disappointing Los Vascos.

BEST WINES: *Carmen Cabernet Sauvignon Reserve, Carmen*

Grande Vidure (another name for Carmenère), Carmen Sierra Los Andes Casablanca Reserve Chardonnay, Carmen Valle Central Merlot, Carmen Valle Central Sauvignon Blanc (Casablanca), Santa Rita Casa Real Cabernet Sauvignon (Maipo), Santa Rita Late Harvest Sémillon (Maipo, Santa Rita Medalla Real Chardonnay (Casablanca), Santa Rita 120 range

Mexico

L.A. Cetto ***

Baja California Founded in 1926 by Italian immigrant farmers who began commercial production in 1938 under the French pseudonym of 'F. Chauvenet'. Winemaker is Italian Carmelo Magoni.
BEST WINES: *Cabernet Sauvignon, Nebbiolo, Petite Sirah, Zinfandel*

New York State

Anthony Road ****

Finger Lakes The first crop was harvested in 1989, fulfilling a winemaking dream shared by John and Ann Martini, and Derek and Donna Wilber. Today, Anthony Road is well known for creating wines of intense flavour.
BEST WINES: *Cabernet Franc, Chardonnay, Late Harvest Vignoles, Semi-Dry Riesling, Vignoles*

Dr Konstantin Frank **

Finger Lakes Ukrainian Dr Frank emigrated to the US in 1951, and by 1959 had not only opened his own winery, but had made the state's first commercial wine from vinifera varieties. His son, Willy, took the reigns of the family business following Dr Frank's death in 1986. Second label: Chateau Frank (for traditional method sparkling wines).
BEST WINES: *Cabernet Sauvignon, Chardonnay, Chateau Frank Célèbre Crémant (Chardonnay-Riesling), Johannisberger Riesling Dry, Riesling Icewine, Salmon Run Riesling*

Fox Run ***

Finger Lakes Under the dynamic, forward-looking ownership of Scott Osborn and Andy Hale since 1993, a remarkable range of wine is made from 125 hectares of vineyards. Poised to become one of the great Finger Lakes producers. Winemaker Peter Bell and vineyard manager John Kaiser have introduced a programme of minimal intervention winemaking and have revitalized the vines by converting to the Vertical Shoot Positioning trellis system.
BEST WINES: *Arctic Fox (Chardonnay-Gewürztraminer-Cayuga), Blanc de Blancs (sparkling), Cabernet Franc, Cabernet Sauvignon, Lemberger, Merlot, Fox Trot Red (Pinot Noir-Gamay-Chardonnay), Reserve Chardonnay*

Glenora ***

Finger Lakes Founded in 1977, Glenora is one of the largest producers of vinifera wines (from bought-in grapes) in the eastern US. Now concentrating on first class, traditional method sparkling wine. Second label: Trestle Creek.
BEST WINES: *Blanc de Blancs, Brut Vintage, Brut Vintage Rosé, Chardonnay, Pinot Blanc, Pinot Noir, Riesling*

Hermann J. Wiemer ***

Finger Lakes In 1973, German-born and Geisenheim-trained Wiemer became one of the first to plant vinifera grapes in the Finger Lakes region and now produces 12,000 cases a year. In response to the demand for vinifera varieties, Wiemer established a separate nursery operation to meet his own and other vintners' needs, and now grows 200,000 grafted vines annually.
BEST WINES: *Brut (sparkling), Bunch Select Late Harvest Riesling, Chardonnay Reserve, Dry Riesling*

Hunt Country ***

Finger Lakes Small winery above Keuka Lake owned by Art and Joyce Hunt who are dedicated to creating wines of elegance. They are now giving much more consideration to site selection and the use of more suitable clones.
BEST WINES: *Cayuga White, Classic Red (Baco Noir-Chancellor-DeChaunac), Johannisberger Riesling, Seyval, Vidal Icewine, Viva Vignoles*

Lamoreaux Landing ***

Finger Lakes Opened in 1990 and named for a 19th century steamboat dock. Mark Wagner (who comes from a grape-growing family) makes his wine from fruit grown on four farms on the east side of Seneca Lake and has already established a reputation as one of the most impressive winemakers of the northeast. Magnificent Greek-style building.
BEST WINES: *Brut Sparkling, Cabernet Sauvignon, Gewürztraminer, Late Harvest Riesling, Pinot Noir, Reserve Chardonnay*

Millbrook ****

Hudson River Region Very classy operation making very classy wines. Owner John Dyson has winemaking interests in Italy (Villa Pillo) and in California (owns Williams Selyem and Pebble Ridge Vineyards).
BEST WINES: *Cabernet Franc, Pinot Noir, Proprietor's Special Reserve Chardonnay, Tocai Friulano*

Palmer ****

North Fork of Long Island Long Island's second largest – and very modern – winery founded by Robert Palmer in 1983. The 250 hectare vineyard is in meticulous condition – immaculate fruit gives immaculate wines. Dan Kleck is the enigmatic winemaker and Chris Kelly the quality-conscious viticulturist.
BEST WINES: *Brut Sparkling, Cabernet Franc, Chardonnay*

Barrel-Fermented, Chardonnay Estate, Merlot Reserve, Pinot Blanc, Riesling, Select Reserve Red Meritage (dominated by Cabernet Sauvignon), White Meritage

Pellegrini ***

North Fork of Long Island One of Long Island's finest producers, retired teachers Bob and Joyce Pellegrini bought a 10-year-old vineyard in 1992 and built a winery, and production has now grown to more than 10,000 cases. Stunning and passionate winemaking from Australian Russell Hearn. Minimal manipulation is his philosophy.
BEST WINES: *Cabernet Franc, Encore (Cabernet Sauvignon-Merlot), Finale (Icewine-style from bought-in Gewürztraminer and Sauvignon Blanc), Merlot, Vintners Pride Chardonnay*

Pindar ***

North Fork of Long Island Founded in 1979, Long Island's largest winery, Dr Herodotus 'Dan' Damianos makes over 60,000 cases a year from extensive, well-kept estate vineyard holdings – 21 varieties are planted. Also home to one of the biggest cats I have ever seen! Owns Duck Walk in The Hamptons, Long Island.
BEST WINES: *Chardonnay Peacock Label, Long Island Winter White (Chardonnay-Riesling), Merlot, Mythology (ageworthy Cabernet Franc-dominated, Bordeaux-style red)*

New Zealand

Ata Rangi ***

Martinborough Wonderful Wairarapa winery producing ultra-premium Pinot Noir and Chardonnay. This premier league winery consistently makes some of the best wines in the region, year in year out. Second label: Mount Riley.
BEST WINES: *Célèbre (Cabernet Sauvignon-Merlot-Syrah blend), Craighall Chardonnay, Pinot Noir*

Babich Wines ***(v)

Henderson Ultra-modern, family-owned winery established in 1916 by pioneer winemaker Josip Babich. Four ranges: Babich Premium, Irongate, Mara Estate (Gimlett Road vineyards) and Patriarch (the most outstanding wine from any given vintage regardless of vineyard or variety, selected by Joe Babich and the winemaker).
BEST WINES: *Irongate Cabernet Sauvignon-Merlot, Irongate Chardonnay, Mara Estate Cabernet Sauvignon, Mara Estate Merlot, Mara Estate Syrah, Patriarch*

Chard Farm ***

Central Otago The location of this winery is such that if you hate heights you would only ever visit it once; the road to reach it is chiselled into precipitous mountain slopes! Worth it, though – the wines are glorious.
BEST WINES: *Chardonnay, Pinot Noir*

C.J. Pask ****

Hawkes Bay Chris Pask, together with one of New Zealand's finest winemakers, Kate Radburnd, have carved a reputation as one of the country's leading wine producers.
BEST WINES: *Cabernet Sauvignon*

Cloudy Bay *****

Marlborough Such is the demand for New Zealand's most famous wine, that my allocation this year was all of three bottles! Cloudy Bay was founded by Australian, David Hohnen of Cape Mentelle, who discovered the enormous potential of New Zealand Sauvignon Blanc by accident. Fellow Australian, Kevin Judd, is the winemaker. The key to their success is the purity of the fruit which they consistently turn into superlative, award-swooping quality wine year in, year out. Veuve Clicquot have had a 70 per cent stake in Cloudy Bay since 1990.
BEST WINES: *Chardonnay, Pelorus (sparkling), Pinot Noir, Sauvignon Blanc*

Collard Brothers ****(v)

Henderson Small can be incredibly beautiful, and nowhere else proves this so well. Some of New Zealand's most stunning and tasty wines hail from here.
BEST WINES: *Hawkes Bay Chardonnay, Hawkes Bay Chenin Blanc, Rothesay Vineyard Chardonnay, Rothesay Vineyard Sauvignon Blanc*

Corbans ***(v)

Henderson New Zealand's second largest winery (producing over 30 per cent of the country's wine) and one of its oldest (1902). Brands include: Cooks (Hawkes Bay), Corbans Cottage Block (premium label), Corbans Private Bin, Longridge (Hawkes Bay), Stoneleigh (Marlborough) and Robard & Butler.
BEST WINES: *Amadeus (traditional method fizz), Cottage Block Chardonnay, Cottage Block Noble Riesling, Private Bin Amberley Riesling, Private Bin Gisborne Chardonnay, Private Bin Marlborough Chardonnay, Private Bin Noble Riesling, Stoneleigh Marlborough Riesling, Stoneleigh Marlborough Sauvignon Blanc*

Delegat's ***(v)

Henderson The Delegat family has been passionate about viticulture and winemaking in New Zealand for over 50 years. Jim and Rosemary Delegat, brother and sister, own extensive vineyards in Hawkes Bay and Marlborough. Their philosophy is to produce wines from the grape varieties for which the region's viticulture is world renowned. Second label: Oyster Bay.
BEST WINES: *Oyster Bay Sauvignon Blanc, Proprietor's Reserve Cabernet Sauvignon-Merlot, Proprietor's Reserve Chardonnay, Proprietor's Reserve Merlot*

Goldwater ****

Waiheke Island Pioneering winery making top-drawer wines. Uses Marlborough grapes for its Chardonnay and Sauvignon Blanc, grown under contract. The red wines have the power to

age quite well (five years or so).
BEST WINES: *Cabernet Sauvignon-Merlot, Dog Point Marlborough Sauvignon Blanc*

Hunter's ****(v)

Marlborough Sauvignon Blanc (oaked and unoaked) has earned international acclaim as a world classic and there is no doubt that Jane Hunter OBE and her team merit this reputation.
BEST WINES: *Botrytized Chardonnay, Gewürztraminer, Late Harvest Riesling, Merlot-Cabernet Sauvignon blend, Merlot-Pinot Noir-Cabernet Sauvignon blend, Miru Miru (sparkling), Pinot Noir, Riesling, Sauvignon Blanc*

Jackson ***

Marlborough Established by two brothers, John and Warwick Stichbury, and named after their great great grandfather Adam Jackson who set up shop from England in the 1840s. First vineyard to go 100 per cent Scott Henry trellising and it is also notable that they do not use irrigation. One of New Zealand's most prestigious single vineyard estates (next door to Cloudy Bay's vineyards). No winery of their own, however.
BEST WINES: *Chardonnay Reserve, Jackson Vintage Brut (traditional method sparkling), Riesling, Sauvignon Blanc*

Kumeu River ***

Kumeu Master of Wine Michael Brajkovich is yet another example of a New Zealander bent on drawing on Old World experience to make the most of excellent fruit. The first New Zealander to pass the prestigious Master of Wine exam, Michael is enormously successful. All of Kumeu River's grapes come from surrounding Kumeu vineyards. Second label: Brajkovich.
BEST WINES: *Cabernet Sauvignon-Merlot, Chardonnay, Mate's Vineyard Chardonnay, Pinot Gris, Sauvignon Blanc*

Martinborough Vineyard ****

Martinborough Larry MacKenna is the man who put the tiny area of Martinborough on the map. With no formal winemaking training, he cut his teeth at Delegat's and Domaine Dujac in Burgundy. He is passionate about Pinot Noir and Chardonnay. He won the 'Best Pinot Noir in the World' award for his 1994 Pinot Noir at the International Wine & Spirit Competition in 1994.
BEST WINES: *Chardonnay, Late Harvest Riesling, Pinot Gris, Pinot Noir, Riesling*

Matua Valley ***(v)

Auckland Brothers Bill and Ross Spence fermented their first Sauvignon Blanc in a tiny shed in Swanson and did much to pioneer New Zealand Sauvignon Blanc. Ararimu is the premium label. Other labels: Judd and Shingle Peak (for Marlborough wines).
BEST WINES: *Ararimu Cabernet Sauvignon-Merlot, Ararimu Chardonnay, Judd Chardonnay, Matua Valley Gewürztraminer, Matua Valley Reserve Sauvignon Blanc, Shingle Peak Sauvignon Blanc*

Montana ****(v)

Various locations New Zealand's largest wine firm with four wineries. Owns Deutz. Hawkes Bay wines are bottled under the Church Road label.
BEST WINES: *Church Road Cabernet Sauvignon-Merlot, Church Road Reserve Chardonnay, Church Road Reserve Merlot, Deutz Marlborough Cuvée Brut (sparkling), Lindauer Brut (sparkling), Montana Awatere Reserve Riesling, Montana Chardonnay, Montana Sauvignon Blanc, Ormond Estate Chardonnay (Gisborne)*

Morton ****(v)

Bay Of Plenty Winery is at Katikati, but the vineyards are in Hawkes Bay and Marlborough. Some of New Zealand's best wines hail from here. Second label: White Label
BEST WINES: *Black Label Brut (traditional method sparkling), Black Label Cabernet Sauvignon-Merlot, Black Label Chardonnay, Black Label Fumé Blanc*

Palliser ***

Martinborough Palliser's first vintage was only in 1989 and it takes a great deal of commitment to quality to establish a reputation in such a short time – they are now one of the region's largest and most successful wineries. Their best wine to date is the trophy-winning Estate Sauvignon Blanc which epitomizes classic Marlborough Sauvignon with its tropical richness and concentration. Pinot Noir is coming on leaps and bounds, and the Estate Riesling and Chardonnay both exhibit consistently high quality. Premier label: Palliser Estate; second label: Palliser Bay.
BEST WINES: *Chardonnay, Pinot Noir, Riesling, Sauvignon Blanc*

Stonyridge ****

Waiheke Island Terrific producer of concentrated, flavoursome Bordeaux-style red wines from very low yields, arguably one of the country's finest. Second label: Airfield.
BEST WINES: *Larose (Bordeaux-style red)*

Te Mata ****

Hawkes Bay With vineyards spanning the Te Mata peak, this long-established, family-owned winery is run by the formidable John Buck. Former accountant, wine retailer, critic and author, he set the standard for others to follow with New Zealand's first Cabernet Sauvignon-Merlot blend 'Coleraine' in 1982. Believing New Zealand capable of matching the great classic regions of Bordeaux, Burgundy and Sancerre, he has emulated and adapted French techniques in search of the highest quality possible and is consistently reaching them. Second label: Awatea.
BEST WINES: *Bullnose Syrah, Coleraine (premium label), Elston Chardonnay*

Vavasour ***

Awatere Valley, Marlborough Fabulous wines since the first release of the 1989 vintage. Drink reds with five years of vintage, whites within three to four years. Second label: Dashwood.
BEST WINES: *Cabernet Sauvignon Reserve, Chardonnay (one of New Zealand's best), Sauvignon Blanc*

Villa Maria ****(v)

Auckland Villa Maria, New Zealand's third largest wine company, have built a reputation for top quality wines across a wide spectrum of styles. Three ranges: Reserve, Cellar Selection and Private Bin. Also owns Esk Valley and Vidal.
BEST WINES: *Esk Valley Merlot Reserve, Esk Valley The Terraces, Vidal Cabernet Sauvignon-Merlot, Vidal Chardonnay, Vidal Sauvignon Blanc, Villa Maria Noble Riesling, Villa Maria Private Bin Sauvignon Blanc, Villa Maria Reserve Cabernet Sauvignon, Villa Maria Reserve Wairau Valley Sauvignon Blanc*

Oregon

Amity ***

Willamette Valley Myron Redford makes well-textured, long-lived Pinot Noir, one of Oregon's top examples.
BEST WINES: *Gewürztraminer, Pinot Blanc, Winemakers Reserve Pinot Noir*

Domaine Drouhin ****

Willamette Valley Winemaker Véronique made her first wine not in Burgundy but in Oregon, after she and her father, Joseph, began their project here in 1988 . From humble beginnings – no water or electricity – they have built a modern winery producing fine, elegant Pinot Noir.
BEST WINES: *Pinot Noir*

Erath ***

Willamette Valley Californian Dick Erath has been a leading producer of textbook Oregon Pinot Noir for over a quarter of a century. From nursery propagation to bottling, Erath is fully involved in the winemaking process, firmly believing that 'great wines are made in the vineyard'.
BEST WINES: *Chardonnay, Pinot Blanc, Pinot Gris, Pinot Noir*

Ponzi ***

Willamette Valley Founded in 1970 by Dick and Nancy Ponzi, this truly is a family winery; daughter Louisa is winemaker, daughter Anna-Maria is marketing director and son Michel is winery controller. Pioneer of Oregon Pinot Gris.
BEST WINES: *Chardonnay, Pinot Gris, Pinot Noir Reserve, Vino Gelato (Ponzi's Italian-style version of a Riesling Icewine)*

The Eyrie ***

Willamette Valley Owned by David Lett who so famously entered his pioneering Pinot Noir 1975 in a blind tasting competition in France, organized by Joseph Drouhin, and came second.
BEST WINES: *Chardonnay, Pinot Gris, Pinot Noir*

South Africa

Backsberg ***(v)

Paarl Pioneers of barrel-fermented Chardonnay in South Africa. Viticulturist Phil Freese (husband of Zelma Long of California's Simi estate) is consultant.
BEST WINES: *Cabernet Sauvignon, Chardonnay, Chenin Blanc (dessert-style), Klein Babylonstoren (Bordeaux-style red), Malbec, Merlot, Pinotage, Shiraz*

Bellingham ****

Franschhoek Currently in the process of replanting vineyards and modernizing its wineries in order to take quality into the millennium. Recent management buy-out from Graham Beck's Kanga Group. Winemaker is Charles Hopkins. Three ranges: Bellingham, Douglas Green and Graham Beck.
BEST WINES: *Cabernet Franc, Cabernet Sauvignon, Cape Gold (Riesling), Graham Beck, Merlot, Pinotage, Sauvenay (Chardonnay-Sauvignon Blanc), Sauvignon Blanc, Shiraz*

Buitenverwachting ***

Constantia Ultra-modern winery producing some of South Africa's best Sauvignon Blancs in addition to Cabernet Sauvignon and Merlot. German-owned, the 200-year-old estate was purchased in 1980 by the Müeller-Maack family who have undertaken extensive replanting and renovations. Buitenverwachting means 'Beyond Expectations'.
BEST WINES: *Cabernet Sauvignon, Christine (Bordeaux-style red), Merlot, Sauvignon Blanc*

Fairview ***(v)

Paarl Charles Back is at the helm of this 400 hectare estate and his attitude is avant garde to say the least. With 14 or so different varieties planted, he is a fan of the unusual and of experimentation. The split is now 80:20 in favour of red varieties. Look out for the new 'Goats Do Roam' blend, to be launched in September 1999. Back also produces some of South Africa's most celebrated cheeses.
BEST WINES: *Cabernet Sauvignon, Chardonnay, Chenin Blanc, Malbec, Merlot Reserve, Pinotage, Sémillon, Shiraz, Viognier, Zinfandel-Cinsaut*

Glen Carlou ****

Paarl Stunning wines from David Finlayson, especially after hooking up with Napa's Donald Hess in 1997.
BEST WINES: *Chardonnay Reserve (sweet), Grande Classique (Bordeaux-style red), Pinot Noir*

Hamilton Russell ***

Walker Bay While everyone else ignored the cool climate Walker Bay area during the 1980s, Hamilton Russell was busy growing Pinot Noir. From the founding of the winery in 1975, Tim Hamilton Russell pioneered Burgundy-inspired Chardonnay and Pinot Noir (the company has been owned by his son Anthony since 1994). These distinguished oak-aged wines are in very short supply. They combine Old World elegance and longevity with bright New World fruit, which gives them an immediate appeal despite their classic styling. Second label: Southern Right.
BEST WINES: *Ashbourne Chardonnay, Ashbourne Pinot Noir*

Hartenberg ****

Stellenbosch Located on the slopes of the Bottelary hills, this estate is at the forefront of quality wine production in the Cape, thanks to award-winning winemaker, Carl Schultz, who has overseen its transformation. Energies are focused on the production of full-flavoured wines.
BEST WINES: *Merlot, Shiraz, Zinfandel*

Kanonkop ***

Stellenbosch One of the top producers of Pinotage with a large local following, thanks to the skills of winemaker Beyers Truter who is considered to be the leading exponent of this grape variety. Sister winery: Beyerskloof.
BEST WINES: *Auction Reserve Cabernet Sauvignon, Auction Reserve Pinotage, Estate Pinotage, Kadette (Pinotage-Cabernet Sauvignon blend), Paul Sauer (Bordeaux-style red named after the founder)*

La Motte ****

Franschhoek Very hi-tech winery making French-style wines, some of South Africa's best. Owned by Hanneli Rupert who also own L'Ormarins, also in Franschhoek. The estate, dating back to 1694, was once owned by Cecil Rhodes. Winemaker is Jacques Borman.
BEST WINES: *La Motte Millennium (Bordeaux-style red), La Motte Sauvignon Blanc (made to a Loire style), La Motte Shiraz (made to a Rhône style), L'Ormarins Chardonnay, L'Ormarins Gewürztraminer-Bukketraube (dessert wine), L'Ormarins Optima (Bordeaux-style red)*

L'Ormarins ***

Franschhoek See La Motte.

Nederberg ***

Paarl See Stellenbosch Farmers' Winery.

Neethlingshof ***

Stellenbosch See Stellenzicht.

Simonsig ***

Stellenbosch In the hands of the dedicated Malan brothers, Simonsig Estate wines reflect the family tradition of excellence and innovation in winemaking dating back to the efforts of pioneer winemaker, Frans Malan, in 1953. Almost half of production is exported. Labels: Frans Malan Reserve, Malan Vintners, Rouge du Cap and Blanc du Cap.
BEST WINES: *Cabernet Sauvignon, Chardonnay, Gewürztraminer (dessert-style), Frans Malan Reserve Pinotage-Cabernet Sauvignon, Kaapse Vonkel (sparkling), Pinotage, Shiraz, Tiara (Cabernet Sauvignon-Merlot)*

Spice Route ***

Malmesbury Project set up by Charles Back of Fairview, Gyles Webb of Thelema, wine writer John Platter and South Africa's first black vineyard and cellar owner, Jabulani Ntshangase, it has become a significant symbol of the new democratic South Africa. The local wine press has already dubbed this quartet as 'The Dream Team' and 'The Spice Boys'! Eben Sadie, Spice Route's gifted young winemaker, has now been offered a partnership in the project, also. The first vintage from this dry-farmed vineyard was 1998.
BEST WINES: *Andrew Hope Merlot-Cabernet Sauvignon, Spice Route Sauvignon Blanc*

Stellenbosch Farmers' Winery (SFW)

Various locations South Africa's second largest winery group and the world's fifth largest. Brands include: Nederberg, Plaisir de Merle and Zonnebloem (premium label). Perhaps the most famous is Nederberg on the strength of the famous annual auction, the highlight of the South African wine calendar.
BEST WINES: *Edelkeur (botrytized), Zonnebloem Blanc de Blancs (sparkling), Zonnebloem Laureat (Bordeaux-style red), Zonnebloem Pinotage*

Stellenzicht ***

Stellenbosch The emphasis is on modern-style, supple reds and fruity Sauvignon Blancs. Hans-Joachim Schreiber also owns the recently renovated Neethlingshof Estate.
BEST WINES: *Lord Neethling (Bordeaux-style red), Neethlingshof Cabernet Sauvignon, Neethlingshof Chardonnay, Neethlingshof Gewürztraminer, Neethlingshof Merlot, Neethlingshof Riesling (botrytized), Stellenzicht Botrytized Sémillon-Sauvignon Blanc, Stellenzicht Cabernet Sauvignon, Stellenzicht Sauvignon Blanc, Stellenzicht Sémillon, Stellenzicht Shiraz*

Thelema Mountain *****

Stellenbosch Owner Gyles Webb enjoys outstanding success with his stunning wines. One of South Africa's top wineries – his wines sell out quickly. Second label: Stormy Cape (UK only).
BEST WINES: *Cabernet Sauvignon Reserve, Cabernet Sauvignon-Merlot, Chardonnay, Merlot, Riesling, Sauvignon Blanc*

Vergelegen ***

Stellenbosch This historic property (1700), replanted in 1989, is now coming into its own as a showpiece of South Africa's recent wine renaissance. André van Rensburg was appointed winemaker in 1997.
BEST WINES: *Cabernet Sauvignon, Chardonnay Reserve, Merlot, Sauvignon Blanc, Sémillon*

Zonnebloem ***(v)

See Stellenbosch Farmers' Winery.

Washington State

Andrew Will ***

Puget Sound Wonderful wines from winemaker Chris Camarda who sources grapes from across the other side of the Cascades.
BEST WINES: *Cabernet Sauvignon, Cuvée Lulu Chenin Blanc, Merlot*

Château Ste Michelle ***

Woodinville Flagship winery of the Stimson Lane Vineyards and Estates Group and the largest winery in the northwest, producing more than a million cases per year. Three distinct ranges: Columbia Valley, Single Vineyard and Reserve. Winemaker is Mike Januik. Also owns Columbia Crest and Snoqualmie.
BEST WINES: *Canoe Ridge Estate Merlot, Columbia Valley Cold Creek Vineyard Cabernet Sauvignon, Columbia Valley Horse Heaven Vineyard Merlot, Columbia Valley Reserve Late Harvest Sémillon*

Columbia Crest ***(v)

Woodinville Although Columbia Crest was originally created as a second label for Château Ste Michelle, the winery has become a success in its own right and is now one of Washington's best in terms of quality and value. The range is split into three tiers: Columbia Valley, Estate and Reserve (the latter being the best).
BEST WINES: *Cabernet Sauvignon, Chardonnay, Merlot, Syrah*

Columbia Winery ***

Woodinville Pioneer of Washington's wine industry for almost four decades, and is setting new standards in wine research and experimentation. The wines are consistently good, most especially the single vineyard examples. Also owns Covey Run in the Yakima Valley.
BEST WINES: *Covey Run Merlot, Milestone Merlot, Otis Cabernet Sauvignon, Red Willow Cabernet Sauvignon, Red Willow Syrah, Sagemoor Cabernet Sauvignon, Woodburne Chardonnay*

Hogue ***

Yakima Valley Like many other growers in Washington state, Mike Hogue was originally a farmer, growing hops, asparagus and spearmint for chewing gum. Having planted a few vines in 1974, Hogue Cellars produced its first commercial wine in 1982. Winemaker David Forsyth emphasizes cool climate varietal character and flavours.
BEST WINES: *Genesis Sunnyside Vineyard Chardonnay, Reserve Cabernet Sauvignon, Reserve Merlot, Riesling, Sauvignon Blanc*

L'Ecole No 41 ***

Walla Walla Valley The story behind the name of this winery stems from the fact that until 1999 the wines were produced in the cellars of the historic town school. They have now moved to a purpose-built winery. Premium, hand-crafted wines with the ability to age are made by Marty Clubb.
BEST WINES: *Barrel Select (Bordeaux-style red), L'Ecole No 41 Chardonnay, Merlot, Sémillon, Windrow Vineyard Cabernet Sauvignon*

Leonetti ****(v)

Walla Walla Valley Cult winery, arguably Washington's finest, making big, powerful wines. Owner and winemaker is Gary Figgins.
BEST WINES: *Cabernet Sauvignon, Merlot, Sangiovese*

Index

Acknowledgements

To list the number of people who have provided help with this book would run into another volume by itself. Suffice to say that I am deeply grateful for the hospitality and friendship offered by those producers whom I visited, and I offer great thanks to the individuals whom I could not see personally, but who kindly responded to e-mails and faxes. Those of you who maintain up-to-date websites provided invaluable – and fascinating – information and I can only say 'please keep it up'. I must also more than acknowledge the assistance of the various generic offices who represent the interests of their country's wine industry at home and within the UK.

Finally, a very, very special thank you to Guy Croton, John Fenton and Karen Neill.